792.9   Shakespeare in the South
Sha

20.00   84-85

DATE DUE

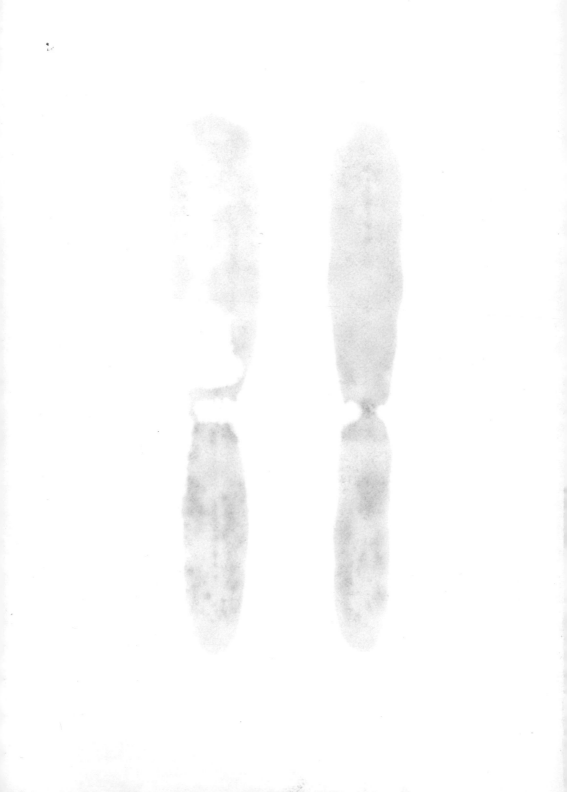

Shakespeare in the South

Shakespeare in the South
Essays on Performance

Philip C. Kolin
Editor

84-85

University Press of Mississippi
Jackson

This book has been sponsored by the
University of Southern Mississippi

Copyright © 1983 by the University Press of Mississippi
All rights reserved
Manufactured in the United States of America

Library of Congress Cataloging in Publication Data
Main entry under title:

Shakespeare in the South.

Includes index.
1. Shakespeare, William, 1564–1616—Stage history—
Southern States.   2. Theater—Southern States—History.
I.   Kolin, Philip C.
PR3105.S47   1983   792.9'5'0975   83-5954
ISBN 0-87805-185-6

Contents

Acknowledgments

I want to express my appreciation to the administration of the University of Southern Mississippi for sponsoring this volume. To President Aubrey K. Lucas and Vice President for Academic Affairs James Sims, I owe a special debt of gratitude, which I happily acknowledge here, for their sustaining encouragement and support of my work. I would also like to thank the University Press Committee, ably chaired by Dr. John Edmond Gonzales, for their help. On behalf of the contributors I would like to thank the festivals, historical societies, and libraries that generously allowed us to use materials from their photo archives. Finally, I want to thank Janeen, Eric, and Kristin who, by the grace of God, assisted me in innumerable ways as this volume made its way toward publication.

Philip C. Kolin

Shakespeare in the South

Shakespeare in the South:
An Overview

Philip C. Kolin

I

Shakespeare was the most popular dramatist on the antebellum southern stage and the most performed playwright in the South since. Yet, surprisingly, no book-length study exists that isolates Shakespearean performances on southern stages or discusses them in detail and in relationship to each other. General histories of the American theater—Garff B. Wilson's *Three Hundred Years of American Drama and Theatre* (Englewood Cliffs: Prentice-Hall, 1973) or volume 8 of the *Revels History of Drama in English, American Drama* (Methuen: London, 1977), for example—pay scant attention to the South in general and even less to Shakespeare's presence there. Theater historians might expect detailed coverage of Shakespeare in the South in books devoted exclusively to Shakespeare in America. But not so. Charles H. Shattuck's *Shakespeare on the American Stage from the Hallams to Edwin Booth* (Washington, D.C.: Folger, 1976) ignores the South. While admitting that Shakespeare in other American cities, New Orleans among them, is "indeed important," Shattuck asserts, "But I have limited my scope mainly to cities of the East and, after the turn into the nineteenth century, mainly to what happened in New York City." Understandably, Shattuck could not have surveyed every regional theater where Shakespeare was performed, and justifiably he concentrated on those theatrical centers—New York, Boston, Philadelphia—from which stars traveled South and to which they returned bedecked with laurel or besmirched with embarrassment. One wonders, though, why a study such as John Ripley's *Julius Caesar on Stage in England and America, 1599-1973* (New York: Cambridge University Press, 1980) mentions only one southern performance in a chapter on "American Productions (1770–1870)." Esther Cloud-man Dunn's *Shakespeare in America* (New York: Macmillan, 1939) offers readers a 25-page chapter entitled "Shakespeare on the Ohio and Mississippi Frontier," but she hardly claims to offer a documented history of performances or a rigorous commentary on tastes. Instead, Dunn supplies a light account of the "crudities" of the theater in the West.

Studies of Shakespeare's reception in the South do exist. A number of books on local and regional theater are pertinent. For example, Hugh F. Rankin's *The Theater in Colonial America* (Chapel Hill: University of North Carolina Press, 1965) surveys the pre-Revolutionary South; the New Orleans theater has been surveyed by Nelle Smither, *A History of the English Theatre in New Orleans* (1944; rpt. New York: Benjamin Blom, 1967), and by John Smith Kendall, *The Golden Age of the New Orleans Theatre* (Baton Rouge: Louisiana State University Press, 1952); Charleston has been studied by Eola Willis, *The Charleston Stage in the XVIII Century* (Columbia: the State Company, 1924), and by William Stanley Hoole, *The Ante-Bellum Charleston Theater* (Tuscaloosa: University of Alabama Press, 1946); theater in Richmond is the subject of Martin Staples Shockley's *The Richmond Stage, 1784–1812* (Charlottesville: University of Virginia Press, 1977); and even Houston and Galveston are covered by Joseph F. Gallegly's *Footlights on the Border: The Galveston and Houston Stage before 1900* (The Hague: Mouton and Company, 1962). These are all valuable studies which offer information about Shakespeare and many other types of dramatic entertainments. Shakespeare, however, does not receive special or separate attention. Chapters are not devoted to him, nor are his plays treated apart from the sweeping and ongoing chronology of which they are a part. Commentary is often sparse; readers will not find an interpretative record of how plays of one decade compare with those performed earlier or later in the same locale. Further, actors are ushered in and out of chapters so quickly that it is hard to discern a pattern in the carpet going from the green room to the stage.

Theater in the Ante Bellum South 1815–1861 by James H. Dormon, Jr. (Chapel Hill: University of North Carolina Press, 1967) strives to offer the kind of documentation and interpretation social and theater historians require. Dormon's purpose is "to bring to light the details of theatrical development of the region and to evaluate the role of the South in the history of the nation's ante bellum theatre." Unfortunately, Dorman excludes Maryland altogether from his study of the southern theater. Moreover, he reserves only a few pages for extended commentary on Shakespeare (pp. 256–58), although he does comment on many individual plays throughout his work. Shakespeare's popularity for Dormon is found not in "the subtleties of his art but in the emphasis on melodrama, oratory and violence that characterized productions" (p. 258). Such a view, while partially valid, does not account for the diverse and complex reception of Shakespeare by southern audiences.

This collection seeks both to document and to evaluate Shakespearean performances in the South from colonial to contemporary times. The thirteen essays here, all of them especially written for this volume, are divided into two parts—"Histories of Shakespearean Performance in the South" and "Some Southern Shakespearean Festivals." My goal in assembling these essays was not to offer a comprehensive analysis of Shakespeare on southern stages. Multiple volumes chronicling Shakespearean productions throughout the South will someday tackle that task. When they appear, I hope that this collection will have influenced their course. A less ambitious though no less rewarding purpose has guided this volume. I want to offer readers—theater and social historians, actors, anyone interested in the South or Shakespeare or both—essays that illuminate the continuity and richness of Shakespearean performances. To reveal that continuity, the essays, through the volume's two parts, fuse past with present. What emerges is a collective view of the South molding yet responding to its own theatrical heritage. The richness of Shakespearean productions is lavishly documented through the numerous references to primary and secondary materials. The texts of Shakespeare's plays—whether in full or much abbreviated form, or in adaptations—reflect the tastes of the times in which they were staged. The South's reception of these plays is recorded in the numerous newspapers, diaries, memoirs, playbills, ledgers, or journals cited throughout the collection. Many of the essays traverse familiar territory but transform the landscape by supplementing or correcting earlier studies. Many more of the essays offer original, sometimes provocative histories.

2

The essays in this collection encourage comparisons between Elizabethan England and the American South, especially during the antebellum period. The two ages had much in common, a fact traditionally emphasized by historians who characterized the South for its Anglophilia. Both epochs saw cataclysmic changes in the social and political fabric of society. England and the South were moving nonstop toward civil war, and in the process both societies saw an erosion of chivalry and idealism. But more useful to the inquiry of this volume, both societies nurtured a great love of theater and a warm fondness for actors. (To be sure, moralizing backbiters attacked theater in both cultures, but with only marginal success.) It is useful to point out a number of parallels between the Elizabethan and southern stages, not to suggest exact correspondences but to provide some points of imaginative departure for the collection of essays that follow.

Both ages produced renowned stars equal to the demands and the triumphs of Shakespearean dramaturgy. Robert Armin, Richard Burbage, and Nathan Field were among the first actors to convey the glories of Shakespearean verse to an audience. Their counterparts who lived in or visited the South—the Booths (Junius Brutus and Edwin), Thomas Abthorpe Cooper, Edwin Forrest, James Hackett—enchanted their audiences, too. Thespians in both ages had enormous stamina and capacity for variety. Their exhaustive schedules found them performing in four or five different plays a week. Luminaries of both stages went on tours, displaying their dramatic talents to different regions of the country.

Both Elizabethans and southerners were delighted by child prodigies. The boy actors of Shakespeare's day were the nonpareil female stars; they were even favorably compared with continental actresses. In the South, Master Joseph Burke, the Marsh Children, and the irrepressible Bateman Twins moved audiences to tears, laughter, and applause. It is an irony of theater history that on Shakespeare's celibate stage boys played women's parts while on the nineteenth-century American stage breeches roles won acclaim for women. Another hallmark of both ages is the vitality of warring companies. In America as in England, actors battled as rival theaters fought for patronage.

Also worthy of comparison are the theater impresarios of both ages. These individuals had shares in the playhouses, managed the stars, and protected the companies from extinction. It is intriguing, for example, to compare the contributions of Noah Ludlow and Sol Smith, the great American theater managers, with their Elizabethan counterpart Philip Henslowe. Southern and Elizabethan theater magnates kept diaries of incalculable worth to theater historians. Such documents record the day-to-day operations of their enterprises, giving specific information on props, plays performed, and receipts and debits.

It is also interesting to note that both theaters were pluralistic, however aristocratic the society in which they were shaped. To the Theatre, the Globe, the Fortune came apparently all classes of London society—groundlings away from their jobs as day laborers, apprentices, law students, merchants, franklins, lords, and ladies. Similarly, southern audiences interested in Shakespeare included all strata of Mason-Dixon culture—slaves and free men and women, riverboat captains and their crews, the petit bourgeois, the landed aristocracy. It is appropriate to note that one of the early playhouses in Vicksburg was called the Citizens Theatre.

In taste as well as in class, southern and Elizabethan audiences invite comparisons. Both groups loved violence; the Elizabethan revenge tragedy shares much with the melodramas on the southern stage. The most popular Shakespearean plays on the southern stage were the most bloody—*Richard III, Macbeth, Hamlet*. Stage blood oozed from both Elizabethan and southern actors. Like their Elizabethan counterparts, southerners liked diverse entertainments, a diversity perhaps perplexing to modern viewers. Elizabethans saw nothing incongruous about viewing a lofty Shakespearean tragedy on Wednesday and on the following afternoon delighting in the gruesome spectacle of bear or bull baiting. In the South as well as in the English-speaking theater in general, Shakespeare frequently shared the bill with burlesque forms of entertainment. Just as the Elizabethans expected an antimasque to follow the sublime masque, southerners waited for pantomimes or singing buffoons to enter as soon as the curtain fell on Shakespeare.

Architecturally, Elizabethan playhouses and southern stages offer intriguing parallels. The Elizabethan playhouse had a yard, galleries, private and elegant boxes, and even places on the stage where dandies, fops, and others who could afford the money and the scrutiny perched themselves. In a broad outline, the various seating arrangements of the southern theatres—with their pits and galleries—are comparable. One of the most notable attempts to blend the two cultures architecturally is the 1976 Mississippi production of the *Taming of the Shrew,* where a Delta riverboat is made to look like an Elizabethan stage complete with music room and decorative façade.

3

The nine essays included in the first part of this volume focus primarily on Shakespeare in some of the leading cultural (and hence theatrical) centers of the Old South—Charleston, Richmond, Annapolis, Baltimore, Mobile, Vicksburg, Natchez, and New Orleans. These antebellum cities witnessed the golden age of Shakespeare in the South. After the Civil War, audiences' tastes changed and Shakespeare sometimes entered desert country. Three essays in this section, however, extend coverage beyond 1865 and up to the 1970s to reveal the tastes of the New South, especially Houston and Atlanta, the western and eastern capitals of the empire. Historically, Houston cannot rival Mobile, New Orleans, or Charleston in Shakespearean productions before 1865. Culturally it was not ready, and hence the emphasis must rightfully fall on twentieth-century productions. Recent performances of *Othello* in Atlanta and Shakespearean comedies in Mississippi reveal the sophistication of southern audiences and also help us to appreciate the legacy of southern theater.

Moreover, recent productions discussed in Part One provide a link to the festivals described in Part Two. Specifically, the essays in Part One document the number of Shakespearean performances, including southern premieres that in some cases were also American firsts, assess the relative popularity of individual plays in the eyes of southern audiences and reviewers, account for outstanding seasons of Shakespearean performances, follow the travels of the stars—American and foreign—who crisscrossed the South, trace the vicissitudes of numerous southern theater entrepreneurs, describe the entertainments—silly or serious—accompanying Shakespeare on stage, and most important of all help us to understand how Shakespeare's regional significance is a part of his enduring and universal appeal.

The first four essays, more precisely, consider Shakespeare in the Southeast, along the Atlantic seaboard where the earliest performances of his work in the South are found. These essays examine Shakespearean productions in the cultural settings of Virginia, Maryland, and South Carolina, while Larry Champion's essay in Part Two offers commentary on some early productions of Shakespeare in North Carolina.

The rightful starting point is Arnold Aronson's essay on Virginia. The first recorded Shakespearean performance in the South occurred in Williamsburg in 1751 when Murray and Kean staged *Richard III*. From this point Aronson divides his history into three sections. In pre-Revolutionary Virginia fourteen of Shakespeare's plays were staged 180 times by actors who wanted to "cater to" the audience's "desire for English culture." The second and third periods of Aronson's history concentrate exclusively on Richmond. He notes that the "golden age of theater in Richmond commenced in the summer of 1790 with the arrival of . . . Thomas Wade West and John Bingnall." Aronson studies their contributions as well as those of Thomas Abthorpe Cooper, Thomas Caulfield, and Junius Brutus Booth, who made his American debut in Richmond. From 1819 to the Civil War Shakespeare was sporadically played, and the more spectacularly the better. The tragedies were the most popular plays because "audiences seemed to expect violent passion and lively action in the drama." In seeing the tragedies Richmond residents were treated to the best performances of the century, for the city "was visited by nearly every major and minor actor in America at the time."

Christopher J. Thaiss's history of Shakespeare in Maryland provides numerous significant parallels with Aronson's. Kean and Murray staged *Richard III* in Annapolis in March, 1752, just one year after their Virginia premiere. As in colonial Virginia, Annapolis offered actors a warm and hospitable moral climate. After the war Baltimore replaced Annapolis as the theatrical center of the state, as Richmond did Williamsburg. Thaiss highlights the major Shakespearean events in Baltimore—the Kean riot of 1826, the William Charles Macready / Edwin Forrest confrontation in 1848, and the ascendancy of and the city's affection for the young Marylander, Edwin Booth. As elsewhere in the South, serious drama was being challenged in Baltimore by spectacle and "prancing animals." Even so, Shakespeare was the most notable attraction for Baltimore audiences who, as in Richmond, preferred the tragedies to the comedies, which were "rarely performed."

Charleston has occupied a leading place in southern culture for centuries. The next two essays in this volume explore the city's Shakespearean heritage; Sara Nalley assesses performances up to 1800, and Woodrow L. Holbein discusses those to 1861. Nalley contends that Charleston's "plays and players were the best in colonial America," an opinion perhaps not shared in Annapolis or Philadelphia or New York. Educated Anglophiles, pre-Revolutionary Charlestonians, like their Richmond counterparts, sought and appreciated good theater including, of course, Shakespeare. Although the first recorded Shakespearean performance in Charleston was in 1763–1764, Nalley suspects that Shakespeare probably was on the boards a decade earlier. Of special importance is the "brilliant" season of 1773–1774, when Charlestonians saw eighteen productions of twelve Shakespeare plays. But that season was not typical of eighteenth-century Charleston. Shakespeare was performed less after than before the war; from 1774 to 1786 there was a lapse in Shakespearean performances. An audience unaccustomed to the plays did not seek them. Moreover, the accompanying spectacle often "outshone the play itself." Also contributing to fewer and poorer performances was the shortage of qualified actors, a condition caused in part by the Vagrancy Act, which fell heavily upon thespians.

Continuing the history of Shakespeare in Charleston, Woodrow L. Holbein organizes his essay around individual histories of the most popular of the twenty-three plays that were staged 600 times between 1800 and 1860. Two of the most popular plays—*Othello* and *The Merchant of Venice*—were also the most controversial, the tragedy because of the race issue and the comedy because it evidently offended Charleston Jewry. Whether special accommodations were made for southern audiences viewing these plays is a matter for discussion. Certainly the history of *Othello* on southern stages is far from settled. Arguing that Charlestonians could accept a Moor but not a Negro on stage, Holbein states, "I doubt that Othello had more than a good suntan when he ceased coming alive on the stage in the Charleston." Readers will want to review the noncontroversial productions of *Othello* in 1774 and 1796 in Charleston and also to contrast Holbein's views with those of Charles B. Lower, included later in the collection. The question of prejudice aside, Charlestonians witnessed some of the great moments in the production of Shakespeare during the nineteenth century the 1825 Booth King Lear, the 1826 Kean Richard III, and Booth's farewell to the city. The visits of these and other great ones to the city are recorded and critiqued in the numerous newspaper reviews Holbein cites.

With the next three essays we enter the Deep and Mid-South, the kingdom of Ludlow and Smith. These essays cover performances in antebellum New Orleans, Mobile, Vicksburg, and Natchez, cities forming a southern theatrical triangle. Actors traveled down river from St. Louis, also part of the Ludlow and Smith empire, and played in Mississippi before journeying to New Orleans, whence they frequently came to Mobile. Sometimes, too, actors traveled east to west, stopping off at Mobile on their way to engagements in New Orleans and points west and north.

Joseph Patrick Roppolo's engaging study reveals that "Shakespeare permeated the American section of New Orleans from 1817 through the Civil War," averaging twenty-five performances per season and doubtless rivaling any southern and many northern cities. *Two Gentlemen of Verona* and *Antony and Cleopatra* were first performed in America on the New Orleans stage. As was true throughout the South, *Richard III* was the city's favorite play. New Orleanians liked their Shakespeare pure and spurned inappropriate costumes, scenery, and diction. Yet adaptations and burlesques, so often a mirror of the times, thrived. In an addendum appropriately labeled "Lagniappe," Roppolo reprints part of a spoof showing Shakespeare getting just revenge on some callous New Orleanians. What Roppolo says of New Orleans might be said of many southern cities: "Shakespeare, in a sense, was not only idolized and popularized but localized."

Like New Orleans, antebellum Mobile boasts an impressive Shakespearean repertoire, as Mary Duggar Toulmin's essay demonstrates. Even though that city may have preceded New Orleans in celebrating Mardi Gras, the first Shakespearean production in Mobile follows that of New Orleans by at least three years. Toulmin mines a rich theatrical landscape in Mobile by following the "engagements of the famous" and tracing the fortunes of the impresarios. Within one month during the 1838–39 season, Ellen Tree, Edwin Forrest, and Junius Brutus Booth played Mobile. Of the 1845–1846 season, Toulmin observes that "probably no theater in the U.S. at the time could have gathered a cast of better quality." In 1857 Edwin Booth made his debut in Mobile. Nor did Mobileans forget their own Mrs. Stuart, in whose behalf they assailed an ungrateful theater owner. But Shakespeare undefiled and peerless was rarely found. His plays shared the bill with such lesser forms of entertainment as ventriloquists, dancers, and equestrian actors, the latter sometimes unloosed when a play dragged. Toulmin notes that performances of the plays were also uneven, audiences having to suffer poor acting and even poorer accommodations. Still, Mobile must rank among the leading southern cities for its performance and appreciation of Shakespeare.

Linwood E. Orange chronicles Shakespeare's fortunes in Mississippi, a period extending one hundred and seventy years and beginning with the first Shakespearean performance west of the Alleghenies. After a harrowing beginning in Natchez, where the stage was built in a graveyard and Hamlet did not want for props, Shakespeare flourished in that river town and upriver in Vicksburg, thanks to the star system and shrewd managers. The years 1836 to 1839 were golden ones for Shakespeare in Mississippi, for as Orange points out, 40 percent of all performances ever done in the state occurred then. After 1840 Shakespearean drama declined on the professional stage, and it was left up to college performers to continue a noble tradition. Of the college productions Orange surveys, two notable ones reveal Mississippi's unique appreciation of Shakespeare. "Under the Green Wood Tree," staged at Ole Miss in 1899 and containing excerpts from *As You Like It* and *A Midsummer Night's Dream*, presented Mississippian Stark Young and also inspired Young's first published drama review, reprinted for the first time from the Ole Miss yearbook in Orange's article. The 1976 production of *The Taming of the Shrew* at the University of Southern Mississippi transformed Shakespeare's Padua and Petruchio's Verona into a Mississippi showboat. Shakespeare in Mississippi thus comes full circle.

Waldo F. McNeir's survey of Houston shows us Shakespeare's reception in the westernmost part of the Deep South. Within the "historical evolution of Houston," McNeir exhaustively though jauntily evaluates Shakespeare's reception in the Bayou City. From the very first wild and woolly production in 1839 to the sophisticated dramaturgy of Sidney Berger, the founder of the Houston Shakespeare Festival, McNeir takes readers on an insider's tour of what was gaudy and glorious in Shakespearean productions in Houston. Of special concern to McNeir are the social and architectural settings in which the directors and players found themselves. Perkins Hall, the Opera Houses (Gray's, Pillot's, Sweeney and Coom's), the Alley Theatre, and the campus of Rice University offered theatrical notables a latitude in Shakespearean staging. Those notables having the greatest influence on the city's Shakespearean entertainments— Edwin Booth, Fritz Leiber, Stockton Axson, Margot Jones, and

Nina Vance, "Houston's most famous theatrical impresario"—play their parts movingly in McNeir's sweeping history, capturing both the spirit and the spite of the town.

Part One closes with perhaps the most provocative essay in the volume, Charles B. Lower's study of how antebellum southern audiences received and understood *Othello,* one of the five most popular Shakespearean plays in the South. Lower counters the standard opinion that southern audiences saw the play in racial terms as a warning against miscegenation and preferred their Othellos not pitch black but tawny, following Kean's precedent, or near white. Reexamining the evidence—reviews, prompt books, actors' comments, and parodies of the play—Lower constructs his case for a black Othello as much from what is said as from what is unsaid. Lower contends that southern audiences did not object to Othello's color and, in fact, perceived Othello as a blackamoor, regardless of the makeup actors wore. (Contemporary reviews cited by Roppolo and Orange further support Lower's contention.) Attempts to "launder" the play have denied southern audiences their sophistication, Lower contends, for they saw the same actors and heard the same lines as northern audiences did. Lower states, "Othello was almost never an objectionable figure in antebellum southern playhouses, and playing him as near-white was not only unlikely but pointless." Turning to a recent and prominent production of the play—the Alliance Theatre *Othello* with Paul Winfield in the title role—Lower draws cultural and theatrical parallels between Othellos of the 1850s and Winfield's Moor.

4

While the essays in Part One document the historical importance of Shakespeare in the South, the essays in the second part concentrate primarily on the South's contemporary contribution to Shakespearean productions. These essays focus on the lively and varied performances of Shakespeare at festivals in North Carolina, Alabama, and Texas, and at a recent experimental program in Florida. Shakespeare festivals are worldwide reminders that Shakespeare, always good box office, is subject to the creative energy or fanciful whim of regional interpretation and taste. Sometimes that influence is intensive, as when Shakespeare's plays are transformed to southern locations, thereby providing a commentary on regional themes, history, landscapes, or language. But the festival directors (encouraged by both reviewers and audiences) do not think of themselves as providing only regional theater; their festivals are justifiably moving toward national prominence.

Before evaluating contemporary productions, Larry S. Champion sketches the early history of Shakespeare in the Tar Heel state, finding that "well over two-thirds of Shakespeare's canon is prominently represented on these early stages." This "vigorous Shakespearean tradition" continues today in Asheville and at the Shakespeare Festival at High Point. Two landmark productions Champion describes are the murky 1974 Asheville version of *A Midsummer Night's Dream,* which was more indebted to Jan Kott than to the fairy magic of an Elizabethan Puck, and the 1976 Raleigh *Twelfth Night* that offered the audience a more conventional interpretation of the play. Also "dedicated to Shakespearean production" in Asheville are the Montford Players, a group well received by a racially and culturally diverse audience. It is the High Point Festival, though, that offers the state's "major Shakespeare attraction." Champion studies its history, financial successes, personnel, and its diverse dramatic styles. One of Champion's most acute observations is that a contemporary southern audience in Appalachia can readily see and hear their cultural and linguistic heritage reflected in Shakespeare's plays. In North Carolina, Shakespeare does indeed appeal to a "cross section of the state's pluralistic society."

In her survey of the Alabama Shakespeare Festival, Carol McGinnis Kay notes that, while Anniston is a most unlikely place to find a Shakespeare festival, successful planning has brought well-deserved fame to the director, Martin Platt, and to the town. Kay examines the repertoire, personnel, and thrust stage, and isolates the "hallmarks" of the festival—extravagant costumes, gorgeous scenery, and a remarkable fidelity to the texts of the plays. (Yet even with its conservative view of the text, the festival has cut lines or inserted "gimmicky additions.") Another characteristic of the festival is that it often relocates the original setting of the plays. The 1973 *Much Ado About Nothing* was placed in the antebellum South; the 1976 *Winter's Tale* and the 1978 *Measure for Measure* were staged in nineteenth-century costume; and the 1977 *Love's Labor's Lost,* which Kay hails as "brilliant," was transformed to the south of France circa 1932. Overall, though, Kay finds these transformations not very successful. She does believe, however, that the company did a dazzling job in staging *King Lear* in 1976 and *Romeo and Juliet* in 1980. Her final judgment is that the "company and the director are clearly capable of comprehending the total range of the Shakespeare canon."

Another unlikely place to find professional productions of Shakespeare is Odessa, Texas. Earl L. Dachslager surveys the history of and the Shakespearean repertoire at the Globe of the Great Southwest. Founded in 1966 by Marjorie Morris and under the able directorship of Charles David McCall, the Southwest Globe has successfully produced Shakespeare in a playhouse that copies many of the features of the original Globe. Dachslager's comments on these productions, especially on the *The Taming of the Shrew* done in "a western style," provide valuable information about Shakespearean plays performed on the westernmost boundary of the South.

In the final essay, Stuart E. Omans and Patricia A. Madden detail the events behind two projects that have changed the presentation of Shakespeare in central Florida. The first of these was the formation of Simply Shakespeare, a traveling troupe composed of students primarily from outside the traditional arts and humanities disciplines. These student-actors created original shows that explored for audiences the relationship of Shakespearean themes to their own lives. These shows have received enthusiastic approval from rural audiences who previously turned away at the very mention of Shakespeare. The second project influencing Shakespearean production in central Florida was the establishment in 1979 of the Shakespeare Institute in Orlando. Funded by the National Endowment for the Humanities, the institute stressed active participation in Shakespeare as an eclectic art and produced *A Midsummer Night's Dream,* together with a Renaissance concert, both played to overflow crowds.

As all four of the essays in Part Two prove, the tastes of contemporary southern audiences differ markedly from those of their nineteenth-century counterparts. During the nineteenth century, as we have seen, tragedy was king. Speaking of Richmond, 1819–1838, Aronson summarizes almost all of the antebellum South's reactions: "It is further clear from the repertoire . . . that Shakespeare's comedies were not popular." In contrast, modern audiences, television trained and pragmatically (if not classically) educated, prefer the comedies to the histories or tragedies. It is significant that none of the Roman plays was staged in Anniston and that Odessa audiences were not feted on the more problematic plays of the canon. That Stuart Omans chose the comic favorite *A Midsummer Night's Dream* to snare Floridians into the riches of the Shakespearean forests is also indicative of this preference.

Shakespeare wrote not of an age but for all time; so goes the panegyric composed by Ben Jonson, Shakespeare's rival and admirer. Yet, ironically, the dichotomy between "age" and "all time" frequently dissolves in theater history. The thirteen essays in this collection prove that Shakespeare's universal appeal is often most profoundly determined by a specific age and region. Extending from colonial Virginia to twentieth-century Atlanta and Houston, the performance and reception of Shakespeare in the South is an incalculably rich and diverse area of study. Given such a warm welcome, Shakespeare may perhaps forgive my quoting, out of context, the following lines which so appropriately summarize his reception: "The southern wind / Doth play the trumpet to his purposes" (*1 Henry IV* 5.1.3).

PART I

Histories of Shakespearean Performance
in the South

Shakespeare in Virginia, 1751–1863

Arnold Aronson

Haste to Virginia's plains, my Sons repair,
The Goddess said. Go, confident to find
An audience sensible, polite and kind.[1]

Virginia is the birthplace of American theater. The performance *Ye Beare and Ye Cubb* in Accomac County in 1665, however insignificant as drama, is the first documented theatrical event in English in the New World. The first building for performances in the colonies was erected in Williamsburg sometime between 1716 and 1718. And when the Hallam Company, the first truly professional touring company in America, left England, they sailed for Virginia, opening in Williamsburg in 1752 with *The Merchant of Venice* preceded by the prologue quoted above. It would be fitting if the first performance of Shakespeare in America were in Virginia as well, but that honor must go to New York City, where *Romeo and Juliet* may have been performed as early as 1730 and where *Richard III* was certainly performed in March of 1750.[2] But even though Shakespeare came late to Virginia, Virginia holds the distinction of being the only colony to have influenced Shakespeare. In 1609 ten ships left England for the Jamestown settlement. One of these, the *Sea Venture,* was blown off course in a storm and was wrecked on the Bermuda Islands, where the crew remained for several months until the ship could be repaired and they could continue the journey. Two accounts of the adventure were published in London in 1610, and it is generally assumed that Shakespeare, who knew and was patronized by several supporters of the Virginia settlement, used this as a basis for *The Tempest.*[3] Thus, in a way, Shakespeare's association with Virginia dates back to the founding of the colony.

But beyond that, Shakespeare had only minimal production in Virginia prior to the Revolution. While theater in pre-Revolutionary

21

Virginia was primarily concentrated in Williamsburg, the number of documentable Shakespearean productions there is limited. It is in Richmond, which in 1779 succeeded Williamsburg as the capital (and hence, cultural center), that any study of Shakespeare in Virginia must concentrate. Indeed, while Norfolk, Alexandria, Fredericksburg, Petersburg, Lynchburg, Staunton, and Tappahanock could boast of theaters through at least part of the eighteenth and early nineteenth centuries, the productions were generally tours emanating from Richmond. But, because Richmond held no significance until after the Revolution, and because its population did not equal the more famous cultural centers in the mid-Atlantic region such as Charleston, Baltimore, or even Annapolis (in 1800, for example, Richmond's population was only 5,737), its importance in the development of American theater tends to be ignored. The most concrete example of this neglect can be found in the several sources that cite Junius Brutus Booth's New York debut as his American debut, when, in fact, the great actor debuted in Richmond. However, the West and Bignall Company, which was based there from 1790 to 1807, may have been the finest company in America at that time, and Benjamin Latrobe's theater, designed for Richmond, would have been among the finest in the world—had it been built.[4]

For the study of Shakespeare in antebellum Virginia we may designate three broad periods: beginnings to 1781, when the Revolution ended and Richmond emerged as the capital; 1781 to 1811, when the tragic Richmond Theatre fire effectively ended legitimate theatrical performance in Richmond and elsewhere for some seven years; and from 1819, when a theater reopened in Richmond, to the Civil War.

Pre-Revolutionary Period

Generally during this period the culture of the colonies reflected that of London. This was more true among the more aristocratic residents of Virginia, with their close ties to the Anglican Church, than among the generally Puritan citizens of New England. Although Shakespeare was certainly popular in England, he did not begin to dominate the stage until the 1740s or so. What little theater existed in pre-Revolutionary America tended to reflect the taste for sentimental drama and moral comedy. Shakespeare was, of course, known in America, and the range and proportion of his plays in production in eighteenth-century America was roughly equivalent to that of London. His works could be found in various personal libraries in Virginia, but he was admired primarily for his poetic language and perceived morality. Thomas Jefferson, for instance, inscribed many of Shakespeare's lines in his own manuscript book of quotations as a student at William and Mary College in the 1760s and later, in 1786, visited Stratford-upon-Avon. But the quotations he chose do not indicate a taste for drama; rather, he seems to have selected them because they are observations on such subjects as the value of life, honor, and virtue.[5] Colonists' tolerance of the stage and appreciation of Shakespeare as one of the greatest playwrights, however, may be seen in a verse printed in the *Virginia Gazette* of May 14, 1767. It was a response to criticism of a clergyman who indulged in "Balls and Spectacles."

> Twixt Sophocles and Grand Corneille
> Twixt Shakespeare and De Vego [sic]
> Twixt Moliere's and Menander's style,
> Decide who will, non ego.[6]

But in terms of actual production, Shakespeare was not seen in Virginia until 1751. The theater at Williamsburg apparently presented contemporary eighteenth-century fare, as did the students of William and Mary College who had been incorporating theatricals in their studies since 1702 and who presented Joseph Addison's *Cato* in 1736. On October 21, 1751, a company of players headed by Walter Murray and Thomas Kean opened a brief stay (no more than three weeks) with a production of *Richard III* at a newly built theater in Williamsburg. The Murray-Kean troupe was organized in 1749 and first performed in Philadelphia. It holds the distinction of being the first touring company in America, but it consisted of essentially amateur players of dubious quality. Being unique, however, they met with relative success, and the Williamsburg theater of 1751 was built specifically for their anxiously awaited arrival, there having been no professional entertainment there since late 1745. *Richard*

III, which had also opened their New York season earlier that spring, was far and away the most popular Shakespearean play of the colonial and antebellum periods. Part of its popularity is attributable to the opportunities it provided the lead actor, and part to the fact that it was the play in which the great David Garrick made his London debut in 1741. As with most Shakespearean works of the time, the play was presented not in the original form but as an adaptation to fit both the acting personalities of the period as well as the dictates of neoclassicism and sentimentality. *Richard III* was done in Colley Cibber's version of 1700, which not only shortened the original, but through simplification tended to make Richard even more evil, hence more appropriate to eighteenth-century sensibilities regarding good and evil. It also provided marvelous moments of theatricality. Interestingly, the name Shakespeare was not yet a guaranteed audience-getter, and the Murray-Kean playbill for *Richard III* made no mention of the playwright although it did list Monsieur Denoier as author of the afterpiece.[7]

The company of Lewis Hallam arrived in Virginia in the summer of 1752 and opened an eleven-month stay in Williamsburg on September 15 with *The Merchant of Venice.* The program noted in small type that it was "written by Shakespeare." Hugh Rankin and others believe that this was really Lord Lansdowne's version *The Jew of Venice,* but Charles Shattuck makes a reasonable argument that it was the version as restored by English actor Charles Macklin in 1741.[8] Aside from the popularity of the Macklin restoration, Shattuck notes that Hallam played the role of Launcelot Gobbo, a role omitted from Lansdowne, and that Lorenzo is played by Mr. Adcock "with Songs in Character."[9] The songs were not in the Lansdowne version, and we are left to speculate what these songs might have been. If nothing else, the evidence points to a typical practice of the time: capitalizing on talents of individual members of the company, something Shakespeare himself did. Arguing for the Lansdowne version, Rankin notes that Patrick Malone played Shylock as a farcical figure, which was more typical of the earlier part of the century.[10]

As for specifics of the production itself, we are left primarily with an anecdote that twelve-year-old Lewis Hallam, Jr., playing Portia's servant, "suffered stage fright and broke in tears from the scene."[11] The company was professional, to be sure, but probably more brave than talented or they would not have left London, where they had met with little success. In Williamsburg they expanded and refurbished the crude theater left by Murray and Kean, but nothing definite is known about this building.[12] An advertisement in the *Virginia Gazette* boasted "Scenes, Cloaths, and Decorations are all entirely new, extremely rich, and finished in the highest taste. . . . The Scenes, being painted by the best Hands in London, are excelled by none in Beauty and Elegance, so that the Ladies and Gentlemen may depend upon being entertain'd in as polite a manner as at the Theatres in London."[13] Although this is clearly puffery, Hallam's Company did bring with them theatrical costumes and scenery designed for touring and they were attempting to cater to the desire for English culture. The Hallam repertoire consisted of twenty-four pieces, of which four were Shakespeare's. Aside from *The Merchant of Venice,* there was *Richard III, Hamlet,* and *Othello.*[14] Their repertoire in New York the following summer also included *King Lear* (in the Nahum Tate version), *Romeo and Juliet,* and *Henry IV.*[15] As advertisements and playbills for the Williamsburg season are lacking, it is not inconceivable that one or more of these was also included.

The November 9 performance of *Othello* was attended by the "Emperor of the Cherokee Nation with his Empress" and several warriors, according to the *Virginia Gazette.* During the afterpiece the sight of actors fighting with swords apparently alarmed the empress, who ordered her warriors to halt the action in order to save the actors' lives.[16] The Hallam Company left for New York following their first Williamsburg season—in debt despite their critical success.

Records of specific productions in subsequent years in Williamsburg and elsewhere in Virginia are lacking, but it is safe to assume that touring companies presented their standard fare. The Murray-Kean Company, for instance, continued to tour and is known to have played Petersburg.[17] David Douglass's London Company of

Comedians toured Virginia between October, 1760, and May, 1761. Their repertoire included Cibber's *Richard III* adaptation; *Macbeth* as adapted by William Davenant with "original Musick as set by Purcell; Witches dance, and all the Decorations proper to the play,"[18] *Romeo and Juliet, Hamlet,* and Shakespeare-Lansdowne's *The Jew of Venice, or The Female Lawyer.*

Williamsburg saw no professional theater from 1763 to 1768. Sometime in late 1767, William Verling, who had acted with Douglass, organized the Virginia Company and opened in Norfolk. Their repertoire was apparently similar to Douglass's, whose troupe was by now known as the American Company. In late March, Verling's actors left Norfolk and opened in nearby Williamsburg on March 31, 1768. *The Merchant of Venice* was in the repertoire, and indications are that Verling interpreted Shylock in a sympathetic manner.[19]

Douglass's American Company continued to tour into the 1770s. There is note of a *Hamlet* in Fredericksburg in June, 1771, and the first Williamsburg performance of *King Lear* on November 12, 1771.[20] Douglass's 1772–1773 Philadelphia season included *Hamlet, Richard III, Cymbeline, The Taming of the Shrew, Henry IV, Othello, The Tempest,* and *The Merchant of Venice.*[21] A painting of Nancy Hallam as Imogene (disguised as Fidele) in *Cymbeline* in Annapolis in 1771 shows her in Oriental clothes—a common eighteenth-century practice.[22] Hugh Rankin calculates that in the twenty-four years prior to the Revolution, fourteen of Shakespeare's plays were presented in the colonies in at least 180 documented performances.[23] Since every major company played Virginia repeatedly, it is reasonable to assume that all fourteen of these plays were performed in the Old Dominion.

In general, it may be noted that Virginia presentations of theater at this time followed English practice fairly closely. Plays were preceded by a prologue and followed by an afterpiece. Miscellaneous entertainments and musical interpolations were freely added. While the theaters were crude at best—generally wooden structures, often converted from prior uses—they attempted to provide a "box, pit and gallery" arrangement, and in Williamsburg, at least, there seemed to be an emphasis on the genteel nature of the proceedings.

Post-Revolutionary Period

Richmond became the capital of Virginia in 1779, was burned by Benedict Arnold in 1781, and was rebuilt and incorporated in 1782. There are references at that time to a theater in "a wooden house" behind Rose's brig, and records of 1785 indicate a playhouse "with front and side boxes and a pit."[24] One of the first actions of the city council was to renew the license of theatrical manager Dennis Ryan.[25] Extant records indicate performances by Ryan's company between June and December, 1784. Ryan's company played a season in New York between June and October, 1783, and it is known that the company consisted at that time of seventeen members and performed fifteen plays, including *Richard III* and *Macbeth*.[26] Presumably, the Richmond repertoire was similar.

In October, 1786, a company headed by Lewis Hallam, Jr., and John Henry—the old American Company of Comedians—played at Alexander Quesnay's new Academy. Ostensibly a school, it had a large stagehouse, flyspace, a trapped floor, and a seating capacity of 1,600.[27] The 1786 New York repertoire for this company included *As You Like It, Hamlet,* the inevitable *Richard III, The Tempest, The Merchant of Venice,* and *Catherine and Petruchio* (David Garrick's adaptation of *The Taming of the Shrew*). Only three titles of the Richmond season are known (none being Shakespeare) but again, the New York repertoire must be similar to the Richmond one.

The next year saw the arrival of a company presumably headed by William Verling of the former Virginia Company.[28] The evidence that remains indicates that their fall 1787 season included *Henry IV, The Merchant of Venice,* and *Romeo and Juliet.* Advertisements for the latter mention "In Act 2nd, a Masquerade and Dance. End of the 4th Act, a Funeral Procession and Solemn Dirge. The Vocal Parts by Mrs. Gifford, Mr. Kidd, and Mr. Wells."[29] While not advertised as such, the production presumably was Garrick's adaptation. The theater, formerly Quesnay's Academy, was now known as the New Theatre on Shockoe Hill. From the standpoint of performance history it is worth noting that advertisements indicated that the doors opened at 5:30 with performances commencing at 6:30. Plays were performed on Monday, Wednesday, Friday, and Saturday.

Fire swept Richmond in 1787. Although the theater seems to have survived, there was little theatrical activity for the following two years other than curiosities such as an Eidophusikon and the display of a camel.

The golden age of theater in Richmond commenced in the summer of 1790 with the arrival of a newly formed company, headed by Thomas Wade West and John Bignall, known as the Virginia Company. Once again, records are incomplete and there is no hard evidence of Shakespeare being performed in this first season. Yet by this date the fourteen Shakespearean plays Rankin cites had become standard eighteenth-century fare. Furthermore, John Bignall, the leading actor, was not yet thirty, and it is hard to imagine his passing up the opportunity to play some of Shakespeare's choice heroes.

West and Bignall definitely presented *The Tempest* "as altered by Dryden" in 1791. This was the John Dryden–William Davenant version with music by Henry Purcell. Davenant had added several characters to the play, including Hypolitus, Dorinda (Miranda's sister), Sycorax (Caliban's sister), and Milcha (Ariel's lover). The latter two are not listed in the program.[30] An advertisement for this production, one of the few extant descriptions of American scenography of this period, described an opening scene of incredible spectacle. The addition of spectacle scenes were not uncommon at this time, but this one seems to have been a fairly sophisticated production or the work, at least, of an ambitious producer.

> The opening discovers a troubled Horizon and Tempestuous Sea, where the Usurper's Vessel is tossed a considerable time in sight, and gives signal of an approaching storm, amidst repeated claps of Thunder, Lightning, Hail, Rain &c and being dashed on a Chain of Rocks (which both sides of the stage strikingly represent) and at the same instant, a dreadful shower of fire, pouring from the distempered Elements, the crew gives signals of distress, the Waves and Winds rise to an affecting degree, and the vessel sinks in full view of the audience. The Scene altogether forming a most awful, but perfect picture of
> A SHIPWRECK.
> This hurricane (which is supposed to be raised by Magic) ceases, a delightful prospect of the Enchanted Island appears, also of the Enchanters Dwelling. Here the business of the play commences; and through the

course of it (which abounds with Poetic Beauties) is represented the strange being CALIBAN, a Monster of the Isle, dressed from Nature, and agreeable to the Authors fancy of that wonderful and truly original character.[31]

It must be remembered that the scene would be depicted primarily with wing and drop scenery and that the sea undoubtedly was created by a series of moving ground rows. Nonetheless, such a scene would certainly delight the audience enormously.

In 1792, as an afterpiece to Frederick Reynolds's *The Sorrows of Werter*, West and Bingall presented *Shakespeare's Jubilee* (or *Shakespeare's Garland*), an allegorical spectacle originally created by David Garrick with music by Charles Dibdin. The Garrick production had run for ninety nights at Drury Lane in London. If the Richmond performance was similar to the original, it opened with comic scenes and characters at Stratford and concluded with a procession of scenes and characters from twenty of Shakespeare's plays. If the Virginia Company's performance was indeed like Garrick's, the audience would seem to have been familiar with at least six more of Shakespeare's plays than they could have ever witnessed in performance. The procession also included the comic and tragic muses on triumphal cars drawn by appropriate attendants and, finally, a figure of Shakespeare with attendants.[32]

The next record of Shakespeare in Richmond is a 1795 New Year's Eve performance of *Romeo and Juliet* "as altered by Garrick." The program described it thus:

in Act First, A Grand Masquerade A la mode Paris, under the direction of Mons. Francisquy. In course of which the minuet Delacour, by Mons. Francisquy and Madame Placide. Un Pas Seul in Character of A Shepherd, by Master Duport. And The Masquerade will conclude with the favorite Alemande by Mons. Francisquy, Madame Placide, and Madame Val. . . .

. . . [In Act Four] a Solemn Dirge and Funeral Procession of Juliet to the Monument of the Capulets, to be conducted by Mons. Placide. . . .

In the Course of the evening, for the first time here, A Triple Hornpipe and Scotch Reel, by Madame Placide, Mons. Francisquy, and Master Duport.[33]

Clearly, the emphasis was on spectacle, and the intrusion of music, song, dance, and theatricality was seen as a positive attribute. In this, the West and Bignall Company was typical of companies throughout America and England.

Romeo and Juliet was enormously popular among eighteenth-century audiences, and the masquerade and funeral procession were standard features that allowed companies to display their theatrical skills. The play was repeated on December 28, 1796. Once again the advertisement emphasized the spectacle, including, of course, "a Grand Masquerade" in the first act, and the fifth-act funeral procession "with a Solemn dirge." This procession is described in detail: "Six boys bearing lighted torches, two banners, Six Mourners, Six Girls, bearing Garlands of Flowers, two Banners, vocal parts of the Dirge, two Banners, Friar Lawrence, The Bier, Capulet and Lady Capulet, Chief Mourners." Altogether, a minimum of thirty-five performers! Of incidental note is that Mr. Prigmore, whose benefit this performance was, "provided stoves to warm the house for that night."[34] Evidently the theater was unheated. One wonders if it was the stoves, which seem to have been kept, that caused the theater to burn on January 30, 1798.

About twenty-five miles southeast of Richmond was the small town of Petersburg, the center of the tobacco trade at the time. By the late 1790s the town had two theaters and the Virginia Company regularly played there.[35] There is a record of *Macbeth* being performed there on February 28, 1797, as a benefit for Luke Robins, the company scene painter.[36] There is no record of *Macbeth* in Richmond during this or subsequent seasons, although that is no proof that it was not presented there. The Petersburg *Macbeth* may have been a new production. The advertisement, at any rate, proclaimed that the scenery was "entirely new for this occasion." It went on to say that the production included "The Cauldron and Witches Dance" and "Banquet in celebration of Macbeth's succession to the throne"—in other words, spectacle.[37]

The Virginia Company was back in Petersburg in the fall of 1797, opening the season on October 27 with *Hamlet*, together with a farce entitled *The Sultan; or A Peep Into the Seraglio*. While theater was apparently thriving in Petersburg and Norfolk, Richmond, despite its position as capital, did not develop rapidly as a theater town. The

1797–1798 season there was brief, and Susanne Sherman notes that the company spent little money on advertising.[38] On November 8, 1797, the company presented "Shakespeare's celebrated comedy of *As You Like It; or Love in a Forest* . . . to which will be added the Musical Farce of *The Farmer; or The World's Ups and Downs.*"[39] Back in Petersburg in the autumn of 1798, their repertoire included *The Tempest* (September 14), in which Ariel, as was the custom, descended in a cloud, and *Richard III* (October 15).[40]

Thomas Wade West died in 1799. By that date the company is known to have performed *The Tempest, Romeo and Juliet, Richard III, As You Like It, Macbeth, Hamlet,* and *The Merry Wives of Windsor.*

By 1791 West and Bignall had established a Richmond-Fredericksburg circuit. Norfolk was added in 1795, Petersburg in 1796, and Alexandria in 1797.

Following the death of West there was a two-year hiatus. Legitimate theatrical activity resumed in 1802 in a temporary theater. No production of Shakespeare is documented, however, until a February 27, 1804, presentation of *Hamlet.* A new theater was opened in 1806 with a seating capacity of 650—less than half that of the previous theater, indicating, perhaps, that Richmond could not support a larger theater (although West and Bignall seem not to have suffered financially at any time). The theater regulations indicate a six o'clock performance time and suggest something of the audience at the time: Cigars were relegated to the "box-lobby." Furthermore, "the music as well as the business of the stage being selected for the evening, it is presumed no particular tunes will be called for during the performance."[41] The practice of interrupting a show for "requests" was not unknown even in New York at this time, and Richmond was clearly no exception. Interestingly, "persons of color" were apparently admitted to the gallery. In the next several seasons until the fire, Shakespeare was represented by *Romeo and Juliet, Hamlet, Macbeth, Othello, Richard III, King Lear* "and his Three Daughters" (the Nahum Tate version with the happy ending and the deletion of the Fool), *Catherine and Petruchio* (as an afterpiece), *The Merchant of Venice,* and *Henry IV.*

Among the more significant events of this period were the appearances of Thomas Abthorpe Cooper. Cooper, a British actor of the Kemble school who came to Philadelphia in 1796, had become the first great star of the American stage. Not only did he help establish the acting style of future American actors—notably Edwin Forrest—but he was largely responsible for the creation of the so-called star system in America in which leading actors would tour and act with resident stock companies. He first performed in Richmond on April 5, 1806, as Hamlet with the West and Bignall troupe. "Crito," a local writer, noted that Hamlet was, "Next to Rolla [in *Pizzaro; or the Death of Rolla*], the favorite and perhaps the greatest character played by Cooper."[42] The critic wrote at length of Cooper's captivating stage presence as well as his naturalness onstage, noting that he never spoke directly to the audience and used pauses effectively. "But it was not Cooper the player and the stranger, who appeared before you, with an eye expressive of curiosity and the blush of anxiety upon his check. It was Hamlet of Denmark. . . . "[43]

Cooper was a great success and returned for six nights in August to perform Macbeth, Othello, Hamlet, and Richard. He was evidently held over, as his Othello was repeated on September 6. The *Richmond Enquirer* of August 29 wrote of Cooper's *Othello*. Noting that Cooper died on the line "and smote him thus" (5.2.356) three lines before Shakespeare has Othello die, the critic wrote: "The dying scene of Mr. Cooper was worthy of the greatness in which he had lived. The *manner* of his death was an evident improvement upon Shakespeare's plan . . . not like Shakespeare protracting his existence, until he had time to make another speech, abounding in a most miserable conceit. . . . "[44] Cooper returned as Othello in June of 1807.

In 1809 Alexandre Placide and J. W. Green took over management of the Richmond theater. Their production of *Macbeth* was the Davenant version with music by Lock. September 22, 1810, saw a production of *King Lear* with William Twaits in the title role. A puff piece in the *Richmond Patriot* suggested that if the play alone were not inducement enough, "the astonishing versatility of talents in the inimitable Twaits" was worth a trip to the theater. "This favorite actor, on that evening plays Lear in the tragedy, and those who have already admired the various and unrivalled excellence of his comic powers will be delighted to find that he is equally qualified for the impassioned scenes of tragedy; equally at home in the sock and buskin."[45]

Thomas Caulfield, a leading member of the company, provided some glimpses of English Shakespearean actors when, on November 14, 1810, he provided a prelude to *The Manager in Distress* consisting of "Imitations of . . . London Performers" including "Mr. Kemble in *Hamlet*," "Mr. Palmer in *Henry 8th*," and "Mr. Aichin in *Henry 8th*."[46] One wonders how familiar Richmond audiences were with those actors or, for that matter, some of the other plays in the prelude.

Another curiosity—rather a mystery—is provided on September 30, 1811, when the role of Othello was essayed by "a gentleman, being his first appearance on any stage." This gentleman apparently appeared in two other non-Shakespearean roles that season. His identity and the reason for his inclusion in the company remain unknown. It is also of some interest that between 1804 and 1806 David Poe performed at Richmond and in 1810 and 1811 Mrs. Poe (Elizabeth Arnold Hopkins) performed. These are, of course, the parents of Edgar Allen Poe, and Martin Shockley speculates that the young Edgar may have appeared on the stage at least once.[47]

On Thursday, December 26, 1811, the theater presented *The Father; or the Family Feud* based on a play by Diderot and a pantomime entitled *Raymond and Agnes; or the Bleeding Nun*. "The curtain rose on the 2d Act of the Pantomime—the orchestra was in full chorus; and Mr. West came on to open the scene—when sparks of fire began to fall on the back part of the stage, and Mr. Robertson came out in unutterable distress, waved his hand to the ceiling, and uttered those appalling words—'The house is on fire.' "[48] Seventy-one people including Governor George William Smith died. The event put a damper, to say the least, on theatrical activity in the region. Clergymen saw the fire as a sign and vigorously renewed their attacks upon the stage; the War of 1812 ended what was left of theatrical presentation.

With the end of this era, Virginians were known to have seen eleven of Shakespeare's plays and possibly thirteen.[49]

New Richmond Theatre

In January, 1819, a touring company under the management of James M. Caldwell played in Richmond for the first time since the fire. It must have been successful, for within six months a new theater, the Richmond Theatre, was erected.

Martin Shockley has chronicled the performances at this theater from 1817 to 1838, when the building was extensively renovated and renamed the Marshall Theatre. During this period playwright George Colman the younger was represented by sixteen plays presented 104 times, while Shakespeare was represented by fourteen plays presented 106 times.[50] Not surprisingly, *Richard III* headed the list, followed, in order of popularity, by *Hamlet, Othello, Macbeth, The Merchant of Venice, Romeo and Juliet, King Lear*. The other productions include *Catherine and Petruchio, or The Taming of the Shrew, Henry IV, Julius Caesar, King John, The Merry Wives of Windsor, Much Ado About Nothing*, and *As You Like It*.[51] Some idea of the theatrical tastes of the time may be garnered from this critique of *King Lear* (seen in the Nahum Tate version) in the *Richmond Compiler* of June 13, 1821. "The drama of Lear is better fitted for the closet than the stage. There is not that scope of high wrought passion about Lear (his old age forbids it), which is calculated to give full play to the genius of the actor. Lear, for instance, is decidedly inferior to Richard or to Othello."[52] It is further clear from the repertoire of these nineteen years that Shakespeare's comedies were not popular. Audiences seemed to expect violent passion and lively action in their drama.

The great theatrical event of antebellum Richmond, though, is the American premiere of Junius Brutus Booth on July 6, 1821, as, of course, Richard III. Booth had left London because of a love affair. Although married and the father of a two-year-old son, he fell in love with a Covent Garden flower girl, Mary Ann Holmes, and left with her for America. He sailed for Norfolk rather than New York in order to avoid acquaintances and possible difficulties because of his

marriage. Booth had been popular in London, considered by some
nearly equal to the great Edmund Kean, so his success in America
was guaranteed. He played until July 20 in Richmond and then went
to neighboring Petersburg. Having missed the Petersburg coach,
Booth walked the twenty-five miles.[53] According to anecdote,
Booth saved his energy through the first three acts of his *Richard III*
premiere, causing managers and audiences to doubt that this was
indeed Junius Brutus Booth. In the fourth act he came alive, leaving
everyone enthralled.[54] Booth's repertoire at the time also included
King Lear.

In July, 1821, Richmond was also treated to a Shakespearean
pastiche, a "Grande Dramatic Olio, from Shakespeare, in five
parts."[55] Somewhat as the Kabuki of Japan or the Peking Opera
strings together several favorite scenes from many plays, Frederick
Brown acted one act each from *Hamlet, Macbeth, The Merchant of
Venice,* and *Coriolanus*.

During this period Richmond was visited by such notable stars as
Henry J. Finn, Charles Kean, Mrs. Hill, Clara Fisher, Thomas
Cooper, William Augustus Conway, and Edwin Forrest. But these
were times of economic depression and legitimate theater did not
fare well. Indicative of its difficulties was the 1831 appearance by
Forrest who, despite his fame, was outdrawn by Madame de Jick, a
trained elephant. The Richmond Theatre was marked by a series of
failed managements and periods of inactivity—no performances
1824–1827, a total of eight performances between 1832 and 1835, and
sporadic performances at all other times.[56] The theater was renovated in 1838 and renamed after Chief Justice John Marshall.

Had there been any doubt about the status of Shakespeare by this
time, the Marshall Theatre laid that to rest. The new drop curtain for
the theater, painted by Signor Guidicini of the Italian Opera House
and Signor Monechesi, a Florentine artist, depicted "The Triumph
of Shakespeare."[57] The scene was described by Richmond sculptor
E. V. Valentine:

> The size of the drop curtain is thirty one by twenty seven feet. The design
> as follows: viz., a monumental facade of sculptural marble (the whole
> width of the picture) rests upon the ground. The monument projects in

the center and contains an octagon opening, while the sides present the portico of a square aperture. The friezes of the monument represent in alto the various emblems of dramatic art, the center of which is a medal-lion head of Minerva. Through the central opening is seen the figure of the Bard of Avon rising triumphantly above the storm of fanaticism. On the right (as viewed) is seen a pyramid against which the lightning falls like the shaftes of malice, harmless. Beneath the central frieze is the word SHAKESPEARE. In the foreground (on the right) between the Bard and the Pryamid, is the figure of Fame, pointing to each object, while that of history is recording the "Never-dying Truth," "We ne'er shall look upon his like again."

To the left of the center are the figures of youthful tragedy and comedy, as having ended a disputation upon the relative merits of the poet. Ad-joining the above group is a bronze candelabra containing the perpetual flame of intellect, the incense of which is wafted to the author of *Hamlet.* To the extreme left, partly hidden by the surrounding drapery is seen the marble figure of the Medician Venue, the eye of the poet being directed to the statue, allegorically, of his copying nature in her truth and beauty. On the drapery over the tableau are the enwreathed names of the triple Grecian poets, representing their mantles falling upon Shakespeare.[58]

Thus, by 1838 Shakespeare was viewed by the owners of the Mar-shall Theatre as the greatest playwright of all time, and Valentine, at least, considered *Hamlet* his most noteworthy play.

The extensive renovations of the theater brought a burst of activ-ity to Richmond's theatrical life, but the enthusiasm soon waned. Not until 1845 could Richmond again sustain regular dramatic fare. But in the fifteen years prior to the Civil War, thanks to such man-agers as William Rufus Blake, John Sefton, and George Kunkel, the city experienced a new golden age of theater. During the 1830s and 1840s the American theater was undergoing a significant transition. The local touring troupes such as the Virginia Company were disap-pearing, to be replaced by stock companies visited by touring stars. The English stars had been replaced, by and large, by well-received, home-grown actors. Among the great or up-and-coming performers of the period were Edwin Forrest, Charlotte Cushman, Barry Sulli-van, Edwin and John Wilkes Booth, Joseph Jefferson, James Hack-ett, and J. W. Wallack, all of whom played Richmond several times, as did such English stars as Charles and Ellen Kean and William Charles Macready. Shakespeare, of course, made up a large portion of the repertoire of these actors—the plays provided good vehicles for the performers and were recognizable to the audience (and known to the supporting actors of the stock company). The Shakespearean repertoire, however, continued to be composed of the same dozen or so plays performed since the earliest days of theater in the colony: mostly tragedies and histories with heroic or histrionic roles for the lead actor.

The 1848–1849 season of the Marshall Theatre provides a good example. Macready played from December 18 to December 22, and his repertoire for the five nights consisted of *Macbeth, Richelieu, Hamlet, Werner,* and *The Merchant of Venice.* He played a brief return engagement after the new year and repeated the role of Shylock on January 3. The rest of the Shakespeare for that season was as follows:

December 27: *Romeo and Juliet*

February 5: *Macbeth* with Mr. and Mrs. James Wallack

February 7: *Richard III* with James Wallack

February 28: *Henry IV* with James Hackett

March 1: *The Merry Wives of Windsor* with James Hackett

April 19 and 20: *Hamlet, Travestie.*

The final piece is identified merely as "interlude dancing by Mlle. Lovarney and Herr Stoepel."[59] What relation it might have had to Shakespeare is open to conjecture. Such a season is typical throughout the 1850s.

From the time of his American premiere, Junius Brutus Booth continued his association with Richmond. His notorious alcoholism, however, necessitated at least one canceled performance in the city. Booth was scheduled to perform the ever-popular *Richard III* on April 1, 1849, but the managers' notes for that evening read, "Mr. Booth was *Drunk* AND DID NOT APPEAR." The plays *Advice Gratis* and *People's Lawyer* were presented instead. An announcement appeared in the newspaper on April 2: "The management respectfully inform the public of Richmond they cannot allow MR. BOOTH to appear again this season after the disappointment he caused last evening to a brilliant audience. Under these circumstances they have fortunately effected a re-engagement of the Popular Comedian, Mr. C. Burke." Booth, of course, did return in subsequent seasons and a year later, on April 21, 1851, his son Edwin made his Richmond debut as a supporting actor to his father's Lear. The performance was repeated on April 25 and 26.[60] Edwin would return to the Marshall as a leading actor in 1856.

Other performers during this period performed Shakespeare in the city. Mr. Hield performed *Romeo and Juliet* in January, 1850, and Wilmarth Waller performed six nights of Shakespearean fare October 15–20, 1851. But aside from the Booths, the most notable performances were undoubtedly those of America's first great actress, Charlotte Cushman, who made her Richmond debut in January, 1852. During a ten-day stay she performed four Shakespearean roles: Rosalind from *As You Like It* (January 20), Lady Macbeth (January 21 and 27), Romeo (January 28), and Katherine from *Henry VIII* (January 30).[61] The latter was one of her most famous roles. She returned in May, 1858, and recreated the roles of Katherine and Lady Macbeth. Her fame commanded increased ticket prices ($1 for a reserved seat).[62] Interestingly, at least one Richmond critic was not overwhelmed by her acting, noting that her 1858 season showed improvement but was still peculiar. "It is useless at this late date to criticize Miss C.'s acting. She has reached the top round of the ladder where criticism will neither benefit nor injure her. Since her last visit to this city she has improved in personal appearance and something in her acting, if a little more smoothness of delivery may be considered an improvement when applied to her peculiar style."[63] She concluded her 1858 season in Richmond with a play entitled *Honeymoon,* followed by the fourth act of *Henry VIII* as an afterpiece.

Under the management of George Kunkel from 1856 to 1861, the Marshall, according to records, saw at least six performances of *Hamlet* and seven of *Macbeth,* among others.[64] But the careers of the younger Booths are of the greatest interest during this time. Most of John Wilkes Booth's career, in fact, was in Richmond.

When Edwin returned to Richmond in November, 1856, it was as a leading actor. Between November 24 and December 6 he played twelve roles, beginning with Richard III and including Romeo, Iago, Lear, and Shylock.[65] He was twenty-three at the time! His youth

Theater bill for *Richard III* with Charles K. Mason at the Marshall Theatre
in Richmond, November 2, 1850
Courtesy Valentine Museum, Richmond

was a disadvantage, at least in the eyes of the reviewers, who felt that more training and maturity would help this otherwise promising performer.

> On Thurs. evening Mr. Booth appeared as "honest Iago," and evinced a right proper conception of the villainous "Ancient," but not withstanding the imputed youth of the character—"four times seven years"—the adolescent appearance of the actor militated against the efficiency of his performance, or rather, we should say alloyed the gratification which it imparted. Mr. Booth is quite a young man, and displays talents not usually developed in one of his years. His juvenility, comparatively speaking, is however, so strikingly apparent, that those who have been accustomed to believe that years of assiduous study and experience constitute the passports to histrionic eminence, are mentally exercised as to the propriety of recognizing in him a graduate of the profession. The idea presses itself upon them that Mr. Booth has received his diploma too soon. For obvious reasons, no one willingly employs a very young physician or lawyer, whether their pretensions to professional skill be well sustained or not. And it is a similar feeling of distrust and reserve which Mr. Booth will have to face and overcome before he successfully establishes his claim to the position where he has been prematurely placed by his over-partial friends, and partly by the dictates of an honest ambition.[66]

Despite this qualified response, Richmond and Shakespeare played a significant role in Edwin Booth's personal life during this appearance. The stage manager of the Marshall at this time was a still-unknown Joseph Jefferson whose ward, Mary Devlin, was the leading lady of the company. Devlin played Juliet to Booth's Romeo—the two were married four years later.

John Wilkes Booth achieved a degree of popularity and recognition for the first time in Richmond. Trying to avoid the shadow of his father and his already successful brother Edwin, Booth was acting in Richmond in 1858 under the name John Wilkes. On October 1, 1858, he used the name Booth for the first time, while playing Horatio to Edwin Booth's Hamlet. At the conclusion Edwin supposedly brought him down to the footlights for the audience's acclaim. Edwin wrote to his father after this performance, "I don't think he will startle the world . . . but he is improving fast, and looks beautiful on the platform."[67] Despite his popularity with Richmonders, John Wilkes Booth was never more than a utility player for the Marshall

Company. As late as February, 1859, for instance, he is listed as Paris to Maggie Mitchell's Romeo in a performance of *Romeo and Juliet*.[68] And whatever his success in Richmond, he found virtually no support in the North.

Edwin Booth's two seasons in 1858 (February 23–March 6 and September 27–October 15) brought a markedly different response from the Richmond critics than two years earlier. His roles this time included Richard III, Hamlet, Lear, Othello, Petruchio, Macbeth, Romeo, Shylock, Henry V, and Benedick.[69] Edwin was favorably compared to his father, and the reviewer for the *Whig* said that his Lear was "one of the most impressive we have ever seen on the stage."[70] (And this of a twenty-five year old!) Edwin Booth returned once more to the Marshall in April and May, 1859, giving ten performances including Lear, Macbeth, Richard III, Hamlet, and Othello.[71]

Aside from providing Edwin Booth his wife, Richmond theater was unremarkable in the years before the war. As a major southern city it was a regular stop on the tour circuit and was visited by nearly every major and minor actor in America at the time. Its repertoire was thus the same as that of most other theatrical cities at the time. No longer an innovator, it was a receiver of theatrical practice. Shakespeare continued to be the most popular playwright, but less than half the canon was represented. The tragic-heroic roles, the great romantic acting parts, continued to dominate. Only *King John* and *Henry V* seem to have been added to the Richmond repertoire at this time.[72]

With the onset of the war, the type and quality of theater in Richmond changed. There were, of course, those who felt that such frivolous activity in wartime was immoral, and there were others who felt that the development of a Confederate culture and literature was as important as any political aspect of the fighting. Most people, however, were simply interested in entertainment as a means of escape from the pressures of war, and theater in Richmond, the capital of the Confederacy, flourished despite a predictable decline in quality. With the outbreak of the war, most of the better actors fled north, and stars from the large northern cities, of course, were unable to tour. John Hill Hewlitt became manager of the Marshall and succeeded in collecting, in his own words, "enough of *fag-ends* of dismantled companies to open the theatre with a passable exhibition of novelty, if not talent."[73] A large part of the repertoire was now devoted to newly written patriotic plays.

On New Year's Day, 1862, the theater burned. For the next year or so theater was provided at Franklin Hall as The Richmond Varieties, but Hewlitt soon left. Elizabeth Magill undertook to rebuild the theater, which reopened February 9, 1863, with great fanfare. The choice of *As You Like It* as the opening bill suggests the importance of Shakespeare and his use as a stamp of respectability. The choice of a comedy, however, probably reflected the desire to avoid the solemn tone of a tragedy and the possible political implications, and may also have reflected a lack of suitable talent for the heroic roles. Ida Vernon and D'Orsey Ogden played the lead roles in this production. While Vernon was probably the best actress in the Confederacy, Ogden had been described by Hewlitt as "a fawning sycophant, with just enough brains to know how to fascinate a frail woman and keep himself from the clutches of the conscript officer."[74]

The enthusiasm for the event was great, but the production was found wanting by otherwise sympathetic critics. The *Examiner* noted that "the present company is probably the best that the troubled times permit, it is useless to look critically at its merits. . . . The play was, however, the least attraction of the spectacle which was the new building itself."[75] The *Illustrated News* said simply, "*As You Like It* was not as we like it."[76] Despite this, the merits of Shakespeare were never doubted—he had become synonymous with culture. As the *Examiner* concluded, "Listening to the poetry of Shakespeare is certainly better amusement than bluff, poker, and rot-gut whiskey."[77]

NOTES

1. Prologue to the first production of *The Merchant of Venice* by the Hallam Company in Williamsburg. Quoted in Barnard Hewitt, *Theatre, U.S.A., 1668 to 1957* (New York: McGraw-Hill, 1959), p. 14.

2. An advertisement of March, 1730, announced that Joachimus Bertrand, a physician, was going to play the Apothecary in *Romeo and Juliet*. There is no evidence of this performance's occuring and the ad may have been a joke. See Charles H. Shattuck, *Shakespeare on the American Stage from the Hallams to Edwin Booth* (Washington, D.C.: Folger Shakespeare Library, 1976).

3. James H. Bailey, "Shakespeare and the Founders of Virginia," *Virginia Cavalcade* 1 (Winter, 1951):9–10.

4. See Brooks McNamara, *The American Playhouse in the Eighteenth Century* (Cambridge: Harvard University Press, 1969), pp. 142–54.

5. Esther Cloudman Dunn, *Shakespeare in America* (New York: Macmillan Company, 1939), pp. 65, 28–33, 95–97.

6. Quoted in ibid., p. 47.

7. Ibid., p. 73.

8. Hugh F. Rankin, *The Theatre in Colonial America* (Chapel Hill: University of North Carolina Press, 1965), p. 54; Shattuck, p. 9.

9. Program reproduced in Hewitt, p. 13.

10. Rankin, p. 55.

11. William Dunlap quoted in Dunn, p. 74.

12. See McNamara, pp. 31–42.

13. Arthur Hornblow, *A History of the Theatre in America*, 2 vols. (Philadelphia: Lippincott, 1919), 1:80.

14. Hewitt, p. 9.

15. See George C. D. Odell, *Annals of the New York Stage*, 15 vols. (New York: Columbia University Press, 1927–49), 1:62ff.

16. Rankin, p. 57; Hornblow (1:87) places the incident in Act 2 of *Othello*.

17. Edward A. Wyatt, "Three Petersburg Theatres," *William and Mary College Quarterly Historical Magazine* 21 (April, 1941):84.

18. Quoted in Rankin, p. 83.

19. Ibid., p. 144.

20. Ibid., p. 164.

21. Montrose J. Moses, *The American Dramatist* (Boston: Little, Brown, 1925; Rept. ed., New York: Benjamin Blom, 1964), p. 31.

22. Reproduced in Shattuck, frontispiece. The painting can be seen at Colonial Williamsburg.

23. Rankin, p. 191.

24. Martin Staples Shockley, "The Richmond Theatre 1780–1790," *Virginia Magazine of History and Biography* 60 (July, 1952):434; see also McNamara, p. 73.

25. Shockley, p. 434.

26. Odell, 1:226–28.

27. McNamara, p. 79.

28. Rankin, p. 200; Shockley, *The Richmond Stage, 1784–1812* (Charlottesville: University Press of Virginia, 1977), p. 21.

29. Shockley, *The Richmond Stage, 1784–1812*, p. 73.

30. Ibid., p. 54.

31. *Virginia Gazette, and General Advertiser*, Dec. 16, 1981, quoted in Susanne K. Sherman, "Post-Revolutionary Theatre in Virginia" (M.A. thesis, College of William and Mary, 1950).

32. Odell, 1:423.

33. Shockley, *The Richmond Stage, 1784–1812*, pp. 111–12.

34. Ibid., pp. 126–27.

35. Sherman, pp. 187ff.

36. *Virginia Gazette, and Petersburg Intelligencer*, Jan. 24, 1797, cited in Sherman, p. 189.

37. Ibid., pp. 189–90.

38. Ibid., pp. 195–96.

39. *The Virginia Gazette, and General Advertiser*, Nov. 8, 1797, quoted in Shockley, *The Richmond Stage, 1784–1812*, p. 134.

40. Sherman, p. 213.

41. Ibid., p. 217.

42. Quoted in Shockley, *The Richmond Stage, 1784–1812*, p. 226.

43. Ibid.

44. Quoted in ibid., p. 239.

45. Quoted in ibid., p. 319.

46. Ibid., p. 327.

47. Ibid., pp. 335, 340.

48. Thomas Ritchie in the *Enquirer*, quoted in ibid., p. 360.

49. The known plays include: *Richard III, Hamlet, Othello, Macbeth, King Lear, The Merchant of Venice, Romeo and Juliet, Henry IV, Catherine and Petruchio (The Taming of the Shrew), The Tempest, As You Like It*, and *The Merry Wives of Windsor*. Possible titles include *Cymbeline* and at least an excerpt of *Henry VIII*.

50. Shockley, "Shakespeare's Plays in the Richmond Theatre, 1819–1838," *Shakespeare Association Bulletin* 15 (Apr., 1940):88.

51. Ibid., p. 93.

52. Ibid., p. 91.

53. Wyatt, p. 85.

54. Eleanor Ruggles, *Prince of Players, Edwin Booth* (New York: W. W. Norton, 1953), pp. 11–12; Stanley Kimmel, *The Mad Booths of Maryland* (Indianapolis: Bobbs-Merrill, 1940), p. 32.

55. Shockley, "Shakespeare's Plays in the Richmond Theatre," p. 90.

56. James H. Dorman, Jr., *Theatre in the Ante Bellum South* (Chapel Hill: University of North Carolian Press, 1967), pp. 143–49.

57. *Richmond Enquirer*, Nov. 14, 1838.

58. Notes of E. V. Valentine in the Valentine Museum Theatre Collection (VMTC), Richmond.

59. Valentine Museum Scrapbook, VMTC.

60. Ibid.

61. Ibid.

62. *Richmond Dispatch*, May 17, 1858.

63. Ibid., May 18, 1858.

64. Nov. 17, 1856: *Hamlet* with J. W. Wallack, Jr.; Nov. 21, 1856: *Macbeth* with Wallack; Jan. 17, 1857: *Macbeth* with Joseph Proctor; May 14, 1857: *Hamlet* with Edwin Forrest; Sept. 16, 1857: *Macbeth* with J. H. Taylor; Oct. 2, 1858: *Macbeth* with Edwin Booth; Oct. 5, 1858: *Hamlet* with Booth; Oct. 6, 1858: *Macbeth* with Booth; Dec. 10, 1858: *Macbeth* with J. W. Wallack, Sr.; Jan. 18, 1859: *Hamlet* with J. A. Neafie; Mar. 15, 1859: *Hamlet* with James E. Murdock; Sept. 16, 1859: *Macbeth* with Wilmarth Waller; Jan. 18, 1861: *Hamlet* with Waller (from files of VMTC).

65. Charles F. Fuller, Jr., "Edwin and John Wilkes Booth, Actors at the Old Marshall Theatre in Richmond," *Virginia Magazine of History and Biography* 79 (Oct., 1971):478n.

66. *Richmond Whig*, Nov. 29, 1856, quoted in Fuller, pp. 478–79.

67. Kimmel, pp. 152–53.

68. Fuller, p. 481.

69. Fuller, p. 479. Stanley Kimmel states that the Oct. 11, 1858, performance of *Henry V* was the American premiere (p. 140). While this is not true, the play had been little performed and this was the Richmond premiere. *Much Ado,* with which Booth ended the fall season, had also been little done in Richmond.

70. *Richmond Whig,* Oct. 15, 1858.

71. Fuller, p. 480.

72. VMTC.

73. Quoted in R. B. Harwell, "The Richmond Stage," *Civil War History* I (Sept., 1955): 295.

74. Ibid., p. 298.

75. *Richmond Examiner,* Feb. 10, 1863, quoted in the *Richmond News-Leader,* Feb. 10, 1953.

76. *The Illustrated News,* quoted in the *Richmond News-Leader,* Feb. 10, 1953.

77. Quoted in Harwell, p. 301. I would like to thank the University of Virginia for assistance in preparing my essay.

Shakespeare in Maryland, 1752–1860

Christopher J. Thaiss

Shakespeare in Annapolis, 1752–1782

Perhaps they felt that their playhouse was too mean for Shakespeare; at any rate, Thomas Kean and Walter Murray did not stage *Richard III*, their first Shakespearean offering in Annapolis, until their "New Theatre" had been refurbished—almost six months into their Maryland season. "The theatre is entirely lined throughout for the reception of Ladies and Gentlemen," read the ad in the *Maryland Gazette* for December 7, 1752, in likely reference to the plastering or planking of the log warehouse turned temporary playhouse, "and they have also raised a Porch at the door to keep out the inclemency of the weather."[1] Unfortunately, neither the lining nor the porch nor two new players, Mr. Wynell and Mr. Herbert as Gloster and Richmond, could save the Murray-Kean venture from collapse after two performances of *Richard III* on December 11 and 16.

Annapolis thus bears the distinction of having witnessed the final attempts of the American colonies' first strolling theatrical troupe. For more than three years, Murray and Kean, whose origins are unknown, brought Shakespeare (the eighteenth-century versions) and the more contemporary English playwrights into the fledgling ports and market towns from Philadelphia and New York south as far as Williamsburg. Though our poverty of knowledge about the troupe bespeaks their lack of funds for playbills or advertisements, and though the scanty public record proclaims their incompetence, these players did nurture the colonists' desire for drama and did give America its first performances of Shakespeare—though *Richard III*, in Colley Cibber's version, seems to have been the only Shakespeare they tried.[2]

The Annapolis to which the players came in 1752 has been called "the most cultivated and dissipated city of the American planta-tions."[3] As Maryland's capital and principal port, Annapolis was the colony's most populous city. Planters, lawyers, petitioners, their families and servants, thronged to Annapolis for the legislative terms in spring and fall, this twice-yearly influx creating social sea-sons with such entertainments as races and balls. But even by 1752 the holiday population was never more than a few thousand, and so, although Annapolis culture desired plays, lack of size and presence of other diversions made the city unable to support for any length of time either a theatrical troupe or a worthy playhouse. The same may be said with even more certainty of Chestertown and Upper Marl-borough, the other Maryland towns to which Murray and Kean brought their struggling players for brief stays between June and December, 1752.

The players were no doubt drawn to Maryland by its moral cli-mate, far more relaxed than that of Philadelphia or New York, where the infant theaters were ever the targets of Quaker and Cal-vinist preachers and pious city councils. Tolerant Maryland, primar-ily Anglican and Catholic, saw no devils on the stage and welcomed the players, but, alas, could not support them.

Eight years passed before the next visit of a touring company to the colony. This time, however, the visitors were the noteworthy London Company of Comedians, led by David Douglass, who had assumed management upon the death of Lewis Hallam, scion of the acting Hallams of London and the first thoroughly professional the-atrical manager in the colonies. Having begun its American career in Williamsburg in 1752—not long before the Murray-Kean troupe passed into oblivion—the Hallam company of British actors had played in Virginia, New York, Philadelphia, and Charleston before leaving for Jamaica in 1754. On Hallam's death from yellow fever, Douglass succeeded both to company leadership and to marriage with Hallam's wife, the leading actress of the troupe. Returning to the colonies in 1758, they played New York and Philadelphia, where, as expected, they encountered stiff religious opposition. Only strong support from the royal governor of Pennsylvania al-lowed the troupe to perform until January 1, 1760, when they packed their trunks for the warmer moral climate of Annapolis. Unfortunately, bitter winter weather precluded their playing until March 3, when Thomas Otway's *The Orphan,* with David Garrick's farce *Lethe* as the afterpiece, was performed with the royal governor in attendance—an honor never before granted the players in the colonies.[4] The governor's presence was probably less attributable to the quality of the theater—though it was the best America had to offer at the time—than to the aspirations of Maryland society to emulate that of London. Plantation families in Maryland, as elsewhere in the South, looked more to England as their cultural center than did the commercial elite, the local merchantry, in the northern cities. Hence, Marylanders relished performances of Shakespeare and of "new" plays that had been given at Covent Garden and Drury Lane only a few years earlier.

Shakespeare was heard the first time in the 1760 season on March 10 as *Richard III,* always an American favorite, was played. No record exists of another Shakespearean performance until April 7, when the Douglass company acted *Romeo and Juliet.* The male lead, as proclaimed by the *Gazettte,* was taken not by Lewis Hallam, Jr., the troupe's rising star, but by "a young Gentleman for his Diversion."[5] The company's frequently allowing stage-struck gentry to take roles shows clearly how the players saw their popularity as being dependent on the whims of their small clientele. It shows something, too, about the tastes of the audience, that this same "young Gentleman" was advertised as Romeo in the April 11 performance. The audience seems to have preferred the novelty of a local hero to the genuine talents of young Hallam.

No amateurs were on stage for the April 9 playing of *Othello,* for which the cast list—the earliest for an American *Othello* still extant—was printed in the *Maryland Gazette.* On that evening, David Douglass, who usually preferred less demanding roles, played the Moor, while Mrs. Douglass, no ingenue, took Desdemona. John Palmer, perhaps the best actor in the company, handled Iago. The most interesting name on the list is that of "Mr. Murray" as the Duke. Might this have been Walter Murray of the old troupe? Most commentators follow George O. Seilhamer's assertion in *The His-*

tory of the American Theatre (Philadelphia, [1888–1891]) that this was so.

Shakespeare was played at least twice more in Annapolis that season: *Richard III* on April 14 (David Douglass's benefit) and *The Jew of Venice* (Lansdowne's version of *The Merchant*) on May 8, This performance featured the novel casting of Douglass as the youthful Bassanio and the nineteen-year-old Hallam as Shylock. The absence of Palmer from the cast may indicate his having already returned to England, which we know to have occurred at about this time.

Soon thereafter the players left Annapolis for Upper Marlborough, where the racing season had begun. During their six weeks' stay the troupe performed Shakespeare at least twice: *Romeo and Juliet* on June 19 and July 1, with Hallam and his mother in the title roles. The theater seems to have been "a neat convenient tobacco-house, well fitted up for that purpose,"[6] this "fitting up" probably a single tier of gallery benches around the pit before the upraised stage.[7]

From Upper Marlborough the London Company played their way to Williamsburg, thence to New England and many adventures that kept the Douglass troupe from returning to Maryland for ten years. No professional drama of any sort came to the colony until February, 1769, when the New American Company, which had formed in 1767, crossed the Potomac from Alexandria and acted through Maryland towns to an opening in Annapolis on the eighteenth. William Verling, whom Douglass had recruited from London in 1765, had fashioned this troupe from other actors restless under Douglass's leadership and from bit players whose backgrounds are no longer known. Most prominent in Verling's company were fellow defectors James Verling Godwin, a dancer-actor, and the explosive Henrietta Osborne, who had thrilled Charleston and Williamsburg audiences with her singing, dancing, and vibrant—sometimes risque—acting, most notably in the "breeches" part of Sir Harry Wildair in Farquhar's *The Constant Couple*. Mrs. Osborne, however, did not travel with the company to Annapolis, she and Verling having quarreled in Williamsburg.[8]

By PERMISSION of his **EXCELLENCY,**
*At the THEATRE, in this City, on Monday next,
being the 7th Inflant, will be prefented, a* TRA-
GEDY *(written by* SHAKESPEARE) *call'd,*

OTHELLO,

MOOR of VENICE.

Duke, *Mr.* MURRAY : Brabantio, *Mr.* SCOTT :
Othello, *Mr.* DOUGLASS : Caffio, *Mr.* HAL-
LAM : Jago, *Mr.* PALMER : Rodorigo, *Mr.* A.
HALLAM : Montano, *Mr.* MORRIS.

Defdemona, *Mrs.* DOUGLASS : Æmilia, *Mifs*
CRANE.

To which will be added, a FARCE, *call'd,*
A   WONDER!
An
Honeft *YORKSHIREMAN!*

No Money will be received at the Door on any
Account ; nor any Perfons admitted without
TICKETS, which may be had at the PRINTING-
OFFICE, and at the Bar of Mr. *Middleton's* Tavern.
BOXES 10 f. PIT 7/6. GALLERY 5 f.
No Perfon to be admitted behind the Scenes.
To begin exactly at VI o'Clock.

Earliest American cast list for *Othello* from the *Maryland Gazette,* Annapolis, April 3, 1760
Courtesy Maryland Historical Society

A Williamsburg recruit, Sarah Jones, took Osborne's place as
Juliet in the opening performance of the Annapolis run. The "New
Theatre" the company used probably occupied a different site from
that at which the London Company had played. According to the
Romeo and Juliet playbill, this new facility featured "Upper Boxes
. . ., the Passage to which, must be from the Stage."

The February 18 performance was the first of three for *Romeo and
Juliet* that season. *Richard III,* the other favorite, also played three
times, Verling himself as Richard. In all, Shakespearean plays were
performed on twelve of the thirty-seven evenings for which plays
were announced. Besides *Romeo and Juliet* and *Richard III,
Othello, Hamlet, Catherine and Petruchio* (Garrick's *Taming of the
Shrew*), *The Merchant of Venice,* and *1 Henry IV* were staged. The
March 6 giving of *Richard III* brought this editorial comment in the

Maryland Gazette: "The Public may be assured, that the Company of Comedians in this City have gained great Applause by their Two last Performances, viz. the tragedies of *Douglas* and *Richard III.*"[9] The company's *Hamlet* was noteworthy not only as the first *Hamlet* in Maryland, but for the amateur who "attempted" the title role. Either this "gentleman" possessed considerable talent or many friends who could purchase tickets to see him, because the ad in the *Gazette* referred to him as "the Gentleman that lately performed Othello" on February 22. He would again assay the Moor on May 13. Another amateur acted Mercutio in the March 11 *Romeo and Juliet;* still another, following *The Merchant of Venice* on April 25, performed tricks on the tightrope, his efforts being overmatched the same evening by those of Douglass refugee Patrick Malone, who stood on his head upon the slack wire, pistols in either hand.

The New American Company's success early in the run increased with the return of Henrietta Osborne by April 8, when she played Polly Honeycomb in the two-act farce of that name, which followed *Richard III.* The same gala evening featured a Mr. L'Argeau, who played "solos on the violin and harpsichord, with several tunes on the Musical Glasses."[10] Mrs. Osborne resumed her place as Juliet on April 20 and drew the loudest praise of the season in a letter to the *Gazette* from one who signed herself "Clarinda": "I will acknowledge the great Pleasure I have felt in Mrs. Osborne's performance of Juliet—Her feeling Manner of Acting. . . . I own she struck my Admiration still more, to find it was in the Power of the same Woman, to express the delicate Sensibility of a Juliet—and the Levity of a Sir Harry Wildair. . . ." Osborne would again show her versatility as Portia (April 25), Desdemona (May 13) and—a challenge—Prince Hal in the first Maryland performance of *1 Henry IV* (May 4). In this performance Osborne shared the lead with Verling's Falstaff and shared the novelty appeal with a Mrs. Parker, who played Poins.

Clarinda's letter did more than praise Mrs. Osborne; it alerted readers to a practice of the New American Company which may partly explain why the troupe, despite the talents of its leading figures, fell apart after the Annapolis season. Clarinda wrote:

I cannot help mentioning a Thing that must always be disagreeable to a sensible Audience. It is the barefaced, illiberal, and very often indecent Insertions of some of his [Verling's] Actors that play the low parts in comedy, or Farce, which is generally substituted for what they have either forgot, or perhaps, which is more likely, never perused—to be imperfect is so great a Fault, that the putting in their Ribaldry, is hardly a greater.

I am afraid the Gentleman, who amused himself with playing HAMLET, forgot to tell the Clowns, *to speak no more than was set down for them;* or if he did tell them, it was only in a Whisper.

Verling did not rush into print to deny Clarinda's claims; however, in a benefit late in the season for a Mr. Darby—one of those who played "low parts"—the ad in the *Gazette* "assured" the customers "of each Performer's being Perfect in their Parts."

A company that must advertise its actors' competence cannot expect to endure, even when that company boasts a Henrietta Osborne. Given, in addition, the financial woes that had plagued Verling and his crew since Williamsburg,[11] one can hardly be surprised that Annapolis saw the last of the New American Company in late May. Thus, for the second time in seventeen years, a theatrical troupe had come to Annapolis to die, Murray-Kean having succumbed in 1752. This time, however, the players left a legacy, in the person of Henrietta Osborne, who, as unpredictable as ever, became a storekeeper near the market square.[12] That she seems easily to have made the transition from touring player to local merchant once more illustrates the southern colonies' moral acceptance of the actors, so unlike their northern neighbors' deep suspiciousness.

Though Marylanders may have anticipated another long dramatic drought, within little more than a year the David Douglass troupe, renamed the American Company in 1766, returned to Annapolis. The troupe had come south from Philadelphia early in 1770 to repair somewhat sagging finances and to escape the anti-theatrical furor aroused by the evangelist George Whitefield. They had found solid support in term-time Williamsburg and towns north. The company timed their arrival in Annapolis to coincide with the Fall Assembly, and players, audiences, and weather cooperated for a successful, though brief, run of six weeks, brief because of what Douglass's ad in the *Gazette* called "the Company's Engagement in Virginia."

A principal reason for the Annapolis sojourn may have been Douglass's bold decision to commit his company to more playing time in Annapolis, this commitment consisting in the building of a "commodious, if not elegant" brick playhouse.[13] No doubt weary of his battles with the pious in Philadelphia and New York and comforted by the expressed support of Maryland's governors, Douglass negotiated with officials to build his theater on West Street on a lot owned by the adjacent St. Anne's Church. Both architectural plans and a subscription patronage plan were quickly drawn up—patrons would receive season tickets worth the amount of their pledge—and construction began before the American company left Annapolis.

Meanwhile, the brief season seems to have sustained Douglass's faith in his plan. Though we know little of what was performed because Douglass had disdained the use of notices in the *Gazette*, that newspaper was the vehicle by which two ecstatic theatergoers expressed their admiration for the American Company. One spectator, "Y. Z.," exclaimed: "The merit of Mr. Douglass's Company is, notoriously in the Opinion of every Man of Sense in America, whose Opportunities give him a Title to judge—take them for all in all—superior to that of any Company in *England,* except those of the Metropolis. The Dresses are remarkably elegant; the Dispatch of the Business of the Theatre uncommonly quick; and the Stillness and good Order preserved behind the Scenes, are proofs of the greatest Attention and Respect paid to the Audience."[14] "Y. Z." reserves highest praise for Nancy Hallam, Mrs. Douglass's niece and her recent successor as romantic lead in the troupe. As Imogen, wrote "Y. Z.," Miss Hallam "exceeded my utmost Idea. Such delicacy of Manner! Such classical Strictures of Expression! The Musick of her Tongue! The *vox liquida,* how melting!" The second enthusiast, an anonymous versifier whose lines follow those of "Y. Z.," supplied even loftier praises for Miss Hallam:

> Hail, wond'rous Maid! I, grateful, hail
> Thy strange dramatic Pow'r,
> To thee I owe that Shakespeare's Tale
> Has charmed my ears once more.
>
> Say! Does she plead, as though she felt
> Thy tender Tale of woe?

> Our eyes, albeit unused to melt,
> With Tears of Pity flow.[15]

Annapolis audiences had good reason to rejoice. Douglass's commitment meant good acting and finely painted scenes[16] for a season every year—in perhaps the finest theater in colonial America (only the Southwark in Philadelphia rivaled it). Although the impending hostilities between England and the colonies would bring the heyday of Annapolis theater to a close in 1773, the three seasons, 1771–1773, saw more performances like those which had drawn the panegyrics of Y. Z. and the local poet. Indeed, in October, 1771, when Nancy Hallam recreated Imogen, another admirer, "Paladour," was poetically inspired:

> Say, HALLAM, to thy wond'rous Art
> What Tribute shall I pay?
> Say, wilt thou, from a feeling Heart,
> Accept this votive Lay?
>
> From earliest Youth, with Rapture, oft
> I've turned great Shakespear's Page;
> Pleas'd, when he's gay, and sooth'd, when soft,
> Or kindled at his Rage.
>
> Yet not till now, till taught by Thee,
> Conceiv'd I Half in his Pow'r!
> I read, admiring now I see,
> I only not adore.[17]

Miss Hallam's characterization inspired not only poets, but a noted painter, Charles Wilson Peale, whose portrait of the actress in the cave scene of *Cymbeline* (3.6) is our finest early rendering of the American theater. Miss Hallam's pose in the painting captures some of the grace that charmed her audiences; her elaborate, vaguely oriental costume indicates not only the current fashion for representing exotic, antique figures, but also the lavishness of a Douglass production at the height of his career. That Peale's painting approaches an accurate view of Miss Hallam on the Annapolis stage is suggested by the verses that appeared in its praise in the *Maryland Gazette* of November 7, 1771: "Thy Pencil has so well the Scene convey'd, / Thought seems but an unnecessary Aid. . . ."

The *Cymbeline* which showcased Miss Hallam in 1770–1771 is the only Shakespearean play which we know to have been performed in

Annapolis in the four seasons, 1770–1773. That at least one other, *The Tempest*, was also staged is suggested by the praise given Maria Storer, another young actress, for her portrayal of Ariel.[18] Annapolis no doubt heard Shakespeare much more frequently than these scattered references imply; the American Company had elsewhere shown their knowledge of a good portion of the canon, and the Annapolis audience, as seen in the extensive records of the 1769 season of the Verling troupe, had shown a keen appetite for Shakespeare. The unhappy fact is that Douglass's policy of avoiding frequent newspaper ads has left us with negligible evidence of the company's repertoire in Annapolis, even though the company's practice in their 1760 run gives us reason to believe that they played almost every night of the week during their three-to-five-week stays in the Maryland capital from 1770 to 1773. Further evidence of their frequent playing comes from the expense diary of the colonies' premier fan of drama, George Washington, who recorded having seen four plays during September 24–28, 1771, four during October 5–9, 1772, and three during September 27–29, 1773.[19] Unfortunately, Squire Washington did not mention which plays he saw.

Of all those who frequented the brick playhouse on West Street perhaps George Washington best realized how shortlived the theatrical gaiety would be. On October 20, 1774, the Continental Congress, in the interest of "frugality, economy, and industry," decreed its "discourage[ment]" of "every species of extravagance and dissipation," including "plays." On hearing the news, Douglass's troupe, performing in Philadelphia—not far from Carpenter's Hall—scrapped their plans for a New York season and boarded a ship for Jamaica, never to return, at least as a company, to the mainland.

When playing ceased with the onset of the Revolution, Annapolis virtually died as a center of theater. In 1774, St. Anne's Church took over the vacant playhouse, still almost new and in far better condition than the old church itself, for its services. Rarely was it used as a theater again. John Henry, chief actor of the American Company in its last years, is said to have brought a troupe there for a brief stay in 1782; Adam Lindsay and Thomas Wall, partners in the first Baltimore theater, played Annapolis at about the same time. The Wignell-Reinagle Company, so important to Baltimore and Philadelphia

theater history, played occasional short summer seasons in Annapolis from 1794 to 1800, thus bringing Shakespeare to the venerable playhouse once more. Nevertheless, only eighteen years later,
according to Annapolis historian Elihu Riley, the theater was razed
to make way for a wagon factory.

Annapolis theater might have continued had not Baltimore succeeded the capital during the war as Maryland's chief port, a year-
round center of trade. However, even without Baltimore's
prominence, Annapolis theater might have succumbed to the great
easing of religious strictures against the drama in Philadelphia and
New York. The history of colonial theater clearly shows that the
best company, Douglass's, only came to Annapolis when the protests grew too strenuous; it is true that the lesser troupes, such as
Verling's, came to Maryland primarily because the northern towns
could not support both them and the American Company. However,
as these towns became cities, even the second-rate companies
would find audiences there.

While it lasted, Annapolis theater contributed several memorable
moments to the history of Shakespeare in America: among them,
Walter Murray's joining the Douglass company for *Othello* in 1760;
Lewis Hallam, Jr., as Shylock the same season; Henrietta Osborne
in breeches as Prince Hal; and, of course, Nancy Hallam as Imogen.
Colonial Maryland also contributed to theater history the *Maryland
Gazette,* whose editor, Jonas Green, supported the stage more
strongly than any other colonial journalist. Green wrote editorials to
support the players, provided space for advertisements, and eagerly
printed letters—and poems—from theatergoers. "Clarinda's" letter
in April, 1769, and the letters and poems in praise of Nancy Hallam
in 1770–1771 are among the most important early pieces of theater
criticism in America. Without them, as without the colonial theater
in Annapolis, America's theatrical heritage would be far poorer.

Shakespeare in Baltimore, 1782–1860

From Shakespeare's golden mine we'll bring the ore,
And land his riches here in Baltimore.

—from the prologue to *Richard III,* spoken
by Thomas Wall at the opening of the
Baltimore theater, January 15, 1782

Though legend has it that Baltimore supported a theater as early as 1773, when the American Company is said to have performed in a converted warehouse at Baltimore and Frederick streets, we have no evidence of drama in that burgeoning port until 1782. On January 15 of that year, Thomas Wall, formerly of the Douglass troupe, and Adam Lindsay, proprietor of a coffeehouse at nearby Fell's Point, presented *Richard III* in a brick theater at the corner of Milk (now East) and Great York (now Baltimore) streets. During the previous year, while the theater was being fashioned from stables on the site, Wall, his wife, and their daughter gave varied programs of lectures, dances, and songs at coffeehouses and even at a sail warehouse in the area. During this time, Wall was also assembling the company which would make his Baltimore theater the first in the new nation to conduct complete seasons in the seven years since the prohibition by the Continental Congress.[20]

Wall's choice of *Richard III* as the opening vehicle was predictable, since it had been the most popular Shakespearean play in America before the Revolution. Gloster gave lesser actors a meaty part that could be played effectively even if its subtleties were lost; the character gave the unsophisticated audiences a villain to jeer, while Richmond gave them a shiny hero to applaud. Moreover, the play was Shakespeare's, so the audience could enjoy the action and feel uplifted as well.

Baltimore audiences supported the Wall and Lindsay "Maryland Company of Comedians" well enough to keep them playing for two seasons, until December, 1782. Certainly, however, the company gave their auditors meager fare. Wall, who had played only minor roles with Douglass, attempted Gloster in *Richard III* and Edgar in *Lear* later in the season, not to mention the leads he took in most of the forty non-Shakespearean performances during that first season. The principal male roles that Wall did not handle were taken by a Mr. Heard, otherwise undistinguished, who seems to have been the audience's favorite, as judged by the proceeds of his benefit performance as Lear on May 17: £102, one of the season's larger takes.[21] The female "stars" seem to have been Mrs. Bartholomew (Lady Anne, Cordelia) and Mrs. Wall (Queen Elizabeth, Regan). The scanty resources of the troupe are evident from the inclusion in many of the cast lists of coffeehouse proprietor Lindsay and the company clerk, Mr. Tillyard. The playbill for *Richard III* indicates that the central role of Richmond, plus the roles of Tressel and Prince Edward, were played by "Gentlemen, for their Amusement."

Just as Jonas Green had boosted the Annapolis theater through his *Maryland Gazette,* so the *Maryland Journal and Universal Daily Advertiser* gave space to such friendly critics as "Cato" (Wall perhaps?) who urged all to attend *Gustavus Vasa* for its "most exalted Ideas of true heroism . . . Every free bosom present at the Representation will feel the patriotic flame rekindled for the Service of his Country" (May 28, 1782).

Despite such efforts, the Wall troupe disappears from the records after December 12. Baltimore's next entrepreneur seems to have been Irish actor Dennis Ryan, sometime player for the Maryland Company, whose name appears in the *Maryland Journal* several times between 1783 and 1786, often in connection with theatrical postponements due to wet weather and impassable streets. Ryan's venture in Baltimore was postponed permanently, the meager record suggests, when two familiar figures, Lewis Hallam, Jr., and John Henry of the (now) Old American Company, tried the Baltimore market with a rival theater constructed between the town and Fell's Point at Pratt and Albemarle streets. Hallam and Henry had entered into partnership the previous year, 1785, after Hallam's return from Jamaica. After returning from England in 1782, Henry played sporadically in Annapolis and elsewhere before 1786. We may presume that the company produced their accustomed play list in Baltimore, including some Shakespeare, in the single autumn season which we know them to have attempted before they headed for Richmond.

Records indicate no interest in Baltimore by theatrical troupes for the next seven years, but good times were coming. Thomas Wignell, by this time the leading actor in the Hallam troupe, resigned in 1792 to found his own Philadelphia-based company with the composer Alexander Reinagle. However, while the pair anticipated the opening of their new theater in 1793, yellow fever broke out, sending Wignell and Reinagle farther south in search of an interim site. They reopened the once-glittering Annapolis playhouse for a brief spell, meanwhile buying the land at Fayette and Holliday streets for the first real Baltimore theater.

Opening on September 25, 1794, with *Everyone Has His Fault,* before what the *Maryland Journal* called a "numerous and brilliant audience," the Wignell-Reinagle company began an association with Baltimore which for most of the next thirty-five years brought the city outstanding drama for two-month-long seasons each spring and fall. The company based its operations in Philadelphia, at the splendid Chestnut Street theater, where it played from December to April. Its summers were spent sometimes in Philadelphia, more often on tour, in Annapolis, Alexandria, and Richmond. Washington became a summer center by 1800.[22] The Baltimore theater, according to William Burke Wood, who succeeded Wignell as manager in 1804, "proved the most safe and profitable scene of our operations."[23]

The company assembled by Wignell surpassed in power and versatility any earlier American troupe and many that followed. Its mainstays included Ann Brunton Merry, who came from England in 1796 and whom many Londoners considered the equal of Sarah Siddons; Mr. Moreton, who excelled in romantic leads (Romeo, Orlando, Ferdinand) but who died while still in his twenties, in 1798; Charles Whitlock, who played older gentlemen; his wife, Elizabeth Whitlock, sister of Sarah Siddons, whose large size and queenly manner suited her for such roles as Lady Macbeth and Queen Gertrude; and Wignell himself, who displayed the canny humility to fill in where needed instead of arrogating the best roles to himself. When it was formed, the company lacked a strong male tragedian, except during James Fennell's short visit in 1794. However, this need was met in 1796, when the British prodigy Thomas Abthorpe Cooper joined the troupe. Cooper, superb in all the major Shakespearean parts, starred as a regular in the Wignell enterprise; he was perhaps the most frequent—and most needed—visiting star in the later years of the troupe under Wood and William Warren. Cooper's theatrical range is evident from observing the playbills of selected seasons. In 1795, before Cooper, the company produced Shakespeare on only six of eighty evenings (*The Merchant, Romeo and*

Juliet twice, *As You Like It, The Merry Wives of Windsor,* and *The Tempest.*) Nineteen years later, in the brief autumn season of 1814, Shakespeare was performed on five of twenty-four nights, with Cooper heading each cast (Gloster, Othello, Romeo, Macbeth, and Shylock). As late as 1828 Cooper was an eagerly awaited attraction in Baltimore; William Wood recognized his worth to the company by devoting to Cooper a chapter of his stage memoirs—the only colleague so honored.

During the years after Wignell's death in 1804, Wood and Warren brought many other stars to Baltimore for brief runs and supported them with a solid repertory company no less skilled than Wignell's. Wood himself took some leading roles but more often played the second male lead, his most famous Shakespearean roles being Edgar and Buckingham. Warren, too, could play Shakespearean leads if called on, but he specialized in older, serious men (e.g., Leonato, Brabantio), though Falstaff was his—and his audiences'—favorite. Mrs. Wood, the former Juliana Westray, was the stock company's leading female performer, though she would support such visiting luminaries as Mary Ann Duff and Lydia Kelly on their seasonal visits. Joseph Jefferson, father of the famous portrayer of Rip Van Winkle, may have been the most beloved member of the company for his versions of Shakespeare's wise fools and foolish wise men: Touchstone, Dogberry, Polonius, and others. Both he and his wife, as well as Mr. and Mrs. William Francis, won large followings during their many years' service for Warren and Wood.

One cannot discuss Shakespeare in Baltimore during the years before 1830 without noting the visits of the stars, e.g. John Howard Payne as Hamlet and Romeo in 1809,[24] James Fennell in six Shakespearean roles in nine nights in 1810, James Wallack as Baltimore's first Coriolanus in 1818, and the comedian James Hackett's imitation of Kean's Gloster *(Richard III)* in 1826. The three most celebrated Shakespearean actors of the time trod the Baltimore stage. George Frederick Cooke, in his sixty-seventh year and his powers greatly diminished by alcohol, visited the city in spring 1811, just months before his death. His visit coincided with Cooper's, and so theatergoers were treated to *Othello* with Cooke as the Moor and Cooper as

Iago, *The Merchant* with Cooke as Shylock, Cooper as Antonio, and *1 Henry IV* with Cooke as Falstaff, Cooper as Hotspur.[25] During his brief stay, Cooke managed to insult the audience by failing to show up for a performance after a night of drinking at an admirer's country home;[26] he even insulted James Madison by refusing to perform during the president's visit to Baltimore, Cooke calling Madison "the comtemptible king of the Yankee Doodles."[27]

Perhaps even more stormy than Cooke's visit were two brief sojourns by the incomparable Edmund Kean. Actually, Kean's first series of performances, April 23–May 15, 1821, were tempestuous only in their grand power. Kean opened in *Richard III* on Shakespeare's birthday, followed as Othello two nights later (with Wood as Iago and Mrs. Wood as Desdemona), then, over the next twenty evenings, acted Shylock, Lear, Hamlet, Othello again, and, as on opening night, Gloster. Not only did Kean play brilliantly before large houses but surprised the company—fed with reports of his outbursts—by his quiet professionalism at rehearsals. However, when Kean returned for eight nights in June, 1826, his reception was violent. Having fled to the U.S. after the disgrace occasioned by his adulterous affair with Charlotte Cox, Kean took on hostile Boston audiences that he had insulted five years earlier. A riot sent him fleeing to Philadelphia, then to New York and Charleston, where his brief runs were relatively peaceful.[28] Nevertheless, when he reached Baltimore in June, trouble erupted once again. Hotheads in the otherwise respectful opening night crowd for *Richard III* began to shout "a violent opposition" which "rendered all Kean's attempts to be heard hopeless." Wood's recollection continues: "The greatest portion of the female auditors retired in disgust from the disgraceful scene, and the play at length ended in noise and confusion. Warren conducted the ladies of the company through the crowd without molestation; Kean was conveyed through the adjoining house to his lodgings safely, but in extreme terror, as might well be expected."[29] Though Kean and the company wanted to try again the next evening, city authorities dissuaded them by admitting the inability of the police to quell the fray that would no doubt ensue. Not only was Kean's visit canceled, but so was the rest of the spring season. The company went to Philadelphia and Kean went north to Canada, thence to England, and never again to the United States.[30]

The third famous tragedian to play Baltimore before 1830 stirred the least controversy, stayed the longest, and had the most profound influence on the Baltimore, if not the entire American, stage. Junius Brutus Booth came to Baltimore in fall 1821, settled in nearby Harford County, continued to appear in Baltimore with almost the loyalty of a Cooper, and produced three actor sons, two of whom debuted in Baltimore and then went on to have lasting impact on the nation.

Just as the colonial players had come seventy years earlier to easy-going Maryland to escape controversy, so Booth, estranged from London by the desertion of his wife for the Covent Garden flowerseller Mary Ann Holmes, came south rather than risk the censure of New York or Philadelphia. However, by opening in Baltimore in autumn 1821, he risked unfavorable comparison with his London rival, Kean, who had thrilled Baltimoreans that spring. Unfortunately for Booth, this seems to have occurred. Wood noted that after a packed house for Booth's Richard III on November 1, crowds fell off sharply for his Othello and Lear.[31] Nevertheless, Booth was back to claim all five Shakespearean leads in the autumn of 1822. Two years later he played Lear for Warren and Wood, then in the spring of 1825 Gloster, Hamlet, and Lear for a rival troupe, under Dinneford, who held forth for one brief season before the arrival of the established players. In the spring of 1827 Booth appeared with the Philadelphia and Baltimore Company, now under Warren's sole management, as Gloster, Hamlet, Shylock, and Lear over a ten-day span. During the next decade Booth continued to play occasional engagements in his adopted city.

Over the more than thirty years of the Wignell-Wood-Warren regime in Baltimore theater, Shakespeare's plays were presented far more frequently than those of any other author—and more frequently than they would again before the 1870s. But the drama of these years can hardly be called predominantly Shakespearean. In no season did Shakespearean performances comprise even a third of the total (eleven nights out of thirty-eight in autumn 1818 was the high); Shakespeare was played an average of only four times per season. Nevertheless, a theatergoer who attended those four nights saw a different play each night, and the dedicated Shakespearean devotee could within a decade see as many as fifteen of Shakespeare's works, from the most frequently presented *(Richard III, Hamlet, Othello,* and *Macbeth)* to the one-night-onlies *(King John, Coriolanus)*. Moreover, he or she would never see any actor but the best as Lear, Hamlet, or Othello. Indeed, Shakespeare nights, so closely linked to the visits of the stars, not only filled the theater, but generated excitement—sometimes near-violence, as with Kean— that made these evenings especially memorable. Retrospective views of the Baltimore stage during the next century would mention the engagements of Kean, Cooke, and Booth; Wood and Mrs. Wood, Warren, Jefferson and Mrs. Jefferson, Francis and Mrs. Francis—these who had built and sustained the theater—would be forgotten, except by historians such as John P. Kennedy, who provides our most vivid memory of Baltimore theater before 1830:

There was a universal gladness in this old Baltimore when the word was passed around—"The players are come." It instantly became everyone's business to give them a good reception. They were strange creatures in our schoolboy reckoning, quite out of the common order of humanity. . . . It was odd to see them dressed like gentlemen and ladies—almost incongruous, we sometimes thought, as if we expected to see them in slashed doublet and hose, with embroidered mantles and a feather in their caps. "There goes Old Francis!" was our phrase; not that he was old, for he was far from it, but because we loved him. . . . And as to Jefferson! Is there anybody now who remembers that imp of ancient fame? I cannot even now think definitely of him as a man, except in one particular, that he had a prominent and rather arching nose. In regard to everyone else he was a Proteus—the nose always being the same. He played everything that was comic, and always made people laugh till tears came to their eyes. . . . No player comes to that perfection now. . . . When our players came, with their short seasons, their three nights in a week," and their single company, they were received as public benefactors, and their stay was a period of carnival. The boxes were engaged for every night. Families all went together, young and old. . . . The elders did not think to frown on the drama, the clergy levelled no canon against it, the critics were amiable. The chief actors were invited into the best company, and I believe their personal merits entitled them to all the esteem that was felt for them. But, among the young folks, the appreciation was far above all this. With them it was a kind of hero-worship, prompted by the conviction that the player was that manifold creature which every night assumed a new shape, and only accidentally fell into the category of a common mortal. . . .[33]

Unfortunately for the actors and for drama lovers, this idyllic scene had already begun to dim by 1826, the year of the Kean riot and, more important, of Wood's retirement. Receipts had fallen off in Baltimore and, years later, Wood noted several reasons that had been suggested to him at the time: lack of a building as elegant as the rebuilt Chestnut Street playhouse in Philadelphia, lack of competition to keep the company always sharp, and too little music and dance to suit the public's taste.[34] Wood discounted the first two reasons. Playbills from throughout the company's existence in Baltimore show its sensitivity to the audience's desire for a lavish theater. Wood and Warren had completely rebuilt the theatre in 1813–1814, increasing its size with a gallery and a third tier of boxes. They advertised for a year its illumination by gas, as they did still another tier in 1828. As for lack of competition, Wood could have pointed to the spring of 1825, when the Dinneford company tried, failed, and merely lowered Wood and Warren's receipts. Competition might have kept quality consistently high, but Baltimore at that time just could not support two companies.

Wood could not, however, discount the third suggested reason: the public's increasing desire for music and dance instead of drama. Writing in 1855, he could merely lament that by 1840 "music divided the seasons with drama, or rather made the drama auxiliary to itself." While light opera, ballad singers, and dancers drew large houses, he said, expenses outdistanced receipts, so that profits were scarce.

Where before 1810 Baltimore theater evenings were divided between the five-act play and the two-act farce, by 1821 songs and dances between the two pieces were commonplace. As early as 1813, a Miss Abercrombie warranted her name in half-inch letters advertising her "Turkish Pas Seul" and "Flag Dance"; the highlight of that season's *Much Ado* was the act 1 "Masquerade, in which will be introduced The Celebrated Tambourine Dance by MISS ABER-

CROMBIE." This same performer was featured in spring 1815 in breeches as Prince John in *1 Henry IV*—shades of Henrietta Osborne! With the production of *Don Giovanni* on October 19, 1824, the turning point in Baltimore theater had definitely been reached. By the fall of 1826, the first season after Wood's departure, drama cast lists were abbreviated on playbills to allow more room for bold-face descriptions of operatic scenes. Spring, 1827, saw two performances of *The Comedy of Errors* advertised for their "many songs, duets, glees, and choruses, selected entirely from the plays, poems, and sonnets of Shakespeare." Spectators were lured to *Macbeth* in the autumn of 1828 by the ad for its "singing witches"; however, the big attractions that season were the opera *The Gnome King*—advertised as appealing especially to children—and the appearance on stage on October 30 of an equestrian act, billed as "The Beautiful Stud."

Though the repertoire drama was fading in Baltimore by 1830, the lively arts as a whole were flourishing. The year 1829 saw the opening of the mammoth Front Street Theatre to rival the old Baltimore playhouse, which now became known as the Holliday Street Theatre. While light opera and frequent plays continued on Holliday Street, the 75-foot-square stage at Front Street allowed many "beautiful studs" to cavort before as many as four thousand spectators. The Front Street also presented musical and dancing acts.

Shakespeare could still be heard at both places during the next two decades from such new visiting stars as Edwin Forrest, Fanny Kemble, Charles Kean and Ellen Tree, and George Vandenhoff, but now the supporting casts came with the main attractions for brief stays and were augmented by hastily prepared locals. Gone were the days when stage-struck youths could look forward to the seasonal return of "their" players. Now they might aspire to the Front Street stock troupe known as the Baltimore Theatre and Circus Company.

Further competition arose in 1844 with the opening of the Baltimore Museum at Calvert and Baltimore streets for plays and concerts in a 500-seat room.[35] Shakespeare was performed there by such ill-suited artists as Kate and Ellen Bateman, "The American Infant Wonders," in "The Trial Scene of the Merchant of Venice"

(1851), with Kate as Portia and Ellen as Shylock! However, the Museum could also present the best, such as Charlotte Cushman the same season in her famous Shakespearean and non-Shakespearean roles.

During the 1840s Baltimore witnessed several memorable Shakespearean performances, by far the most important the December, 1848, confrontation between Edwin Forrest and William Charles Macready. Just nine days after the American hero, Forrest, had ended his latest battle against his English rival in Philadelphia, where they had played the same roles on the same nights at separate theaters, both actors brought their companies to Baltimore for three head-to-head performances: *Macbeth* (December 11), Bulwer's *Richelieu* (the thirteenth), and *Hamlet* (the fifteenth). On December 14, Forrest played Othello; Macready, Shylock. Forrest held forth at the smaller, more prestigious Holliday Street Theatre; Macready, at the huge Front Street, known for its prancing animals. On December 12, the *Baltimore American and Commercial Advertiser* reviewed the openings of both actors:

> *Mr. Macready.*—This distinguished tragedian made his first appearance at the Front Street Theatre last night before one of the largest audiences ever gathered within the walls of that spacious establishment. He was received with a burst of applause that lasted several minutes, and which broke forth again and again throughout the course of the play. His representation of the character of Macbeth was a masterpiece of the histrionic art; a most happy conception, embodied with perfect skill. On the conclusion of the play he came forward at the call of the audience, and in a few brief remarks returned his thanks for the flattering reception. . . .
>
> *Mr. Forrest.*—This gentleman commenced an engagement last night at the Holliday Street Theatre in the character of Macbeth. Some time before the raising of the curtain the house was packed in every part, the doors opening from the boxes into the lobby being completely thronged with spectators. Upon his appearance he was greeted with the most deafening rounds of applause and prolonged cheering which he promptly acknowledged. His impersonation of the character of Macbeth throughout, which was frequently interrupted by the hearty plaudits of the audience, was strongly marked by his great genius. . . . At the close of the performance he was called before the curtain and greeted with three continuous cheers, to which he responded in a brief speech, apologizing

for his inability, through exhaustion, from saying more than to return his heartfelt thanks for the very kind reception he had met with. . . .

Though many had come out of curiosity, expecting an incident, maybe even a riot like that which had greeted Kean in 1826, that evening and the rest of the week became triumphs for both men and one of the most glittering moments in Baltimore theater history. Six months later the same actors would occasion perhaps the darkest moment in New York theater history, the Astor Place riot, in which thirty-one would be killed.

The year 1849 brought a new theater, the Howard Atheneum at the corner of Charles and Baltimore streets; the year also brought the decline of the venerable Holliday Street, plagued by financial losses and legal squabbles among its owners. Meanwhile, at the Front Street, in the reins of actor-impresario William E. Burton, *Julius Caesar,* rarely seen in Baltimore earlier, was staged by a truly remarkable cast: John R. Scott as Brutus, Edwin Forrest as Antony, Junius Brutus Booth as Cassius, and Mrs. John Drew as Portia— with Burton himself, plus the younger Joseph Jefferson and the great comedian John E. Owens in minor roles.[36]

Owens became manager of the Howard Atheneum after 1850, and he brought Shakespeare to Baltimore in the early years of this last decade before war. Of special note was Laura Keene's run in 1853, just after her sudden rise to stardom in New York and her even more sudden departure from that city.[37] Keene, a strong manager as well as a virtuoso performer, assembled a fine supporting cast for her portrayals of Portia, Rosalind, and other characters who suited "her looks, her gentility, and her deft comic touch."[38] Keene played once more in Baltimore, in 1856, but at the Holliday Street, not the Howard, which failed the season after Keene's first visit and was converted into a warehouse.[39] Before its closing, however, the last managers, Joseph Jefferson and John Sleeper Clarke, presented John Wilkes Booth as a sixteen-year-old Richmond. His premature debut was one of many embittering experiences for the younger brother, who blamed Clarke for encouraging him to appear before he was ready. Booth claimed that Clarke—who later married Booth's sister Asia—had merely wanted the Booth name to support his sagging enterprise.[40]

With the close of the Howard, the decline of the Holliday Street, and the near abandonment of serious drama at the Front Street, Shakespeare in Baltimore had almost disappeared by 1854—two years after theater in Maryland had turned a century old. But just at this moment there emerged into prominence two men who would become the greatest names in Baltimore dramatic history: John T. Ford, who at twenty-five became manager of the Holliday Street, and Edwin Booth. While Ford was rejuvenating the once-famous playhouse, the rival Front Street in 1856 featured for the first time in the East the young Marylander Booth, who had been acting for several seasons in San Francisco, after having played stock in Baltimore five years earlier.[41] Baltimore saw Booth as Richard III and as Hamlet, the role with which he would later be most closely identified.[42] Within a few years Ford and Booth would begin an association that would bring Booth to Baltimore at least once a year until 1890. As owner-manager of Ford's in Washington, Ford would also be associated by fate with Edwin's brother John, whose capital crime would land Ford in jail for several months on suspicion and make Edwin ashamed to play in Washington ever again. Since the great Booth would not play in the capital, his visits to Baltimore after 1865 would bring special trains of Washington admirers to the Holliday Street and to Ford's Grand Opera House, which would open in 1871 and herald the most glittering era of Baltimore theater.

Though Edwin Booth's name would come to be most closely linked to the development of the New York stage, the actor himself always considered Baltimore his home, remembering it as the city, and Maryland the state, which had given refuge to his father, when he had fled disgrace in England and scorn in the North. During his long career, Booth would see Baltimore much as Wood and Warren's company viewed it before 1830, and much as the colonial players had viewed Annapolis: as a place where enthusiastic audiences welcomed actors and actresses, appreciated good theater, and overlooked bad nights and indecorous behavior. Just a short journey from Philadelphia, Maryland offered a southern ambience and a theater-loving populace irresistible to the troupes. No wonder David Douglass had built a brick playhouse in Annapolis in 1770 and John T. Ford built a grand opera house in Baltimore in 1870—to compete with the Holliday Street, his own theater. No wonder that in the 1870s Baltimore would become a favorite try-out city for new productions on their way to the harsher climate of New York.

In terms of the Shakespearean repertoire, Marylanders, throughout the century from 1752 to 1860, were as unsophisticated in their tastes as they were accepting of the actors. They liked *Richard III* best of all the histories, *Romeo and Juliet* best among the tragedies. They liked *1 Henry IV* for Henrietta Osborne or "Miss Abercrombie" in tights, and *Othello, Macbeth,* and *The Merchant of Venice* for their villains, the more wicked and grotesque the better. *Hamlet* was infrequent, especially before 1810; *Lear* and *Julius Caesar* were almost never seen. The comedies were rarely acted, their romantic nuances not to the taste of spectators for whom fat Falstaff was the comic favorite. Ironically, the most famous Shakespearean performance of the colonial period, Nancy Hallam's Imogen, came in a play that would be staged in Baltimore only twice in the next one hundred years. For the most part, Shakespeare in Maryland, 1752–1860, was not the very best available in America, but with commitments from strong companies and bright stars it was often very good and, on occasion, wonderful. More important, without the hospitable, albeit unsophisticated, audiences of Maryland, even the strong companies might have failed, thus setting back for decades the growth of the American theater.

NOTES

1. Kathryn Painter Ward, "The First Professional Theater in Maryland," *Maryland English Journal* 9 (Spring, 1971): 78.
2. We know that *Richard III* was played in New York twice in Mar., 1751, and in Williamsburg on Oct. 26 of that year. See Hugh Rankin, *The Theater in Colonial America* (Chapel Hill: University of North Carolina Press, 1960), pp. 32–37.
3. Elihu Riley, *Annapolis, the Antient Capital of Maryland* (Annapolis, 1901).

4. Rankin, p. 86.

5. Mary Childs Black, "The Theatre in Colonial Annapolis" (M.A. thesis, George Washington University, 1953), p. 32.

6. Andrew Burnaby, *Travels through the Middle Settlements in the Years 1759 and 1761*, 2nd ed. (London, 1776), p. 64.

7. Rankin, p. 88.

8. Ibid., p. 146, cites the *Virginia Gazette*, Jan. 12, 1769.

9. *Maryland Gazette*, Mar. 8, 1769.

10. Ibid., Apr. 5, 1769.

11. Rankin, p. 145.

12. Black, p. 87.

13. Rankin, p. 219, n. 2.

14. *Maryland Gazette*, Sept. 6, 1770.

15. The versifier was discovered by historians to be the Rev. Jonathan Boucher, certainly no Puritan! See Rankin, p. 219, n. 2.

16. Crafted by Thomas Nicholas Doll, scene-builder for Covent Garden.

17. *Maryland Gazette*, Oct. 10, 1771.

18. Ibid., Nov. 7, 1771.

19. Black, pp. 82–94.

20. Lynn Haims, "The First American Theatre Contracts: Wall and Lindsay's Maryland Company of Comedians, and the Annapolis, Fell's Point, and Baltimore Theatres, 1781–83," *Theatre Survey* 17 (Nov., 1976): 179–94. The Maryland Historical Society maintains playbills for the 1781 entertainments and the spring, 1782, play season.

21. Records of the Maryland Company of Comedians, Mr. Tillyard, Clerk. Maryland Historical Society MS.

22. William Burke Wood, *Recollections of the Stage, Embracing Actors, Authors, and Auditors During a Period of Forty Years* (Philadelphia: Henry Carey Baird, 1855), p. 66.

23. Ibid., p. 271.

24. Ibid., p. 127, recalls the "crowning triumph" of Payne's benefit, which grossed $1,160, the highest take of the decade.

25. Ibid., p. 134.

26. Ibid.

27. Donald Kirkley, "Recalling the Old-Time Theatres," *Baltimore Sun*, Oct. 31, 1934.

28. See Charles H. Shattuck, *Shakespeare on the American Stage from the Hallams to Edwin Booth* (Washington: Folger Shakespeare Library, 1976), p. 43.

29. Wood, p. 321.

30. Shattuck, p. 43.

31. Wood, p. 271.

32. Four—Monday, Wednesday, Friday, Saturday—was the standard number, plus occasional Tuesday and Thursday performances.

33. Cited by Mildred Greenfield, "The Early History of the Theatre in Baltimore" (M.A. thesis, Johns Hopkins University, 1953), p. 32.

34. Wood, p. 304.

35. Greenfield, p. 51.

36. Kirkley, "Recalling the Old-Time Theatres."

37. Garff Wilson, *A History of American Acting* (Bloomington: University of Indiana Press, 1966), p. 119.

38. Ibid.
39. Greenfield, p. 51.
40. Eleanor Ruggles, *Prince of Players: Edwin Booth* (New York: Norton, 1953), p. 100.
41. Ibid., p. 48.
42. Greenfield, p. 56.

Shakespeare on the Charleston Stage, 1764–1799

Sara Nalley

Charleston, South Carolina, has a rich theater heritage dating from the eighteenth century, when according to historians the city was one of America's leading theater centers.[1] Chroniclers of Shakespeare in America often acclaim Charleston's early tradition of Shakespearean performance, citing the season of 1773–1774, when twelve of Shakespeare's plays were staged in the city.[2] The view that sometimes emerges is that of a wealthy, aristocratic city, hospitable to the arts and strong in its support of great drama, including the plays of Shakespeare. If such a view is not entirely inaccurate, it is certainly incomplete. A survey of Shakespearean production in eighteenth-century Charleston will show that the 1773–1774 season was atypical, and that Charleston's early theater history is, in fact, more varied and more troubled than that one brilliant season suggests.

Charleston's theater tradition began in 1703, when Anthony Aston, an English actor, played in "Charlestowne."[3] No further theatrical activities are documented until 1735, when a season of Thomas Otway's *The Orphan* and John Dryden's *The Spanish Fryar* was presented along with opera, pantomime, and dance. The prologue delivered at the first performance of *The Orphan* on January 18, 1735, suggests that Charlestonians knew and respected Shakespeare. It offers this plea for tolerance:

> And if important Mortals, cramm'd with Thought,
> Condemn what Addison and Shakespear wrote,
> Fond of our Peace, averse to all Disputes,
> We straight submitt, and ask—the Price of Boots.
> The good and wise may say, "Abuse has been,"
> But from th'Abuse ne'er argue to the Thing.[4]

Few Charlestonians of 1735 would have been likely to "condemn what Shakespear wrote." Charleston was, in the years before the

Revolution, a wealthy, cosmopolitan city. Leading citizens customarily sent their sons to England to be educated, first to Westminister or Eton and then to the universities or Inns of Court. There the young men acquired English tastes in literature and theater, which certainly included Shakespeare. On their return to Charleston, they maintained ties with English styles through the complete sets of contemporary English magazines held by the Charleston Library Society, organized in 1748.[5] Hennig Cohen notes that editions of Shakespeare's works were frequently offered for sale in pre-Revolutionary Charleston newspapers and that local writers quoted extensively from Shakespeare.[6]

But while Charleston gentlemen undoubtedly knew Shakespeare from their English travels and their reading, they left no records of Shakespearean performance in Charleston before 1764. Accounts of the seasons of 1736 and 1737 show productions of Otway, Joseph Addison, and George Lillo, but no Shakespeare. In the *South Carolina Gazette,* the bill for the May 26, 1737, performance of *The Recruiting Officer* announced "the Song of Mad Tom in proper Habiliments, by a Person that never yet appear'd upon the Stage."[7] Eola Willis speculates that the song was from *King Lear* and thus might be considered an early instance of Shakespearean performance in America,[8] but such a suggestion cannot be proved. Nor is there evidence to support Louis Marder's puzzling claim that "the first professional production of Shakespeare in the United States was the performance of *Richard III* at the Dock Street Theatre in Charleston in 1737."[9] The standard sources of information provide no hint of such a production. Furthermore, in 1737 the theater was called the New Theatre in Queen Street, not the Dock Street Theatre, and the performers there were probably amateurs, not professionals. Certainly, the United States did not exist in 1737.

If Charleston performances of Shakespeare went unrecorded, it is much more likely that they occurred in the season of 1754–1755, when Lewis Hallam's Company of Comedians played in Charleston. The repertoire of Hallam's troupe included *King Lear, Romeo and Juliet, Henry IV,* and *Richard III,* as well as two plays they had staged in Williamsburg in 1752, *The Merchant of Venice* and

Othello. The journal of Ann Manigault, wife of a prominent Charleston merchant, and the *South Carolina Gazette* record eight performances by Hallam's company in Charleston in 1754 and 1755. No Shakespearean plays are mentioned in either source, but, as Hugh F. Rankin observes, it is possible that Hallam did not find it necessary to advertise all his plays, for the General Assembly was meeting in Charleston at the time and the city was crowded with potential theatergoers.[10]

Charleston's next theater season, in 1763–1764, provides the first record of Shakespearean performance in South Carolina. Hallam's successor, David Douglass, arrived in Charleston from Virginia in November, 1763, to build a new theater on Queen Street for his troupe, the American Company.[11] Ann Manigault's 1764 journal notes that early in the season she saw the company perform William Congreve's *Love for Love,* Nicholas Rowe's *Jane Shore,* Lillo's *The Conscious Lovers,* and other plays. Finally, she wrote, "April 12. Romeo and Juliet," and a month later, "May 10. To the Play. King Lear."[12]

A letter from Alexander Garden to David Colden suggests that Douglass's company had performed *Romeo and Juliet* earlier in the season, prior to the April performance Ann Manigault saw. Headed "Charlestown Feb[ry] 1st 1764," Garden's letter offers a first-hand account of the season.

> [Douglass] has met with all imaginable Success in this place since their theatre was opened, . . . since which time they have performed thrice a week & Every night to a full nay a Crowded house. . . . Mr. Douglass has made a valuable acquisition in Miss Cheer who arrived here from London much about the time that Mr. Douglass arrived with his company. Soon after that, she agreed to go on the stage where she has since appeared in some Chief Characters with great applause particularly Monincia [*sic*] in the Orphan & Juliet of Shakespear & Hermione of the Distresst Mother. Her fine person, her youth, her Voice, & Appearance &c conspire to make her appear with propriety—Such a one they much wanted as Mrs. Douglass was their Chief actress before & who on that account had always too many Characters to appear in.[13]

Douglass's decision to add Shakespeare to his 1764 program might well have been due to the arrival of Margaret Cheer. No cast lists are available, but it is likely that Miss Cheer appeared in *King Lear* as

well as in *Romeo and Juliet,* for both Cordelia and Juliet are roles
she played later in Philadelphia. She did not return to Charleston
with Douglass for his next season in 1766, and Douglass offered no
Shakespeare. Once again, the choice of plays was probably dependent upon the availability of talent rather than a reflection of audience tastes; the 1766 company had only nine actors, too few for
Shakespeare, and six of these were inexperienced players.

During the next several seasons the American Company played in
New York and Philadelphia, leaving Charleston without theater.
Before Douglass returned to Charleston in the summer of 1773, he
had added a number of talented players to his troupe, and some of
the original group had gained needed experience. The company that
joined him in Charleston for the opening of a new theater on Church
Street on December 22, 1773, was a solid one. It included John
Henry, Lewis Hallam, Jr., Nancy Hallam, Maria Storer, Mr. and
Mrs. Owen Morris, Miss Wainwright, and Mrs. Douglass, all performers with extensive Shakespearean experience. John Henry and
Nancy Hallam, in particular, had won high praise for their performances of Shakespeare.[14]

With this troupe, the strongest company yet to appear in Charleston, Douglass presented in 1773 and 1774 the season that is often
cited as evidence of the city's early theatrical prominence. The ambitious program offered a total of fifty-nine performances. Twelve of
Shakespeare's plays were staged: *Hamlet, Cymbeline* (two performances), *Romeo and Juliet* (two performances), *The Merchant of
Venice, Richard III, The Tempest* (three performances), *Henry IV,
Othello, King Lear, Julius Caesar, Macbeth,* and *King John.* In
addition, the season included four performances of David Garrick's
Catherine and Petruchio, a version of *The Taming of the Shrew.*[15]
All except *Romeo and Juliet* and *King Lear* were apparently having
their first Charleston productions. Eola Willis cites the April 20,
1774, production of *Julius Caesar* as that play's first American pro-
duction, but Charles Shattuck reports an earlier production in
Philadelphia.[16]

The complete list of plays offered in this remarkable season is
available only because two South Carolina newspapers printed, at

the close of the season, a "Catalogue of Plays that have been performed here this season, by the American Company of Comedians, under the Direction of Mr. David Douglass."[17] The list is prefaced with this comment: "The choice of Plays hath been allowed to be very judicious, the Director having selected from the most approved English Poets such Pieces as possess in the highest degree the Utile Dulce, and while they entertain, improve the Mind by conveying the most useful Lessons of Morality and Virtue."

The Shakespearean season that "improved the minds" of Charlestonians in 1773 and 1774 was, in its variety, on a par with those of London, New York, and Philadelphia. Cohen provides an analysis of comparable seasons in those cities, noting that London audiences could see fifteen Shakespearean plays in the 1773–1774 season, while Charleston theatergoers were offered twelve. Available records from New York and Philadelphia indicate that neither city had a season of Shakespeare to equal Charleston's in the early 1770s.[18] It is safe to assume that these Charleston productions did not match the artistic levels of those seen in London, where David Garrick was managing and acting at the Drury Lane. Certainly, though, Charleston's plays and players were the best in colonial America. The American Company was made up of seasoned professional actors who had performed Shakespeare to good notices in Philadelphia, New York, Annapolis, and Williamsburg over a period of years.

The Charleston production of *King John* on May 19, 1774, was apparently the last professional performance of Shakespeare in colonial America. In October, 1774, the Continental Congress passed a resolution to "discountenance and discourage every species of extravagance and dissipation," including "shews, plays, and other expensive diversions and entertainments,"[19] thus putting an end to theater until after the war.

The Revolutionary War years were harsh ones in Charleston. Not until 1783 was theater again recorded in the city, and never again in the eighteenth century was there a season to equal the one of 1773 and 1774. In the years after the war, Charleston saw fewer productions of Shakespeare than in the outstanding prewar season, and contemporary reports suggest that these postwar performances were no longer equal in artistic quality to those seen in New York and Philadelphia. These trends first become evident in the accounts of the season of 1786.

Neither the amateur performances of 1783 nor the short season of Dennis Ryan's American Company in 1785 included Shakespeare. Not until 1786, when James Godwin built a new theater he called Harmony Hall, was Shakespeare again seen in Charleston. Godwin had no acting company and thus opened the season with concerts and the popular one-man *Lecture on Heads*. But by October he had recruited enough performers to attempt *Richard III,* with "two Parties of Volunteer Companies" enacting the battle scene.[20] The evening was not an unqualified success. The *Morning Post* reported that Godwin played Richard "with great and well earned applause," but the unidentified "Gentleman" debuting as King Henry was accused of "a sort of strut across the stage which even tragedy, altho always on stilts, could not bear." Miss Barrett, as Lady Anne, and the volunteer soldiers fared no better.

> The little she has been able to remember was dealt out in such a languid unimpassioned manner, as not to be heard even by the gentlemen in the orchestra; a variation in her action and attitudes would also be well. In the scene between Richard and Lady Anne, from the inanimation of the beauteous mourner, it resembled exceedingly the story of Pygmalion who fell in love with a statue.
>
> Owing to the smallness of the stage and a crowd behind the scenes the Battle of Bosworth's Field turned out a very la! la! performance indeed, resembling in nothing, what was done "in our great Harry's days."[21]

Richard III was repeated at Harmony Hall on October 31, this time followed by "a Methodist Field Preacher's Harangue in a Barrel,"[22] an entertainment which perhaps made up for the deficiencies of the main play.

In January, 1787, Godwin acquired two new actors identified in playbills only as Mr. Smith and Mr. Shakspeare, both of whom had performed Shakespearean roles in Baltimore. With these reinforcements he once again attempted *Richard III* on January 8, followed by *Henry IV* on January 16. The review of *Henry IV* was guardedly favorable, though it suggests that Godwin had not solved his production problems.

The strong coloring in which the inimitable Bard has drawn most of his characters renders a correct representation exceedingly difficult; there was, however, in the play of last night more than usual equality in point of merit. . . .

The jolly Knight had a most able representative, every period producing loud appeals of laughter from the audience.

It will not be amiss when the play is brought forward again to provide a stump of a tree on which Falstaff may rest the body of Hotspur, during his conversation with the Prince.

. . . .

If animadversion produces reformation, it may not be amiss to mention the long waits between the acts.[23]

The remainder of Godwin's season included a repetition of *Henry IV* and a production of *The Merchant of Venice,* which featured the "breeches roles" popular in the eighteenth century. It was advertised as "an admirable play," promising "the introducing [of] Portia and Nerissa in breeches, . . . a happy thought [which] must ever be pleasing as it tends to show female virtue triumphing over false delicacy, by assuming the garb of a man, from motives of tender affection to a husband. . . . Miss Gordon, who performs Portia, is an elegant figure."[24]

Godwin closed the season with two showings of *Romeo and Juliet,* with Smith playing Romeo and "a young lady for her amusement" as Juliet. The young lady was probably a stage-struck amateur who dared not risk her reputation by having her name used, a casting practice common in eighteenth-century America.

A summary of this first postwar Shakespearean season shows that, of forty performances given, eight were Shakespeare's plays. Shakespearean production thus accounted for one-fifth of the season, somewhat less than in the 1773–1774 season when one-third of the dates offered Shakespeare. The fact that Shakespeare appeared less frequently on Charleston playbills after the Revolutionary War was certainly due in part to the unavailability of experienced players, but it probably also reflected the tastes of a new generation of audiences.

The Charlestonians who composed theater audiences in the late eighteenth century were less accustomed to theater than their English-educated counterparts of mid-century. Charleston had recovered from the war and was once again a wealthy city, but South Carolina historian George Rogers, Jr., notes that, whereas in the 1750s wealth had fostered an interest in the arts, the concerns of wealthy Charlestonians in the 1790s tended to be less sophisticated.[25] Charles Fraser, whose 1854 *Reminiscences of Charleston* includes an account of the opening of the theater in 1793, observes that most Charlestonians in the audience had never seen theater: "Theatricals had been so long discontinued here, that the rising generation were strangers to the fascinations of the stage."[26]

Indeed, for some years prior to 1793 Charleston's entertainment was limited to lectures, concerts, and balls. In March, 1787, the South Carolina legislature passed a vagrancy act that subjected actors, along with beggars and fortune tellers, to a penalty of ten to thirty-nine lashes on the bare back. The law was repealed in 1791, opening the way for Charleston's most active theatrical decade of the century.

The 1793 theater which Fraser recalled was built by Thomas Wade West and John Bignall, who were responsible for reviving Charleston theater after its period of prohibition. West had had a respectable career as a Shakespearean actor in London, playing Bassanio, Hotspur, Richmond, Hamlet, Edmund, and Petruchio. His wife had performed with him in *Henry IV, King Lear,* and *Catherine and Petruchio.*[27] Most of the other actors in the company they brought to Charleston were relatively inexperienced, though, and, in the opinion of theater historian George O. Seilhamer, inferior to the performers in the Old American Company, then playing in New York.[28]

Though West and Bignall opened the new theater on February 7, 1793, Shakespeare did not appear on its bill until March. The delay was perhaps due to a need for more experienced actors. A. A. Chambers, who had performed secondary roles in Shakespearean plays at Drury Lane and the Haymarket, arrived in Charleston in early March and played the title role in *Richard III* on March 11. In April he appeared as Orlando in *As You Like It*, as Laertes in *Hamlet,* and as Ferdinand in *The Tempest.* In May he was Mercutio in *Romeo and Juliet.* West and Bignall were performing major roles as

The Charleston Theatre opened in 1793 by Thomas Wade West and John Bignall. After 1833, the building was used by the Medical College.
Engraving and drawing by C. Simons. Courtesy South Carolina Historical Society

well. In all, the company offered five productions of Shakespeare in a fifty-performance season.

West and Bignall opened their next season in January, 1794, this time offering only four Shakespearean plays in a season of seventy performances. Again, the managers probably had personnel problems. Chambers left Charleston at the end of March, leaving West and Bignall without a leading actor. Another factor in the selection of the program was the necessity for competing with the newly opened French Theatre on Church Street, where manager Alexandre Placide was presenting "Harlequin-pantomimes, rope-dancing with many feats and little amusing French pieces."[29]

Throughout the remaining years of the eighteenth century a variety of managers struggled to attract audiences to the Charleston

Theatre, built by West and Bignall, and the City Theatre, as Placide's French Theatre came to be known. The lengthy play lists of the years 1794 to 1799 show from three to seventeen performances of Shakespeare each season, fewer than in the exceptional 1773–1774 season. The most popular Shakespearean play of the postwar period was *Richard III,* with *Romeo and Juliet* and *Hamlet* close behind. Of the plays in the 1773–1774 program, *Julius Caesar* and *King John* were not repeated after the war. The only additions to the prewar offerings were *As You Like It* and *The Merry Wives of Windsor.*

Newspaper accounts of these and other Shakespearean plays provide ample evidence that productions of Shakespeare in eighteenth-century Charleston followed the pattern of the times: that is, as in other American and English cities, Shakespeare's plays were presented in Charleston in drastically cut or rewritten versions, they were invariably accompanied by afterpieces and variety entertainment, and both the main play and the afterpiece were given spectacular productions. The performances Ann Manigault saw in 1764 were no doubt of David Garrick's version of *Romeo and Juliet,* in which Juliet wakes in the tomb before Romeo's death, and Nahum Tate's rewriting of *King Lear,* which ends with Edgar and Cordelia married. A Charleston bill for *Romeo and Juliet* in 1796 advertises "a grand Funeral Procession, with a Solemn Dirge, in which Mrs. Pownall will sing the celebrated Song, from Handel's Oratorio of Judas Maccabeus, Return O God of Hosts."[30] The procession and dirge, also Garrick's innovations, were standard in eighteenth-century productions of *Romeo and Juliet. Richard III* as performed in this period was Colley Cibber's revision, which incorporates portions of *Henry IV, Henry VI,* and *Richard II. Hamlet*'s settings utilized eighteenth-century stock scenery; it was advertised at the City Theatre in 1796 with "a Parlour Scene finished in a masterly manner, . . . which exceeds any thing heretofore exhibited in this city."[31]

All Shakespearean plays, whether they were rewritten or not, were severely cut, a fact which explains how an audience having viewed *Romeo and Juliet* could then sit through the rest of the bill offered by the City Theatre on February 12, 1796. Following the main play, it promises these acts:

> In the course of the Evening's Entertainment, a dis-
> sertation on HOBBY HORSES, by Mr. Jones.
> Likewise, a COMIC SONG, called the FROLICS OF
> QUEEN MAB.
> A COMIC SONG, called MURDER in IRISH,
> And a COMIC SONG called A TWIGGLE and a
> FRIZ, in the character of a Hunch Backed Barber,
> By Mr. Jones.
> (A Little Merry He)
> To be sung by Master JONES, being but three years
> and a half old.
> To which will be added, the Musical FARCE of
> THE AGREEABLE SURPRIZE.
> To conclude with Mr. Jones, in the character of
> HARLEQUIN, will FLY from the back of the stage,
> to the extent of the Gallery, and down again.[32]

The main play of the evening was always accompanied by an afterpiece, usually a farce, as well as by singing, dancing, or other entertainment. During the 1790s managers often used the afterpieces and variety entertainment to satisfy the public's growing appetite for spectacle. A popular afterpiece was *Shakespeare's Jubilee,* devised by Garrick. The piece presented scenes and characters from a number of Shakespeare's plays, along with comic and tragic muses and a grand procession. It was performed on a bill with *Romeo and Juliet* in Charleston in 1793 "with all the necessary decorations, Inn Yard, Music, Banners, &c."[33]

By 1799 the accompanying entertainment sometimes outshone the play itself. On April 10, 1799, the Charleston Theatre advertised "the favorite and much admired comedy called *As You Like It,*" but it was the afterpiece that received most of the newspaper space:

> (for that night only)
> DANCING on the TIGHT ROPE
> By Mr. Placide.
> Who will dance a HORNPIPE, also, Display
> a FLAG, in several attitudes, and play on the
> Violin, in different ways.
> In the course of the entertainment,
> Mr. Placide will balance a Peacok [sic] Feather

> also blow the feather in the air, throwing
> A SOMERSET
> And catch the feather in equilibrium on his
> forehead.

The bill also offers "an entire new Pantomime," closing with this promise: "Mr. Placide respectfully informs the public that he has neglected no expense to render the last scene of the Pantomime one of the most brilliant that has ever yet appeared."[34]

Certainly, though, spectacle was not restricted to the afterpieces. The procession customarily included in *Romeo and Juliet* has already been noted. *Macbeth* as staged in 1796 included "a chorus of witches, while Hecate and Malkin, the attending Spirit, ascend into the Clouds."[35] Dryden and Davenant's version of *The Tempest* was staged six times in eighteenth-century Charleston. The notice for May 12, 1794, describes its wonders in detail.

> The opening discovers a troubled horizon and tempestuous sea, where the usurper's vessel is tossed a considerable time in sight, and gives signals of an approaching storm, amidst repeated claps of thunder, lightning, hail, rain, &c. being dashed on a chain of rocks, (which both sides of the stage strikely [*sic*] represent) and at the same instant, a dreadful shower of fire, pouring from the distempered elements; the crew gives signals of distress, the waves and winds rise to an affecting degree, and the vessel sinks in full view of the audience: the scenes altogether forming a most awful, but perfect picture of A SHIPWRECK.
>
> This hurricane (which is supposed to be raised by magic) ceasing, a delightful prospect of the Enchanted Island appears, also of the Enchanter's Dwelling: here the business of the play commences. . . .
>
> . . . .
>
> [The Play] terminates . . . in A VIEW of a CALM SEA on which Neptune and Amphitrite appear in a shell-chariot, drawn by sea-horses. . . . The piece concludes with the spirit Ariel's appearing in a chariot of clouds.[36]

Clearly, eighteenth-century Charleston audiences shared with theatergoers elsewhere in America and in England a taste for "improved" Shakespeare and for spectacular productions. It is likely, though, that most of Charleston's performances were not as good as those in London, New York, and Philadelphia. Shattuck observes that the English actors who journeyed to America in the eighteenth century were perhaps competent but surely inferior to the best on the London stage.[37] And, unlike the actors who played in Charleston in 1773 and 1774, Charleston performers in the 1790s were not America's best, for the strongest companies were in New York and Philadelphia.

Accounts from the period sometimes praise local players in the effusive style of the day, but derogatory comments appear frequently, indicating that it was not unusual for Charleston audiences to be subjected to an actor's reading his part, mumbling inaudibly, relying on the prompter, or performing while intoxicated. Even when none of these atrocities occurred, performances were sometimes unacceptable. Of W. H. Torrans's portrayal of the title role in *Richard III* in 1797, a local critic reported, "His pronunciation was neither correct nor emphatical, and his gestures were generally awkward and unnatural. . . . The Play, upon the whole, was miserably represented."[38]

A letter printed in the local newspaper in 1795 suggests that Charlestonians were resigned to second-rate performances. "It is not certainly in Charleston that we ought to expect to see at the Theatre, the first of the profession; the emoluments are not sufficient to pay the salaries of the first rate actors. . . . In every profession, mediocrity is more than half the world arrives at: if, the present Company of Comedians exceeds the generality, they are certainly entitled to commendation."[39]

The practice of bringing in star actors for limited engagements, begun on a limited scale in the 1790s, probably gave Charleston audiences an occasional opportunity to see better acting than the local actors could offer. The first to arrive was James Chalmers, who played Richard III, Shylock, Hamlet, Romeo, and Petruchio in 1796. The local press pronounced him "the best performer in top-comedy that ever graced the Charleston boards."[40] Most of his Shakespearean roles were in tragedy, though, and Seilhamer rates his tragedy as inferior to his comedy.[41] When he played a return engagement in 1799, a critic offered this review: "The part of Hamlet 'take it for all in all' was well supported by Mr. Chalmers. In some of the scenes he was excellent; in others his voice and gestures were too much empassioned. Hamlet's beautiful soliloquy on death was well delivered; and that on his mother's marriage was pronouced with an emphasis that riveted attention."[42]

The star system also brought to Charleston Elizabeth Kemble Whitlock, sister of the English actress Sarah Kemble Siddons. With her husband Charles, Mrs. Whitlock appeared at the City Theatre in 1797, playing Rosalind in *As You Like It,* Queen Elizabeth in *Richard III,* and others. Contemporary accounts describe her as a large, unattractive woman, less talented than her famous sister. Charleston loved her, though, and her reviews were strong. "A Friend in Truth" (who might have been a friend of a rival company) wrote a long letter to the newspaper in which he details the weaknesses of the City Theatre company and compares the new actress with her colleagues: "Mrs. Whitlock . . . is a brilliant, set in tin—her companions, by their impervious dullness, repell the rays necessary to display her lustre."[43]

If the importing of actors in the 1790s could not lift the quality of Charleston's Shakespearean performances much above the mediocre, it did pave the way for the great actors who visited the city in the nineteenth century, when Thomas A. Cooper, Edmund Kean, Edwin Forrest, William Charles Macready, and Edwin Booth played Shakespeare in Charleston.[44]

By the end of the eighteenth century, then, Charleston had seen one fledgling season of Shakespeare, in 1764; it had seen, in 1773 and 1774, one brilliant season, equal in variety and in quality to any offered in America; and it had seen a series of seasons, from 1786 through 1799, in which Shakespearean productions declined in popularity and in artistic quality. Clearly, to select the 1773–1774 season to characterize Charleston's early history of Shakespearean production is misleading, for that season was atypical. It was preceded by many years of theatrical activity in Charleston, but those years included only two documented performances of Shakespeare. The years following 1774 were marked by a strengthening of theatrical organization and by spectacular productions, but also by a decline in the predominance of Shakespeare and by mediocre performances. In the production of Shakespeare's plays, only in 1773 and 1774 does Charleston deserve to be ranked with America's leading theater cities.

But if eighteenth-century Charleston did not always have first-rate productions of Shakespeare offered to a cultured and appreciative public, it did have Shakespeare: eighty-two documented performances of fifteen different plays, and probably many more that went unrecorded. It is a record few southern cities can match, and one that supports Charleston's claim to a significant, if not a preeminent, place in the early history of Shakespeare on the American stage.

NOTES

1. See Barnard Hewitt, *Theatre, U.S.A., 1668 to 1957* (New York: McGraw-Hill, 1959), p. 43; and Garff B. Wilson, *Three Hundred Years of American Drama and Theatre: From Ye Bear and Ye Cubb to Hair* (Englewood Cliffs, N.J.: Prentice-Hall, 1973), p. 38.

2. See Hennig Cohen, "Shakespeare in Charleston on the Eve of the Revolution," *Shakespeare Quarterly* 4 (1953): 327–30; Louis Marder, "Shakespeare in America until 1776," *Shakespeare Newsletter* 26 (1976): 2; and George C. Rogers, Jr., *Charleston in the Age of the Pinckneys* (Columbia: University of South Carolina Press, 1980), p. 110.

3. The city's name was changed to Charleston in 1783. The modern spelling will be used throughout this essay.

4. *South Carolina Gazette,* Feb. 8, 1735.

5. Rogers, pp. 98–100.

6. Cohen, pp. 327–28.

7. *South Carolina Gazette,* May 21, 1737.

8. Eola Willis, *The Charleston Stage in the XVIII Century* (Columbia: The State Company, 1924), p. 31.

9. Marder, p. 2.

10. Hugh F. Rankin, *The Theater in Colonial America* (Chapel Hill: University of North Carolina Press, 1965), p. 72.

11. Mary Julia Curtis, "The Early Charleston Stage: 1703–1798" (Ph.D. diss., Indiana University, 1968), p. 61. Curtis's thorough research supplied much of the factual information on Charleston theater for this essay.

12. "Extracts from the Journal of Mrs. Ann Manigault, 1754–1781, with notes by Mabel L. Webber," *South Carolina Historical and Genealogical Magazine* 20 (1919): 207.

13. *The Letters and Papers of Cadwallader Colden: Collections of the New York Historical Society for the Year 1922* (New York: New York Historical Society, 1923), 6: 281–82.

14. For contemporary accounts of their acting, see Charles H. Shattuck, *Shake-*

speare on the American Stage from the Hallams to Edwin Booth (Washington: Folger Shakespeare Library, 1976), pp. 13–15.

15. Hereafter *Catherine and Petruchio* will be included in statistical accounts of Shakespearean production.

16. Willis, p. 74; Shattuck, p. 16.

17. *South Carolina Gazette,* May 30, 1774.

18. Cohen, p. 329.

19. Quoted in Shattuck, p. 15.

20. *Charleston Evening Gazette,* Oct. 11, 1786, quoted in Willis, p. 119.

21. *Charleston Morning Post,* Oct. 19, 1786, quoted in Willis, pp. 119–20.

22. Curtis, p. 149.

23. *Charleston Morning Post,* Jan. 17, 1787, quoted in Willis, p. 134.

24. [*Charleston Morning Post*], Feb. 16, 1787, quoted in ibid.

25. Rogers, p. 109.

26. Charles Fraser, *Reminiscences of Charleston* (Charleston: John Russell, 1854), p. 20.

27. Curtis, p. 175.

28. George O. Seilhamer, *History of the American Theatre* (1888–91; rpt. New York: Benjamin Blom, 1968), 2: 329.

29. *City Gazette and Daily Advertiser,* Mar. 26, 1794.

30. Ibid., Feb. 11, 1796.

31. *South Carolina State Gazette and Timothy and Mason's Daily Advertiser,* Jan. 18, 1796.

32. *City Gazette and Daily Advertiser,* Feb. 11, 1796.

33. *State Gazette of South Carolina,* May 31, 1793.

34. *South Carolina State Gazette and Timothy and Mason's Daily Advertiser,* Apr. 10, 1799.

35. *City Gazette and Daily Advertiser,* Mar. 16, 1796.

36. *South Carolina State Gazette and Timothy and Mason's Daily Advertiser,* May 12, 1794.

37. Shattuck, p. xi.

38. *City Gazette and Daily Advertiser,* Mar. 27, 1797.

39. Ibid., Nov. 21, 1795, quoted in Curtis, p. 326.

40. [*City Gazette and Daily Advertiser*], Jan. 4, 1796, quoted in Willis, pp. 296–97.

41. Seilhamer, 3: 190.

42. Willis, p. 439.

43. *South Carolina State Gazette and Timothy and Mason's Daily Advertiser,* Apr. 26, 1797, quoted in Curtis, p. 377.

44. For an account of Shakespeare in nineteenth-century Charleston, see W. Stanley Hoole, "Shakspere on the Ante-Bellum Charleston Stage," *Shakespeare Association Bulletin* 21 (1946): 37–45.

Shakespeare in Charleston, 1800–1860

Woodrow L. Holbein

Between 1800 and 1860 the citizens of Charleston, South Carolina, had the opportunity to see approximately 600 performances of twenty-three of Shakespeare's plays, from the ever-popular *Richard II* and *Hamlet* to *Love's Labor's Lost* with its one performance.[1] The tragedies (*Hamlet, Macbeth, Othello, King Lear, Romeo and Juliet, Julius Caesar, Anthony and Cleopatra*, and *Coriolanus*) had 338 performances; the comedies (*Love's Labor's Lost, The Winter's Tale, Cymbeline, Twelfth Night, The Tempest, The Merry Wives of Windsor, Comedy of Errors, As You Like It, Much Ado About Nothing*, and *The Merchant of Venice*), 140 performances; and the histories (*King John, 1 Henry IV, Henry VIII*, and *Richard III*), 114. No other dramatist could rival this interest. One would like to say that the popularity of Shakespeare reflected the genteel, cultured society of Charleston. However, the attraction of the performers—both from the stock company and the visiting stars—more than likely accounted for Charlestonians' enthusiasm for Shakespearean drama.

On April 14, 1806, Thomas Abthorpe Cooper started a limited engagement but remained until May 16. With his appearance Charleston became a major stop for almost all of the famous tragedians—English and American—and each had a repertoire of Shakespearean roles. Cooper, Edmund Kean, Junius Brutus Booth and his son Edwin, William Charles Macready, Anna Cora Mowatt, and many more in conjunction with the stock company performed Shakespeare's tragedies: *Anthony and Cleopatra*, 4 times; *Coriolanus*, 10; *Julius Caesar*, 11; *King Lear*, 26; *Romeo and Juliet*, 64; *Othello*, 64; *Macbeth*, 76; *Hamlet*, 83. The reviews in local newspapers offered not only continuing praise for outstanding performances but also expressed continuing fascination in the tragic Hamlet, in the terror, horror, and passion of Macbeth, in the young

Sketch of the Charleston Theatre on Broad and New streets, 1793–1833
Drawing by Emmett Robinson

star-crossed love of Romeo and Juliet, in the rage of Lear, and finally in the villainy of Iago and in the insane jealousy of Othello, with the Moor's color sometimes an issue.

From January 1, 1800, to the closing of the theater in 1860, *Hamlet*, not surprisingly, was the most popular tragedy. Not only did stock companies perform it repeatedly, but many of the visiting actors did, too. When Cooper portrayed Hamlet before a Charleston audience on April 14, 1806, it was the beginning of a long and generally warm relationship. When he made his last appearance as Hamlet in Charleston on March 27, 1835, he had performed Hamlet ten times over a period of twenty-eight years. In a review in the *Courier* of Cooper's first performance of *Hamlet*, Thespiad called Cooper "a very great and indeed extraordinary performer," but he also said that "Mr. C's Hamlet . . . is a showy piece, in some places brilliantly coloured, . . . but it wants uniformity. In some parts he appeared to us to be mistaken, in others faint, and in others again extremely great." Although Thespiad did not provide details, he found Cooper's scenes with Ophelia and with Gertrude in the closet scene "of the highest order of excellence."[2]

On November 2, 1818, Henry J. Finn's characterization of Hamlet before a Charleston audience provided material for one of the more unusual dramatic reviews. In his review in the *Southern Patriot*, Launcelot asked Mr. Ticklepitcher for opinions of the interpretation of Finn's portrayal of Hamlet. Ticklepitcher stated that Finn "struck off some passages with good taste, and much success but the general conception of the part is quite incorrect." Not liking the ghost scenes, Ticklepitcher stated that when the Ghost departed for the "shades, I should have liked Mr. Finn's soliloquy much better had he given it in a burst of horrour and indignation, . . . and when Hamlet said 'But bear me stiffly up' and then *rising* at the word *up*— a ludicrous effect!" Ticklepitcher approved of Finn's reading of the play, especially the following: "Most performers read the line 'My father's spirit in arms?,' but Finn read it 'My father's spirit? in arms!' "[3]

Junius Brutus Booth first appeared in Charleston in *Hamlet* for his benefit performance on December 7, 1821. The reviewer in the *City Gazette* stated that Booth would have to study many years before he could unfold all the beauties in that "philosophical and arduous character," for in the ghost scene Booth delivered the words too quickly and created "no true sense of horror." In giving advice to the players Booth sat in a chair, but the critic thought it would have been more natural to stand and "infinitely more graceful to have exhibited by gesture the wholesome advice he was then giving." However, the reviewer accepted Booth's mode as defensible and, citing Booth's reading of "My father's spirit!—in arms?" thought the actor had read the line rapidly, "My father's spirit in arms!" "without the pause which gives so pregnant a sense to the exclamation." In the death scene Booth evidently fell to the floor too soon, for he had to rise again to stop Horatio from taking his life. Booth's scene with Ophelia and the closet scene were his best: "Pregnant with force and feeling." In summary, Booth had "a fine countenance and youthful appearance, and melancholy guise in Hamlet, imparted to it interest, even when he failed."[4] Although J. B. Booth had six more engagements in Charleston, he performed Hamlet only twice: February 24, 1844, and March 25, 1852.

William Charles Macready had two engagements in Charleston during January, 1844, and January, 1849, appearing as Hamlet three times. He opened his first engagement on January 8, 1844, with his portrayal of Hamlet to a "large, fashionable and intelligent audience" and repeated the role on January 19. After Macready's opening performance, Dr. John Beaufain Irving provided detailed accounts of Macready's Hamlet. Having completed his education at Rugby and Cambridge, Irving had been a junior at Rugby when Macready was in the sixth form. Although he may have been slightly biased, Irving considered Macready's engagement not only successful, but also the high point of theater in Charleston before the Civil War. Judging Macready's Hamlet as faultless, Irving stated that the actor "artistically preserved and exhibited the distinctive feelings which agitate the bosom of *Hamlet the Dane*."[5] Irving seemed to praise everything, but he thought the closet scene was the crowning glory of the whole performance.

> In the first interview between Hamlet and the Ghost, Mr. Macready was accustomed to make the *terrible* graces superior to the tender; in his second interview, though not deficient in the former, the latter predominate. In his bearing towards the Ghost, he is now *reverential*, rather than *awe-stricken*. He pursues the melancholy shade to its exit, with filial love, and a tearful eye; and then his complete prostration on the vanishing of the Ghost—from its *novelty*, and as the *natural* result of a previous high state of excitement, was sure to be felt and acknowledged by his audience. . . . His whole manner and countenance, when turned towards his mother, were such, as if he was struggling within himself, to bear in mind the injunction of his father, not to think, by any act of his of punishing his mother, but to leave her to Heaven and her own conscience![6]

When Macready returned five years later, he received similar good reviews, although on the day of the performance of *Hamlet*, January 15, 1849, a brief item in the newspaper so upset him that he recorded in his *Diary*, "Looked at a paper, in which it is observed that 'some people think that the Hamlet of Vandenhoff senior superior to Macready's.' What ignorant and conceited dunces in literature and art these people are! It is the fact!"[7]

Whether ignorant or conceited dunces, Charlestonians had en-

joyed *Hamlet* through the years, but *Romeo and Juliet* also pleased
them with its young lovers and, occasionally, with a woman in a
breeches role. *Romeo and Juliet* was a popular attraction in Charleston, with sixty-four performances from May 6, 1803, to April 2,
1860;[8] however, only a few received reviews. Thomas Abthorpe
Cooper portrayed Romeo, one of his major roles, six times from
1806 to 1832. A review by Momus of the April 14, 1818, performance
shows that some of the audience had feared Cooper would fail as a
lover, but this performance dispelled any misgivings. "Those who
have thought that Mr. Cooper could not *make love,* were unde-
ceived when they beheld him in the character of Romeo. Without
being particular, we may observe that the garden scenes were in a
style melting, touching effect."[9] When Cooper became too old to
play Romeo, he turned to the role of Mercutio. The third and last
time he played it, his own daughter was Juliet.

Probably the most interesting productions of *Romeo and Juliet*
starred a woman as Romeo. Miss Lydia Kelly played Romeo on
March 2, 1829, nine months before her December 11, 1829, performance at the Park Theatre in New York City for her benefit.[10] According to the accounts in the Charleston newspapers, "This enchanting
actress . . . has acquired much fame" in her short visit to Charleston.[11] One reviewer noted that "a very crowded and fashionable
audience graced the theatre" for a performance that met the public
expectation.[12] Six other performances saw women Romeos. On
March 3, 1836, Mrs. J. Barnes played Romeo while her daughter,
Miss Charlotte Barnes, played Juliet. Twice in 1839 Mrs. McClure
portrayed Romeo (February 28 and March 2). Mrs. Melinda Jones
performed Romeo three times. The second performance, on March
2, 1854, was of particular interest, for she had the lead opposite
Anna Cora Mowatt's Juliet. In her last appearance as Romeo in
Charleston, Mrs. Jones starred opposite her daughter Avonia Jones.

The most successful and popular Juliet was Anna Cora Mowatt,
who appeared five times in the part on a Charleston stage. During
her first season (December, 1845, and January, 1846), Mrs. Mowatt
presented Juliet three times. When she made her first appearance on
December 10, 1845, Mrs. Mowatt had "been on the stage scarcely

six months," according to a reviewer, who was overwhelmed with admiration for the actress:

> With the winning beauty of the balcony scene, in which her tones seemed to come directly from her heart in snatches of music,—the ardor of youthful love tempered by the instinctive modesty of innocence,—and a rich ideal atmosphere thrown overall;—or with the beautiful affectionateness of the first scenes with the nurse,—or the sweetness of sentiment, undisturbed by a single tone of sentimentality in her interviews with Romeo,—we are struck with the variety of power she displayed in the delineation. . . . Her whole conception of the character was as perfect as it could be, and the faults were merely of detail, which a little more practice will remedy.[13]

When she again appeared in Charleston on December 8, 1846, her Juliet was said to be "almost perfection itself. We have before us the Juliet of Shakespeare . . . : the *beau ideal* of all that is sweet and gentle and lovely in women."[14] Her third performance, on March 2, 1854, with Mrs. Melinda Jones as Romeo, went unreviewed.

Between 1800 and 1860 *Macbeth* proved almost as popular as *Hamlet,* with at least seventy-six performances and with approximately thirty-five different Macbeths, including Edmund Kean, Charles Macready, Thomas Abthorpe Cooper, Edwin Forrest, Edwin Booth. A permanent member of the resident company generally portrayed Lady Macbeth. Between 1807 and 1824 Mrs. Alexandre Placide and Mrs. Charles Gilfert performed Lady Macbeth eighteen times. During the same period only two other ladies appeared in the role.

Thomas Abthorpe Cooper appeared in the leading role more than anyone—male or female—over a longer period, fourteen performances from April 16, 1806, until his last appearance on March 2, 1830. During the twenty-six years Cooper repeatedly received praise not only for individual scenes but also for his overall performance. On April 21, 1806, one reviewer said that Cooper's Macbeth "was throughout the whole character, with very few and very trivial exceptions, uniformly great and excellent."[15] In 1819 "the merit of Cooper . . . does not lie so much in detail, . . . but in the *general effect,* in the genius which prevails and illuminates *the whole.*"[16] In 1828 Cooper's performance "evinced no marked declension of his powers in picturing the dark and terrific passions which make up Macbeth."[17]

In his early appearances in Charleston, Cooper must have startled the audiences in the scenes surrounding the death of Duncan. In ·1806 Thespiad stated that "in the scene preparatory to the murder, the air drawn dagger part included, he could not be surpassed." In the death scene Cooper evidently stretched his talents to their limits. "The horrible and terror in *highest* state were so genuinely painted by him in countenance and action, that nature for a time appeared to have interposed her arm in creating a copy from even her most faithful imitator, Shakespeare."[18] By 1819 Cooper seemingly had perfected the final episode of the death scene for theatergoers in Charleston. A critic for the *Southern Patriot* vividly described Cooper and the spell he cast after murdering Duncan.

> The deed appears so to have congealed the mental powers of the murderer that Macbeth, as personated by Cooper, walks across the stage, backwards with his eyes fixed upon the door of the chamber in which the king and *guest* should have slept—his countenance like marble—his looks—wild—his gait bewildered—finding his way from the horrid scene 'without his eyes'—until the touch of Lady Macbeth recalls him to recollection, and he starts, as it were, into life and thought with a universal tremour and exhaustion of frame. . . . Its effect upon the audience was electrical.[19]

The audience reaction to his appearance on December 12, 1828 (just two years prior to his final performance as Macbeth) clearly expressed the appreciation and popularity that Cooper had sustained since 1806. "When Mr. Cooper first appeared, every person in the Pit, by a simultaneous movement arose, and the most enthusiastic cheering rang through the house. We have never witnessed a warmer expression of feeling on any similar occasion."[20]

After Macready opened his engagement in Charleston with *Hamlet,* he made his second appearance on January 10, 1844, as Macbeth. Dr. J. B. Irving, who continued his glowing review of his schoolmate, praised Macready's "usual discrimination" and his consistency. Providing some details of the banquet scene, Irving pointed out that Macready made a change in the scene for the Charleston audience. "Instead of the *Ghost of Banquo* walking on with his hand pointed to his gashed throat, he caused him to rise through a trap door immediately at the seat designated for himself."[21] In a revealing comment about Charleston audiences, Macready said that he "acted Macbeth with great care and energy; before an applauding audience the performance would have made a great sensation."[22] He implied that the audience did not react to his performance as he felt it should. Nevertheless, judging from reviews, Charlestonians appreciated Macready.

When Mr. and Mrs. Charles Kean appeared as Macbeth and Lady Macbeth on February 4, 1846, Kean's improvement during his twelve-year absence from Charleston was a topic of conversation. A better Macbeth and Lady Macbeth had not been seen together; "the mournful conviction of despair, which possesses *both hearts,* in spite of the attainment of all their ambitious desires, was a highly touching and holy moral, in which passion is overcome by woe!"[23] Another review paid respects to Charles Kean but concentrated on the performance of Mrs. Kean, who gave a "perfect delineation of the[se] passions. The deep lines of thought—thought intent upon evil—suggested by the letter of her husband, . . . were expressed in her features with a fidelity to nature that we have never seen surpassed."[24] Probably Lady Macbeth's sleepwalking scene received the most praise.

But above all, the scene of sleep-walking was so truthful and so awful a picture, that the audience were borne beyond themselves, and felt as though they were in presence of no mimic stage, but witnesses of stern reality. . . . Silence, universal silence pervaded the Theatre, from the pit to the gallery—a pin could have been heard to fall. . . . And when she left the stage, one long, loud burst of enthusiastic applause at once rewarded the skill of the actress and relieved the heavy oppression that the scene had thrown the audience.[25]

In addition to Kean, George Barrett, Henry Wallack, William A. Conway, Edwin Forrest, John Oxley, and Edwin Booth were some of the many actors who played Macbeth in Charleston.

On May 13, 1807, *King Lear,* "Not performed in Charleston these ten years," was staged in Charleston. This was the first of twenty-six performances, probably of an altered version and generally with a traveling star. Although Cooper made Charleston a regular stop, he portrayed King Lear only twice (May 13 and 16, 1807), probably using George Colman's version of Tate's adaptation of *King Lear*. Nahum Tate had eliminated the Fool and the King of France, created a romance between Cordelia and Edgar, and restored part of the kingdom to Lear. The Colman version of Tate's adaptation dropped the romance between Cordelia and Edgar and eliminated Gloucester's imagined leap from the cliff of Dover. Criticizing the unnecessary revisions, deletions, and alterations, one reviewer stated that "the plays of Shakespeare are, in these days of taste, so altered, so lopped, so bedizened in the dress of modern foppery, that the 'Bard of Avon' in the closet, and the Shakespeare on the stage, are like 'Poor Tom,' and the son of Gloucester—the identity is scarcely recognized through the disguise."[26] He did regret the omission of the Fool but he could "not give up easily, the best descriptive passage in the play—"How fearful/And dizzy 'tis to cast one's eyes so low"—and condemned the survival of Cordelia and Lear. Although the reviewer gives details of the performance, it would be difficult to determine whose version or adaptation, Colman's or Tate's, the Charleston audience saw.[27] When Junius Brutus Booth played Lear on December 3, 1821, the reviewer in the *City Gazette and Daily Advertiser* criticized him and Tate for altering Shakespeare; "we put in our *veto* against the vile alteration which this play has undergone—not surely to suit an English or American audience." When Lear rages against the elements, "we could find very little of one of the old bard's most sublime flights of eloquence; and the few lines of it, reserved by the Prompter, or by Mr. Tate, who has sadly mangled the whole play, were uttered by Mr. Booth with an expression of much anger. . . . 'Tis too beautiful, too sublime, to be torn to pieces, either by the curtailment of the managers, or by the passions of the performer."[28] When Booth performed Lear on March 25, 1825, newspaper notices included Aranthe but not the Fool in the cast, Booth probably continuing to perform Tate's adaptation. Since the managers stopped after 1825 providing a cast list in theater notices, we have no way of identifying which version of *King Lear* audiences saw unless a reviewer cited the fact. For example, when John Vandenhoff performed Lear on January 31, 1838, the reviewer only noted, "We are sorry, however, that several scenes usually performed in Lear, were omitted in last night's representation, thus depriving it of some portion of that symmetry which is so necessary to preserve its unity."[29]

J. B. Booth appeared in Charleston as Lear eight times from December 3, 1821, to March 27, 1852. In his first performance "complete success crowned his personation of one of the most arduous characters on the stage."[30] Another review praised Booth's performance as "original, frequently great, in some instances it was electrical."[31] Booth, the reviewer continued, held the audience spellbound in the curse scene. "Lear's curse was as bitter as a curse could be—his alienation of mind was gradual and thrillingly felt—his recollection of Cordelia shot through the audiences, like the lightning from Heaven. We speak here without qualification—it was a great and masterly stroke of acting." In March, 1825, Booth appeared on Friday, the twenty-fifth, and because of "the distinguished marks of approbation" and "in compliance with numerous requests," repeated the play on Monday, the twenty-eighth.[32] These performances were probably his finest depiction of Lear for Charleston, as the following comments indicate: "Mr. Booth's performance, forcible and impressive, evinced a mind active and well-disciplined."[33] "Mr. Booth has never been equalled on this side of the Atlantic. . . . The applause throughout . . . was unbounded, and followed in such rapid succession, as in many instances to delay the performance."[34] "In tremulous frame, the sunken voice, and the lines of venerable age, yet with a soul alive to undeserved cruelty, the ungratefully treated old man appeared that the author has described so masterly."[35] On March 27, 1852, just eight months before his death, J. B. Booth made his final appearance in Charleston as King Lear. Although warmly praised, it was not one of his best performances. Nevertheless, Booth still retained much of the energy, fire, and spirit that had captivated the first Charleston audience. The curse scene continued to electrify audiences. "When Lear is excited to his highest pitch of wrath and indignation—when his irritable nature is aroused by the ingratitude of his daughters—when he pours out on them the concentrated bitterness of his spirit, in a

tide of curses and imprecations—Mr. Booth imparted an awful gran-
deur to these passages by the force of his action."[36] His son Edwin
traveled with him on this last tour, but there is no indication he
performed in the tragedy. Edwin, however, returned to Charleston
to bring Lear to life for one night, April 5, 1859, but no reviews shed
light on his performance of a role that his father had immortalized
for Charlestonians.

Othello proved popular in Charleston. From the first performance
on January 30, 1809, until its last on March 21, 1860, theatergoers
saw sixty-four performances of *Othello* with Thomas Abthorpe
Cooper, William A. Conway, Edmund Kean, Edwin Forrest, J. B.
Booth, William C. Macready on stage. Performances of *Othello* appeared slowly, however, because of City Council restrictions. When
Cooper appeared for his second engagement in Charleston (April,
1807), Alexandre Placide, the theater manager, requested permission of the City Council to stage *Othello* but the council denied the
request.

A letter in the *Times* for May 9, 1807, on the "Failure of Council to
permit Othello on Stage," signed by Juvenis, offers many intriguing
observations about the performance of *Othello,* or at least its intended performance. Juvenis accepted, reluctantly, the right of the
City Council to watch "over us with . . . parental solicitude" but
asserted that the council may have gone too far in "refusing to
permit Shakespeare's inimitable play of *Othello*." The council's objection to the play was that it "contained sentiments incompatible
with the real interests of this country." Juvenis disagreed, pointing
out that Alexandre Placide, in obtaining a license, consented not to
admit "persons of a particular description"—undoubtedly
Negroes—and complied with the condition for the license.
Moreover, for this performance, the play had been "revised, corrected, and (I may add) adapted to Carolina, as every paragraph,
which, by the most scrupulous, might be thought improper, has been
entirely stricken out; so that not a sentiment remains, which could
be distorted or interpreted into a meaning inimical to the true interest of the community."[37]

One can only speculate what kind of adaptation a South Carolina audience needed. In *Travels through Lower Canada, and the United States of North America, in the Years 1806, 1807, and 1808* John Lambert throws light on the situation. In a brief description of the theater, Lambert expected the "Charleston stage [would be] well supplied with *souty* negroes, who would have performed the *African* and *savage* characters in the dramatic pieces." Instead of being *"real negroes,"* the performers would not even "condescend to *blacken* their faces, or dress in any manner resembling an African."[38] (I wonder if the adaptation of *Othello* meant a "white Moor"?) According to Lambert, Charlestonians feared that the Negroes would develop a sense of importance as individuals and would attempt to imitate white men. For this reason *Othello* "and other plays, where a black man is the hero of the piece, are not allowed to perform, nor are any of the negroes, or people of colour permitted to visit the theatre."[39]

On January 30, 1809, Cooper performed the first nineteenth-century Othello in Charleston. Since *Othello* had been denied to Charleston, the announcement created unusual interest and as a result "all parts of the house were filled with anxious expectants."[40] Cooper received customary praise for his conception of the character. Cooper appeared sixteen times in *Othello*, five as Iago, including his last appearance on January 8, 1838. The reviewer of this performance pointed out that Cooper continued to captivate an audience, especially with his soliloquy beginning "That Cassio loves her": "we thought we could perceive in every lineament and change of voice the development of the dark intellect and subtle, plotting spirit of mischief in Iago that balances probabilities of success with the chances of failure, in mentally working out a plan of demonical wickedness. It was truly a masterpiece of acting, the vivid embodyment of deep calculating cunning, sharpened by concentrated hate."[41]

On February 6, 1819, Mr. I. Cleary, having just arrived from a tour of England, made his first appearance in Charleston as the Moor. Generally, Touchstone and C. (the reviewers) praised him, but both criticized his facial expressions because of makeup. Touchstone stated that "we think considerably more effect would have been produced had the color on Mr. C.'s face been less dinghy, and laid on smoothly—its darkness was too murky to shew well and distinctly the workings of the passions on his face, which wanted outline." C. more clearly defined Othello's color in arguing that "Moors are not black."

> His countenance [Cleary's] is expressive, though the motions of the muscles of his face could not be well discerned, through the pitchy die with which he covered the Moor's visage. The Moors are not black, they are two shades darker than the Spaniards; and mellow into *brown* rather than black. Passages from this very play of Shakespeare may be urged against this position; but what Othello says of Desdemona's beauty, which by her supposed lapse from virtue, had now become 'begrim'd and black as his own face'—must be put down as much to the intention and force of passion which sought *that contrast* as to the metaphorical language of the poet.[42]

C. probably provided the answer for the audience's acceptance of a black or tawny Othello on an antebellum stage. In commenting on the costumes of the performers, C. also shows his desire to place Othello among the ranks of whites rather than blacks. C. expresses wonder at the various costumes "all differing from each other, and none of them attending to the *fact,* that Othello, though a Moor, was in the Venetian service." Since Othello had married a Venetian lady and abhorred the Turks and Ottomites, he should not be clothed in a "Turkish Robe, nor with the tunic of the Caliph of Bagdad." As the commander of the Venetian forces, "the *Venetian* uniform of that age would be the most appropriate costume."[43] Although the issue of color that had kept *Othello* off the stage during the first decade of the nineteenth century still influenced Charleston, antebellum audiences evidently could accept a Moor in a Turkish costume, but not a Negro.

After Cleary's characterization of Othello, the racial issue apparently never appeared in the local newspapers. *Othello* continued to be popular in Charleston with such performers as Edmund Kean, Edwin Forrest, Junius Brutus Booth, William Charles Macready, and Edwin Booth, who starred as Iago as late as March 2, 1860. However, only a few reviews of any significance appeared. Kean drew high praise, Forrest and J. B. Booth played before full houses, while Edwin Booth received only a brief mention for his efforts. Only Macready received detailed commentary and this from Dr. J. B. Irving, who wrote of the "force and feeling" of Macready, especially in the third act "when Iago first wakes him to suspicion, nothing could be finer, and more truthful to nature than those impassioned feelings of the heart which he evinced." Irving saved the highest praise for the fifth act. Macready exhibited "as great *intensity* of conception, as anything he did during his Charleston engagement. His manner of stabbing himself—his tottering toward the bed where Desdemona lay—his manifest anxiety to reach it ere he died—as if this was the only penitence left to him, but called forth from every part of the house a simultaneous outburst of enthusiasm."[44]

With Edwin Booth's performance as Iago on March 21, 1860, Shakespeare's *Othello* on the antebellum Charleston stage ended. The play started the first decade in controversy over color and ended just before the Civil War with no reference to race. However, I doubt that Othello had more than a good suntan when he ceased coming alive on the stage in Charleston.

During the antebellum period, 141 performances of Shakespeare's comedies had played in Charleston: *Love's Labor's Lost*, 1; *The Winter's Tale*, 1; *Cymbeline*, 2; *Twelfth Night*, 3; *The Tempest*, 5; *Merry Wives of Windsor*, 13; *Comedy of Errors*, 13; *As You Like It*, 21; *Much Ado About Nothing*, 36; *The Merchant of Venice*, 46. Obviously the roles of Rosalind and Orlando, Beatrice and Benedict, Portia, and, especially, Shylock were favorites for performers and audiences alike. Of the comedies, *The Merchant of Venice* probably had the most interesting stage history in Charleston. On January 16, 1800, it appeared before a Charleston audience, but was not to play again until April 22, 1811. During the eleven-year lapse, at least two performances were scheduled—on April 28, 1802, and November 14, 1803—only to be canceled. Although the manager gave no reason for the first cancellation, evidently some members of the Jewish community in Charleston requested the removal of *The Merchant of Venice* from its scheduled performance.[45]

After a request for *The Merchant of Venice* by Momus on March

22, 1811, in the *Charleston Times,* Shakespeare's play had a permanent place both with the company and with touring stars, such as Henry Wallack, Junius Brutus Booth, Edmund Kean, Charles Kean, and William Charles Macready. Evidently Momus anticipated some objections, for he commented on the alteration of the text for the performance of April 22, 1811: "The *harshness* of some expressions will be ameliorated; verbal alterations will be made in those few passages, which we are certain the genius of Shakespeare could only have stooped to utter, totally, with the overwhelming prejudices of a dark and bigotted age; and no offence can possibly be given to that portion of the community, who, without these objections, would listen to this beautiful production with pleasure and administration."[46] Prejudice and anti-semitism may have influenced the drama, but they were not mentioned in the limited reviews during the period.

The first review of any significance of *The Merchant of Venice* appeared in the *Southern Patriot* of November 25, 1815; Thespis assessed Thomas Hilson's Shylock, which he had seen the night before. For Shylock "there is a certain *unnatural* atrocity . . . which renders *disgust.*" In Shylock "there is no trace of nobleness. . . . 'Tis all demonical and black atrocity." Hilson gave powerful evidence of a Shylock "with all his atrocity, with all those features of disgust."[47] Hilson completely dominated the performance and depicted a villainous character too strong for comic purposes, setting the tone which probably prevailed on the Charleston stage.

In his first appearance in Charleston, Henry J. Finn recreated the Shylock that he had played in New York. Although a reviewer in the *Southern Patriot* considered *The Merchant of Venice* one of Shakespeare's worst plays and, in particular, the trial scene as ridiculous, he liked Finn's earnestness. To illustrate Finn's effective style and passion, the reviewer described Shylock's reactions: "His [Shylock's] exclamation, when he hears Antonio's bankruptcy confirmed, "Thank God! thank God!" the act of dropping on his knee, his pause; filled up . . . by the terrible expression of his countenance, representing all the horrid joy of malice—and the tone of the voice in which the exclamation was uttered, were all in a style of acting highly effective and striking."[48] Finn returned to Charleston sixteen years later and performed Shylock again on November 27, 1834, but no one reviewed his performance.

Of the other performances only brief reviews remain. *The Merchant of Venice* was popular on the stage even if some performances went unreviewed. When Mr. and Mrs. Charles Kean appeared in Charleston together, one commentator stated that Charles Kean resembled Edmund Kean, "that Mr. C. Kean's voice, manner, and attitude, and that the stage business is almost identically the same."[49] On February 11, 1846, Mr. and Mrs. C. Kean performed *The Merchant of Venice* to a full house, and a reviewer stated that "this is the best character that Charles Kean plays."[50] Unfortunately, details of C. Kean's performances of Shylock in Charleston are missing. On November 24, 1855, a performance of *The Merchant of Venice* by Grattan Dawson as Shylock elicited comments on Dawson's overacting, thus suggesting the usual interpretation of Shylock by the average performer. Dawson's "Shylock was not good":

He exhibited more agony than would have been necessary for a half-dozen Shylocks. There are times when the character requires intense emotion, and when the rolling up the eyes until the whites only are visible, and a clutching with the fingers, and a hissing voice through teeth that are closed, from excess of feeling, are all very proper; but not so always; to every character there must be some relief, and it is particularly necessary, to a proper appreciation of the villainy of Shylock that it should be lightened by its humor, and shaded by its pathos. Mr. Dawson got into a frenzy at the beginning, and never seemed to find his way out again.[51]

Although *The Merchant of Venice* started the antebellum period in controversy, the role of Shylock offered too many opportunities for members of the stock company and the traveling stars not to be played often.

Although *As You Like It* had only a limited number of performances (twenty-one), several actresses starred as Rosalind—Lydia Kelly, Clara Fisher, Fanny Fitzwilliam, Mrs. Charles Kean, Charlotte Cushman, Anna Cora Mowatt, and Fanny Morant. Their accomplishments surpassed meager reviews of them. For her performances of February 22 and 24, 1854, Mrs. Mowatt was called "one of those dainty Shakespearean treats . . . and we would gladly see presented as often as possible."[52] When Fanny Morant appeared on stage in Charleston on November 8, 13, and 30, 1855, the *Mercury's* critic stated that she represented Rosalind "with a spirit, a delicacy and a grace, that fairly enraptured the audience."[53] The reviewer for the *Charleston Standard* said that "it was one of the greatest triumphs on the Charleston stage."[54]

Much Ado About Nothing was popular both for stock company and touring stars. It first appeared on February 25, 1804 and its last of thirty-six performances in the city occurred on March 23, 1860. In the review of the first nineteenth-century performance of the play, Thespis provided some early commentary on Shakespeare as well as Benedict and Beatrice.

> Like all the plays of the great Bard it has some considerable defects, but those are so entirely overbalanced by the beauties of the piece at large, and particularly by the parts of Benedict and Beatrice, that they vanish like small specks of cloud passing between us and the sun. In no characters in the English or any other language is there such a display of elegant vivacity and refined wit which excites the internal smile of delight rather than the broad loud laugh of mirth. A congeniality of temper, intellect and disposition occasions an apparent disagreement between Benedict and Beatrice, which never fails to display itself in a war of words whenever they meet. . . . Perhaps no poet that has ever lived—not Homer himself, has exhibited more genius or more art in painting character than Shakespeare has in making these two.[55]

Cooper appeared in Charleston as Benedict seven times, starting on May 27, 1807, and ending with his final performance on January 15, 1838. The more interesting performances were probably the four during the 1830s in which he costarred with his daughter. When they made their last appearance in Charleston, a reviewer exuberantly praised Miss Cooper and her aging father:

> Mr. Cooper in Benedict, if we allow for the absence of that buoyance which belongs to an earlier period of life, showed no diminution of that power of varied expression which has always characterized his performances. Into the soliloquy where he first learns the love of Beatrice for him there was thrown the sympathizing influence which thoroughly identifies the performer with the character he performs. The gradations from the very first revelation of the fact that he was adored, to the moment that the idea has been realized to his mind that he was really beloved by her who

had made him the mark of too trenchant wit, were marked by consummate judgment and effective personation. . . . Mr. Cooper displayed all these changes with a spirit fully conversant as well with the broad lights as the delicate shades of the character.[56]

In addition to the performances given by the stock company, many other traveling stars brought Benedict before the Charleston audiences—Henry Wallack, John Dwyer, Thomas Caldwell (prior to his move to New Orleans), Vincent DeCamp, George Vandenhoff, and Edwin Booth just before the Civil War. Of the women who depicted Beatrice, Clara Fisher, with Cooper as Benedict; Mrs. Charles Kean, with her husband; and Anna Cora Mowatt were the star attractions. When Anna Cora Mowatt made her first appearance as Beatrice on December 9, 1846, one reviewer commented that she "fully equalled the expectations which had been raised by the laudatory paragraphs of the Northern critics."[57] When she appeared on February 20, 1854, the reviewer praised her "exuberant gaity," "eccentricity, overflowing vivacity," and "her sparkling stream of wit and raillery."[58]

Of the other comedies, *The Tempest, Twelfth Night,* and *Cymbeline* appealed mostly as novelty attractions for the benefits. On April 1, 1811, the performance of *The Winter's Tale* was to be the first in the United States. The *Times,* however, carried a notice that afternoon stating that "owing to the inability of the company, and the impossibility of procuring a sufficient number of correct copies of *The Winter's Tale,* as revised and corrected for Representation, it is unavoidably withdrawn."[59] Undaunted, though, the company acquired the correct copies and prepared *The Winter's Tale* on April 17, 1811, its first performance in the United States. Unfortunately, no one reviewed the performance.

From 1800–1860, Shakespeare's histories were performed 113 times: *King John,* 4; *Henry VIII,* 7; *1 Henry IV,* 20; *Richard III,* 82. Except for those covering performances of *Richard III* few reviews appeared. Although the company brought *King John* forward only four times, three were benefits; a reviewer of a performance on June 9, 1823, placed *King John* after *Richard III* for "its action, character, and dialogue." The reviewer further stated that "the action of the piece is uninterrupted and events succeed and grow . . . with the apparent rapidity of hours, instead of years." The reviewer's evaluation of the character of King John and the interpretation of it seems perceptive. "King John appears with all the failings of a man— cunning but bold; ambitious, but hesitating; resolved, yet horror- stricken." Generally, the reviewer praised all the members of the company, but he called particular attention to the "artificial" scene between Hubert and Prince Arthur. "So young a boy could not have made so pretty a speech as Arthur did to Hubert, about the fire, the tongs, and the tenderness of the organ of sight . . . not the voice and passion of a terrified and bewildered child."[60]

The first performance of *1 Henry IV* on February 7, 1806, was inauspicious. Thespiad disappointedly stated that "the first part of *Henry the Fourth* . . . was played, or rather attempted, on Friday evening last."[61] Only a few of the actors evidently took their roles "seriously," especially the drinking with Falstaff. Although the company staged the play several times, no particular actor, with the exception of James Hackett, received the cachet of distinction for his portrayal of Falstaff. Although Hackett acted Falstaff six times before a Charleston audience, only one reviewer focused on his acting. While Hackett gave "pointed and forcible expressions to *some* of the jolly Knight's comic peculiarities," the reviewer pre- ferred to see him in "characters in which his imitation is natural, because it is founded less on study than on observation, and a quick perception of the ridiculous in living originals." Moreover, the re- viewer felt that Hackett's power as an actor came from "*direct imitation* and not in working out by continuous study an *ideal* repre- sentation." Too many of the other characters performed by Hackett were heard in his Falstaff.[62]

On November 29, 1821, Junius Brutus Booth made his first ap- pearance in Charleston as Richard, a role he continued to act until his final performance of March 29, 1852; his son Edwin appeared as Richard on February 20, 1858, and made his final performance of Richard eight years later on March 29, 1860. The father and son had excited the Charleston stage for almost forty years. The comments on the Richard of J. B. Booth's first ten performances clearly established the actor's supremacy. One critic expressed disappointment over the first three acts, especially the first monologue in "which Gloucester lets forth the secret man of blood and ambition . . . in which Mr. Booth completely failed," but observed that the audience may have been unaccustomed to Booth's style of acting. In Act 4, Scene 2, when Richard told Buckingham, "Shall I be plain?—I wish the bastards dead," the reviewer had "never seen a more lively expression of enquiring, searching, and finally decided and open villainy." The tent scene must have enthralled the audience. It was "uncommonly effective—the horror of his countenance, and fixture of his eye; . . . his gradual recovery from this well depicted temporary phrenzy—was as fine a piece of execution and judgment as we ever recollected to have witnessed."[63] In another review of the same performance, we learn that Booth's "tent scene and his death received three distinct rounds of applause, a circumstance unusual in our Theatre."[64] Of the performance on March 18, 1825, Spectator gloriously praised Booth's depiction of Richard.

> Such talent preserving in its keeping the general portrait of the "crook'd back tyrant"—such genius flashing over and illuminating particular passages, might well command the admiration and loud applauses this gentleman received. To detail the performance would be superfluous; the places which struck us with greatest force and pleasure were the emphatic prompting and open declaration to Buckingham, to commit the murder; the soliloquy, while the murder of the young Princes is going on; and the power of eye and countenance with which Richard's hasty and rapid orders are given to Tyrell. In a succeeding scene, his reading was uncommonly fine in the encounter with his mother; and the dialogue with Elizabeth was distinguished for its taste and expressiveness. The fourth act was full of impetuosity and power. The unrivalled countenance of Mr. Booth came into full play, and his mind conquered every obstacle, in giving to him the faculty of imparting interest to every incident connected with the character. The fifth act rose still higher in energy and impressiveness.[65]

The reviewer in the *Southern Patriot* of March 29, 1838, hailed Booth's performance of Richard as "the most finished specimen of acting ever seen on these boards. . . . His performance is instinct with genius." The tent scene "is among the finest exhibitions of histrionic power we have ever witnessed."[66] On March 29, 1852, Junius Brutus Booth acted his final Richard on the Charleston stage.

The reviewer for the *Charleston Evening News* fittingly summarized the achievement of Booth's long career when he stated that "he was the Richard of Shakespeare."[67] His son Edwin accompanied him to Charleston for the performance of *Richard III,* but no reference lingers about his appearance in the play. Later, Edwin Booth returned and performed Richard five times, with his last performance on March 29, 1860, eight years after his father's farewell to the role in Charleston. The single review of all Edwin Booth's performances of Richard in Charleston stated that "certainly the mantle of the father has fallen upon no unworthy shoulders. . . . We doubt if there is another man living who could do the tent scene better."[68]

When the manager of the Charleston Theater announced in January, 1826, that he had engaged Edmund Kean for a limited appearance, reviewers expressed concern, for Kean had recently become unpopular in Boston for refusing to play before small houses and for making disparaging comments about Boston audiences. Just before his arrival in Charleston, an audience in Baltimore had booed and hissed Kean off the stage. Although probably every major traveling star who had visited the city played Richard, Edmund Kean's was the most significant *Richard III* in Charleston. When he made his first appearance on March 13, 1826, J. B. Irving believed the event would live forever in the memory of anyone who witnessed it. Because of the incidents in Boston and Baltimore, Kean must have been alarmed as he walked onto the stage. Irving stated:

> His anxiety behind the scenes was very great. When dressed for his part, the "Duke of Gloster," looking through a hole in the curtain, he saw . . . that the Theatre was full and but *one lady* there—he turned to a friend and observed, "I hope it bodes no evil." Everything was done to reassure him. No sooner, however, did the play begin than he was satisfied of the *good intentions* of his audience. Applause followed applause, even before he entered, and it had a talismanic effect upon him—those eyes of his of magical brightness, *flashed lightening;* and his bosom heaved and his whole soul seemed stirred and ready for a mighty effort! As he stood at the wing, ready to go on the stage, he muttered something in a tone of triumph—a moment after, and he was at the footlights with an air I shall never forget. The welcome given him was long and warm. He did not begin the opening soliloquy with the usual words, "now is the winter of our discontent," &c. He told me afterwards he could not, for he felt after

such a reception, he must omit them, and commence as he really did, with this line, so appropriate to his then position and circumstances:— "Now are our brows bound with victorious wreaths."[69]

When Kean took his benefit on April 10, 1826, he acknowledged his indebtedness to Charleston, claiming, "I pant for an opportunity of better expressing my obligations to a community, which has equal claims upon my gratitude and admiration."[70] Although one could compile a long list of performances he would like to have seen, I would place Kean's 1826 visit together with Booth's farewell to Charleston near the top. Both events were great theater.

With the firing on Fort Sumter, a rich era of theater history ended. For sixty years antebellum Charleston society supported theater. Charlestonians watched the melancholy Hamlet come alive on the stage; they saw Romeo and Juliet love and die, with Romeo played by a woman possibly before the event in New York; they witnessed the horror of self-destruction by the ambition of Macbeth and Lady Macbeth; they complained of the altered *King Lear* but still enjoyed a performance by a "star"; they followed Othello's destructive passion of jealousy that often seemed to transcend color. They saw the first performance of *The Winter's Tale* in the United States; they may have overcome some of their prejudices in watching Shylock in a frenzy; they applauded the witticisms of Beatrice and Benedict. Seeing Booth, they were present at the finest performances of Richard in America. The people of Charleston thoroughly enjoyed drama; more importantly, they enjoyed Shakespeare.

NOTES

1. The performance totals come primarily from William Stanley Hoole, *The Ante-Bellum Charleston Theatre* (Tuscaloosa, Ala., 1946) and the Charleston newspapers.
2. *Charleston Courier*, Apr. 21, 1806.
3. *Southern Patriot* [Charleston], Nov. 7, 1818.
4. *City Gazette and Daily Advertiser* [Charleston], Dec. 11, 1821.
5. John Beaufain Irving, "Dr. Irving's Reminiscences of the Charleston Stage," ed. Emmett Robinson, *The South Carolina Historical and Genealogical Magazine* 51 (1950): 204, 205.
6. Ibid., p. 206.

7. William Charles Macready, *The Diaries of William Charles Macready, 1833–1851*, ed. William Toynbee (1912; rpt. New York: Benjamin Blom, 1969), 2:416.

8. In addition to Shakespeare, on May 11, 1857, opera fans had an opportunity to see part of Vacci's opera *Romeo and Juliet* when Madame Elena D'Angri as Romeo and M'lle Mathilde D'Angri as Juliet did the third act of the opera. I believe this was the only operatic version of *Romeo and Juliet* in Charleston between 1800 and 1860.

9. *Southern Patriot*, Apr. 18, 1818.

10. George C. D. Odell, *Annals of the New York Stage* (New York: Columbia University Press, 1927–49), 3:448.

11. *Southern Patriot*, Mar. 3, 1829.

12. *City Gazette and Daily Advertiser*, Mar. 4, 1829.

13. *Southern Patriot*, Dec. 11, 1845.

14. Ibid., Dec. 9, 1846.

15. *City Gazette and Daily Advertiser*, Apr. 21, 1806.

16. *Times* [Charleston], Feb. 10, 1819.

17. *Southern Patriot*, Dec. 13, 1828.

18. *Charleston Courier*, Apr. 21, 1806.

19. *Southern Patriot*, Dec. 15, 1828.

20. *City Gazette and Daily Advertiser*, Dec. 15, 1828.

21. *Charleston Daily Courier*, Feb. 25, 1858.

22. Macready, p. 248.

23. *Southern Patriot*, Feb. 5, 1846.

24. *Charleston Evening News*, Feb. 5, 1846.

25. Ibid.

26. *City Gazette and Daily Advertiser*, May 18, 1807.

27. Ibid.

28. Ibid., Dec. 5, 1821.

29. *Southern Patriot*, Feb. 1, 1838.

30. *Charleston Courier*, Dec. 6, 1821.

31. *City Gazette and Daily Advertiser*, Dec. 5, 1821.

32. Ibid., Mar. 25, 1825.

33. *Southern Patriot*, Mar. 29, 1825.

34. *City Gazette and Daily Advertiser*, Mar. 28, 1825.

35. *Southern Patriot*, Mar. 26, 1825.

36. *Charleston Evening News*, Mar. 29, 1852.

37. *Times*, May 9, 1807.

38. John Lambert, *Travels through Lower Canada, and the United States of North America, in the Years 1806, 1807, and 1808* (London: n.p., 1810), 2:374.

39. Ibid., p. 374.

40. *Charleston Courier*, Feb. 6, 1809.

41. *Southern Patriot*, Jan. 9, 1838.

42. Ibid., Feb. 9, 1819.

43. Ibid., Feb. 10, 1819.

44. *Charleston Daily Courier*, Feb. 25, 1858.

45. *Charleston Courier*, Nov. 14, 1803.

46. *Times*, Apr. 18, 1811.

47. *Southern Patriot*, Nov. 25, 1815.

48. Ibid., Oct. 31, 1818.

49. *Evening Post* [Charleston], Feb. 11, 1832.

50. *Mercury* [Charleston], Feb. 11, 1846.

51. *Charleston Standard*, Nov. 13, 1855.

52. *Charleston Daily Courier*, Feb. 23, 1854.
53. *Mercury*, Nov. 9, 1855.
54. *Charleston Standard*, Nov. 13, 1855.
55. *Charleston Daily Courier*, Feb. 29, 1804.
56. *Southern Patriot*, Jan. 5, 1838.
57. *Charleston Evening News*, 10 December 1846.
58. *Charleston Daily Courier*, Feb. 28, 1854.
59. *Times*, Apr. 1, 1811.
60. *City Gazette and Daily Advertiser*, June 11, 1823.
61. *Charleston Daily Courier*, Feb. 11, 1806.
62. *Southern Patriot*, Mar. 13, 1838.
63. *City Gazette and Daily Advertiser*, Dec. 5, 1821.
64. Ibid., Dec. 1, 1821.
65. *Southern Patriot*, Mar. 19, 1825.
66. Ibid., Mar. 29, 1838.
67. *Charleston Evening News*, Mar. 30, 1852.
68. *Charleston Daily Courier*, Feb. 22, 1858.
69. Irving, p. 196.
70. *Southern Patriot*, Apr. 11, 1826.

Shakespeare in New Orleans, 1817–1865

Joseph Patrick Roppolo

I

Snow fell in New Orleans on January 12, 1852.[1] As the courtyards filled with what one small Creole Negro servant believed was sugar, a policeman looked at the snow-whitened iron lace of the balconies and at the burdened palms in the French Quarter and muttered, "This weather is most tolerable and not to be endured."

He was paraphrasing Shakespeare, of course—Dogberry the Constable, to be exact; but, in quoting Shakespeare so aptly, he was doing nothing unusual, for in nineteenth-century New Orleans Shakespeare was quoted frequently—and deliberately—and was much used as a point of reference on those occasions when direct quotation would not serve. Few murders were discussed in the press without at least passing reference to Othello, Macbeth, or Lady Macbeth. Few handbags or pocketbooks disappeared without the comment "who steals my purse steals trash"—made, usually, by the press rather than by the victim.

Shakespeare was employed even in the Confederate cause, if I read between the lines correctly. During the occupation of New Orleans by Federal troops, a lady asked for, and received, in her newspaper's "Notes and Queries" section, identification of this passage: "O, it is excellent / To have a Giant's strength, but it is tyrannous / To use it like a giant." If the Federal officers—among them a general nicknamed "Spoons"—saw in the request any reflection on their activities, official or unofficial, there is no record of it. (General Benjamin Butler, Federal occupier of New Orleans, used his "giant's strength" to confiscate fine silverware for Union use.)

Any news event in connection with the theater itself led, naturally, to profuse use of Shakespearean quotations and allusions. When, for example, on January 31, 1844, it was announced that live lions and tigers were to appear on the stage during a presentation of

Mungo Park, the *Daily Picayune* muttered editorially, "Masters, you ought to consider with yourselves: to bring in, God shield us, a lion among ladies, is a most dreadful thing; for there is not a more fearful wild fowl than your lion living; and we ought to look to it" (*A Midsummer Night's Dream* 3.1. 30–35). The lions and tigers, tame, old, and toothless, were brought forth nevertheless.

In matters of criticism and interpretation, the press found Shakespeare essential in making its points. Barton, the comedian, for example, "would make the ghost of Hamlet's father laugh." Ad libbing caused the *Daily Picayune*'s critic to comment in 1825 that were *he* in charge, matters would be conducted differently. He would post in a conspicuous place in his theater Hamlet's charge to the players: "Let those who play your clowns / Speak no more than is set down for them." Apparently this critical suggestion was no more effective in New Orleans than it had been in Shakespeare's London, for it appeared frequently thereafter.

The newspapers, and presumably their readers, took their Shakespeare seriously. Any deviation by an actor from what was considered standard procedure brought forth immediate attacks; and if an accused actor replied, lengthy controversy might result. Lawrence Barrett found this out to his sorrow during the season of 1863 when a quarrel developed over the reading of the line "But in that sleep of death, what dreams may come / When we have shuffled off this mortal coil / Must give us pause." Barrett, apparently, read the line without a pause after "coil," which the *Daily Picayune* critic found offensive. "We well remember, Macready's reading of the passage in question," he wrote. "[The line] was spoken as a solemn soul-piercing interrogatory, while the words which follow—*'must give us pause'*—came as the low subdued prelude to further self-communing on that momentous theme—the dreams which arise in that sleep that knows no waking. This reading gives a new, speculative and spiritual meaning to the passage and affords the actor an opportunity to display the transcendent power of this craft." Barrett, incidentally, did not benefit by this criticism. Two days later the critic noted disapprovingly that the actor was persisting in his "fault."

It is worth noting that no letters from readers protesting the abundant use of Shakespeare appeared in the press of that period. It can be presumed only that few or none were written, that the average newspaper reader was actually interested in Shakespeare and familiar with the plays, and that editors and readers alike found Shakespeareana of every variety newsworthy. Certainly the press missed few opportunities to present not only casual quotations and pointed criticism but also long and detailed studies and reminiscences, ranging from the hilarious to the deadly serious. Here, by way of demonstration, are random headings taken from the newspapers: "The Text of Shakespeare," "The Nationality of Othello," "Hamlet in a Hobble," "To Sleep, To Die," "White's Shakespeare," "Two Ghosts to One Hamlet," and "Hackett's Belly." Even that relatively nonliterary magazine *DeBow's Review*, published in New Orleans and dedicated to the proposition that "Commerce is King," offered its readers such Shakespearean items as an article entitled "The Plays of Shakespeare," a critical treatment of *Much Ado About Nothing*, and "Shakespeare as Physician and Metaphysician."

In a paper which should be heavy with dates and statistics, all of these items from the policeman in the snow to Shakespeare in *DeBow's Review* may seem trivial, but they go far, I believe, toward proving my thesis: Shakespeare permeated the American section of New Orleans from 1817 through the Civil War. The people—not merely the Anglophiles and the intellectual snobs—knew him, accepted him, and loved him. This thesis could be documented further by references to the teaching of Shakespeare in the American schools in New Orleans, by reference to the numerous and highly popular Shakespearean readings by unknowns and by famous actors and actresses, and by quotations from epitaphs on stones and monuments still standing in New Orleans cemeteries. But the point has been made. Let us pass instead to the record of Shakespearean performances in New Orleans from 1817 through 1865.

2

The first Shakespearean play to be performed professionally in New Orleans was *Othello*—a strange choice surely in a city in which the Negro population, slave and free, almost doubled that of the white.[2] If the theater manager and beneficiary, one A. Cargill, had any fears concerning the reception of the play on that June 2, 1817, evening, they were not in evidence; and there were, apparently, no adverse reactions, for Cargill repeated the play in January, 1818.

Cargill was head of a small theatrical troupe which in 1817 was, according to the *Gazette* (March 22, 1817), providing "National Amusement" for the English-speaking segment of the New Orleans population. These amusements included "a number of Moral, Patriotic and Humorous Recitations and Songs" and such plays as Isaac Pocock's *The Miller and His Men,* the farce *Animal Magnetism, The Weathercock,* and *The Village Lawyer.*

Apparently, Cargill had ambitions beyond the presentation of such light entertainment, for on May 30, 1817, he advertised that his company would present Shakespeare's *Othello* on the occasion of his own benefit. The advertisement shows no awareness on Cargill's part that he was making history, that he was, in fact (as far as the records show), introducing Shakespeare to the New Orleans stage.

A player named Jones was assigned the role of Othello; Cargill himself played Iago, and a Mr. Robinson was Roderigo. Neither Desdemona nor any other member of the cast was mentioned in the advertisements.

As was the custom, the evening's entertainment was to be long. In addition to *Othello,* the bill included William Macready's *The Village Lawyer* and other entertainment, notably "the favorite song of the American Soldier, or [The] Battle of New Orleans," with Cargill as the vocalist. The performance began possibly at 6:30 P.M., almost certainly by 7:00 P.M., for the hours of theatrical entertainment were regulated by city ordinance, and the mayor seems to have insisted that the ordinance be observed. By midnight, or perhaps a little earlier, it was over, since Cargill in his advertisements had assured "the ladies and gentlemen who may honor the theatre with their presence on that evening" that "the scenery will be so managed as to cause no unnecessary delay."

What happened during the five or more hours of that first presentation of Shakespeare to an American audience in a French playhouse in the Vieux Carré of New Orleans can only be surmised, for the contemporary records are remarkably devoid of comment. The audience must have been small, for Cargill, advertising another benefit for himself in the *Courier* and the *Gazette* in October, 1817, says that he was "disappointed in receiving his benefit last spring." Apparently there was no trouble over the miscegenation theme, nor was there New Orleans sentiment against the play itself, for *Othello* was repeated on January 5, 1818, in the same theater by the same company. It was to be repeated ninety-six times—a total of ninety-eight performances—in the years through 1865, to become, statistically, the fourth most popular Shakespearean play in New Orleans.[3]

The first *Othello* was followed by the first New Orleans performance of *1 Henry IV* on December 15, 1817. Again this was a Cargill production in a French playhouse, the St. Philip Street Theatre in the Vieux Carré. For this play, however, there was more ballyhoo than there had been for the initial performance of *Othello*. As early as December 2, New Orleanians were advised that "Shakespeare's celebrated tragedy, Henry IV, or The Humours of Sir John Falstaff," was in preparation. Cargill was to play the King, Robinson was to play Prince Hal, and Jones was to play Falstaff. A Mr. Voss, "lately from the eastern theatres," was assigned the role of Hotspur. Originally scheduled for December 5, the performance was postponed, but the ballyhoo continued; there was, in fact, an unusual amount of plugging to get a good house, not merely of American playgoers but of French. The play was heralded in the *Gazette* (December 9) as "one of Shakespeare's best tragedies," and that newspaper added, significantly, "We know not one in the whole catalogue of plays more suited to the temper and natural affability of Frenchmen. . . ." French newspapers, too, like *L'Ami des lois* (December 12), carried announcements.

There are no detailed reviews of this initial performance, but Cargill, certainly, must have been satisfied with the patronage, for on December 18, 1817, he repeated *Henry IV* "in consequence of the particular request of a number of citizens of New Orleans."

After these two performances, New Orleans was to see *1 Henry IV* fifty-three times through 1861, (The play seems to have been a casualty of the Civil War, for it was not performed after April 11,

Three New Orleans theaters circa 1842—the Orleans, New American
Theatre, and the St. Charles Theatre
Courtesy Special Collections, Tulane University Libraries

1861.) In total number of performances, *1 Henry IV* ranks ninth among Shakespearean performances in New Orleans.

With the advent of *Othello* and *1 Henry IV*, the floodgates were open. After these plays came initial performances of twenty-one ·more Shakespearean plays or adaptations: *The Merchant of Venice*, February 21, 1818, by a company headed by Noah M. Ludlow; *Catherine and Petruchio* (an adaptation of *The Taming of the Shrew*), March 6, 1818; *Romeo and Juliet*, March 10, 1818; *Richard III*, March 14, 1818; *Hamlet*, January 17, 1820; *Macbeth*, February 21, 1820; *Much Ado About Nothing*, March 24, 1820; *As You Like It*, April 14, 1820; *King Lear*, March 2, 1821; *Julius Caesar*, April 11, 1821; *King John*, April 14, 1823; *The Merry Wives of Windsor* (the first production on the stage of an American playhouse, rather than a French playhouse, in New Orleans—James H. Caldwell's Camp Street Theatre), January 30, 1826; *The Comedy of Errors*, March 31, 1828; *Henry VIII*, January 17, 1831; *Twelfth Night* (which has a significance peculiar to New Orleans, for Twelfth Night, January 6, marks the traditional date on which the Mardi Gras season begins), April 11, 1831; *Two Gentlemen of Verona*, December 28, 1831; *The Tempest*, April 5, 1833; *Antony and Cleopatra*, March 8, 1838; *Coriolanus*, April 13, 1844; *2 Henry IV* (never performed in full), February 24, 1849; and *The Winter's Tale*, January 15, 1848.

Two of these New Orleans premieres deserve special attention because, as far as the records show, they were also American premieres. *Two Gentlemen of Verona* was presented in Caldwell's American Theatre in New Orleans on December 28, 1831—fifteen years before the Keans gave New York audiences their first opportunity to see the play.[4] The New Orleans cast was apparently drawn from the stock company. It was strong but not superlative, and the play has the dubious distinction of being the only Shakespearean play in New Orleans records which, having been performed once, was never performed again.

The second of the American premieres in New Orleans was that of *Antony and Cleopatra* at the St. Charles Theatre on March 8, 1838, with Ellen Tree as the Egyptian Queen. From this distance in time, play and theater seem well matched. The ornate chandelier, the

heavy curtains, and the numerous gas lights of the St. Charles undoubtedly added to the lushness of the stage sets and of Shakespeare's poetry. And with such attractions as the "glorious Ellen"
and William Hield (as Antony), it is no wonder that the audience was
both large and fashionable—in fact, one of the best of the season.
Caldwell, with good reason, considered *Antony and Cleopatra* a
success, and the play was repeated the following evening. Eight
years later, the play opened in New York.[5]

The most popular of Shakespeare's plays in New Orleans through
1865 was *Richard III*, which is listed 170 times. Not every listing, of
course, indicates a complete performance, for *Richard III* was one
of the most frequently mutilated of the Shakespearean plays. It was
often offered in fragments merely to permit a star to make his
"points," and on more than one occasion *Richard III* appeared as
pure horse opera, with advertising emphasis on "Richard on Horse-
back" in "terrific combat."

Trailing *Richard III* in popularity were *Macbeth*, with 147 listings,
Hamlet with 127, *Othello* with 98, *The Merchant of Venice* with 89,
and *Romeo and Juliet* with 88.

These figures, it seems to me, must be taken as proof of the
popularity of Shakespeare in New Orleans, for we are dealing here
not with the intangible percentages of a pollster but with plays,
which, whatever their merit, were offered as box-office attractions
to a public that paid cash to see them. Even alone, the figures are
impressive: twenty-three Shakespearean plays were performed approximately 1,200 times in a period of forty-eight years—from the
initial performance of *Othello* in 1817 to the close of the Civil War in
1865—an average of twenty-five Shakespearean performances a season.

More to the point, perhaps, is the fact that Shakespeare's plays
sometimes achieved long runs in a period when two successive performances of any play were regarded as evidence of success, entitl-
ing a local author to a third-night benefit.[6] Audiences, managers
were quick to learn, rarely "suffered" more than one performance of
a play in any week. In 1854, *The Tempest*, by these standards, was
spectacularly successful at Placide's Varieties in New Orleans,

Playbill announcing the arrival of Thomas Abthorpe Cooper as Macbeth at the New American Theatre, New Orleans, March 28, 1827
Courtesy Special Collections, Tulane University Libraries

achieving an almost unbroken run of twenty-two performances between February 23 and April 10. This was followed almost immediately by at least nine successive performances of *As You Like It*—a run broken only because the Varieties' season was drawing to a close. In addition to the runs there were also scattered performances of the two plays, so that they alone in the space of a little more than two months accounted for forty evenings in the theater. No amount of Shakespearean snobbery or love for things British could force a manager to sacrifice so many evenings simply to British Literature and Art. No, the public came—and by public I mean not only the Ladies and Gentlemen (in capitals) but the merchants, the steamboatmen, the small farmers, the visitors, the prostitutes, the free men and women of color, and the slaves.[7] And the public paid.

On the other hand, I cannot argue that it was Shakespeare alone who drew the public to the theater. It was, in addition to the play itself, excellent direction, superlative playing, novelty, and spectacle (as the reviews attest) which drew throngs to *The Tempest* and *As You Like It*. But these ingredients are not necessarily foreign to Shakespeare, and it is, of course, a truism to say that Shakespeare well played is better (even at the box office) than Shakespeare played in large part by the prompter.

It is significant that the record runs achieved by these two plays were achieved without benefit of stars, but stars were responsible in large part for the continuing popularity of such plays as *Richard III*, *Macbeth*, and *Hamlet*. And the roster of stars, British and American, who appeared in Shakespearean roles in New Orleans is impressively lengthy. It includes James H. Caldwell, self-styled father of the English language theater in New Orleans; Noah H. Ludlow and Sol Smith, prominent figures in the theatrical history of New Orleans, Mobile, St. Louis, and the Southwest; and Jane Placide, the beautiful center of several romantic storms. It includes also Avonia Jones, whose first name itself was a tribute to Shakespeare; the eccentric and erratic—and frequently drunken—Junius Brutus Booth; William Charles Macready; James Anderson; Edwin Forrest; James H. Hackett, whose portrayal of Falstaff was unrivaled; George Vandenhoff; the venerable Thomas Abthorpe Cooper, for whose retirement tears were shed on stage in a New Orleans theater; the Keans; the Wallacks; Josephine Clifton; J. E. Murdoch; James R. Anderson; Julia Dean; Annette Ince; Edwin Booth; Edwin's brother, John Wilkes Booth, who on Good Friday, 1864, was winning New Orleans with his uneven but often "remarkably fine" acting.

Often the attraction of a star was combined with novelty or even sensationalism in a Shakespearean production. Thus, Mrs. Ann Sefton appeared frequently in the role of Romeo—and won high praise. Ludlow and Smith appeared more than once as the singing witches in *Macbeth*—roles which must have delighted them. Henry Placide and Tom Placide, brothers with a remarkable family resemblance, appeared together as the two identical Dromios in *The Comedy of Errors* with great popular success over a number of years. The pinnacle of praise for them was reached when a patron, seeing the play for the first time, asked loudly, "But when is *Tom* going to appear?" Tom, of course, had already been on and off a dozen times.[8] Charlotte Cushman, who began her career as a singer with a "prodigious" voice, was converted to tragedy in New Orleans and astounded her first audience with a Lady Macbeth not to be seen, the critics warned, by those with tender hearts or weak stomachs. Yet Miss Cushman, like Mrs. Sefton, could play Romeo wonderfully well.

Of all the novelties introduced in the antebellum period the most popular (and the most wearisome to the historian) were the child prodigies. Marsh's Juvenile Comedians and the Bateman Children played interminably, season after season, offering, among other items, bits and pieces of Shakespeare to enthralled audiences. Ten-year-old Kate Bateman as Shylock and eight-year-old Ellen as Richard III were so successful in 1853 that their engagement at Placides Varieties was extended for more than a month. Thirteen-year-old Joseph Burke played the violin, directed the orchestra, acted in farces, and impersonated Richard III, Hamlet, Shylock, and Romeo, with the support of adult actors. He was, according to the press, phenomenally successful.

The juveniles were not alone, however, in their exploitation of Shakespeare. The adults, too, hesitated not at all to offer isolated scenes or acts that would show them to advantage. It must be admitted that this custom, general over America, brought little criticism, but the critics often were loud in their protest against any departure from the text and against radical interpretations of character. They condemned also those "illusion shattering" occasions when costumes or scenery were inappropriate or when actors failed to remember their lines. Not even actor-managers were above reproach, as Ben DeBar discovered when he read in the *Daily Pica-yune* in 1853 that he was "a good Dogberry, and only lacked letter perfectness in the language. That dignitary must say just what is set down for him to say—no more and no less." Plunkett, a stock company actor, was advised by the same newspaper in 1858 to "make himself what he calls himself, gray haired, and what Benedick calls him, 'the white beard.'"

Stereotyped modes of fighting and incidental mishaps sometimes rendered serious scenes ridiculous. The *Picayune* on January 2, 1858, asserted that Charles Dickens's account of the fight between the short sailor and the tall sailor in *Nicholas Nickleby* was "no great caricature" of the fights in *Richard*, *Macbeth*, and *Henry IV* as usually performed on the stage, and cited the night on which, in each of two fights, "Douglas vs Blunt, and Harry vs Harry," the sword was knocked out of the winner's hand, so that "the disarmer had to permit the disarmed to take *his* sword and put *him* to death." There were also references to the frequent appearance of Shakespeare's heroes with bound-up fingers, cut thumbs, and patched frontlets.

Not even properties were beyond misadventure. During the long run of *The Tempest*, already mentioned, the pasteboard Ariel apparently became temperamental, for the press refers to its "frequent blunders" and cites one of the worst: during an "interesting point" the flying Ariel fell flat upon the stage. The newspaper recommended that the theater "get rid of this unmeaning and troublesome effigy" in the interests of art.[9]

The demand for artistic perfection, as exemplified by the Ariel incident, was nowhere more apparent than in productions of Shakespeare; and when perfection or near-perfection was achieved by star, artist, mechanic, and company the praises were prompt and loud. I need here cite only the long run of *The Tempest*, which, in addition to letter-perfect playing (always excepting Ariel) and skilled direction, had the advantage of fifteen new sets, including the rocky pass, the interior and exterior of the cave of Prospero, the deep glen, the dragon tree, and the crag-crowned beach. Most effective and sensational was the shipwreck scene, "not usually presented," which was offered "fully and faithfully," including the storm at sea;

the vessel afloat, with the passengers and crew seen and heard "in converse"; and the "actual" wreck of the vessel, "as accurately as is consistent with limited space."[10] With such elaborate staging, Shakespeare, critics and audiences felt, was receiving only his due, for Shakespeare was acknowledged King of Playwrights. Cut and mangled, his lines could be lisped by babies, but always Shakespeare was Shakespeare, and carelessness and ineptness were not to be tolerated on the stage.[11]

Such seriousness might, of course, be interpreted as Bardolatry—and it may have been, in part. But it indicated also an acceptance of and a familiarity with Shakespeare that, perhaps paradoxically, often could be playful. It is possible to joke—lightly of course—about something that is, however honored or sacred, a part of one's everyday life; so it was that neither critics nor audiences objected to a "Hamlet Travestie" with Young Cowell as Hamlet and Mr. [*sic*] Holland as Ophelia. Nor were there objections to an "Othello Travestie" in which Iago was represented as an Irishman—a bit of casting of particular interest to residents of the Irish Channel in New Orleans. Shakespeare, in a sense, was not only idolized and popularized but localized.

The success of the farces and travesties I cite only as added proof of familiarity with Shakespeare and a fondness for him. For who, knowing his Shakespeare, could resist a comic "Shakespearean Festival—or The Distressed Doorkeeper"? Perhaps even the policeman whom I left in the snow in my opening comments went to see "Shylock, or The Merchant of Venice Preserved." If he did, I envy him.

Lagniappe

Shakespeare himself, in person, visited New Orleans once—just once.

That was in 1841, while a "rehearsal" (before a full audience) was in progress in the original, ornate, and magnificent St. Charles Theatre.

The venerable bard, long dead, descended on a cloud to the stage of the playhouse and in ringing tones (for he had been an actor, too) announced to the startled performers the purpose of his visit. He was, he said, "curious to know / How gets the drama on below."

His curiosity was satisfied quickly. He learned, among other things, that theater audiences were afflicted with a pervasive lack of taste, that ballyhoo had replaced quality, and that sensationalism was preferred to art.

As for his own plays, this author of "certain rather antiquated dramas" was told bluntly that he "did not draw." He was, as we might put it today, poison at the box office.

Hurt and bewildered, Shakespeare groaned, "I do not draw, and so am dead?"

"Why, no," he was told. "We see some signs of life. Properly harness'd for the strife, / With horses thru the fifth act pricking, / You sometimes are alive and kicking!"

When Shakespeare argued that even without horses his plays are classic and deserve attention, he was dealt another blow: "Sir," he was told, "we admit your claim, / and very often quote your name. / You are the stage's bene-FAC-tor, / Yet still *depend*, sir, on the *act-or*."

With such information it is no wonder that Shakespeare despaired. "Heigh ho," he said, "I'm very glad that I am dead. / It's clear I shouldn't earn my bread. / I ruin those who still stick TO me, / And most of those who praise ess-CHOO [eschew] me. / Necessity makes strangest courses. / Shakespeare—once more— is holding horses."

And with this bitter allusion to the days when as a youngster he supposedly worked his way into the theater by holding the horses of patrons, Shakespeare left the nineteenth century to its own very dubious devices.

Once off the stage Shakespeare became merely Ben DeBar, an actor, and the curtains closed to the applause and delighted laughter of an audience which had just witnessed the first performance of a new piece written expressly for the occasion by the well-known playwright Joseph M. Field.

If the audience was aware that it had just been slashed to pieces by a skillful satirist, it gave no indication; but the editors of the *Daily Picayune* demonstrated their awareness of what they must have considered just criticism by reprinting the play, *G.A.G., or, The Starring System,* in its entirety—the first and only time in the history of the *Picayune,* as far as I have been able to discover, that it published a complete play.[12]

Certainly, much of the criticism in *G.A.G.* was laughably pointed. Some of it was even true.

NOTES

1. *New Orleans Daily Picayune,* Jan. 12, 13, 1852.

2. New Orleans, according to the *New Orleans City Guide,* American Guide Series (Boston: Houghton-Mifflin, 1938), was founded in the spring of 1718. The city, therefore, was ninety-nine years old when *Othello* was presented. The population in 1810 included 8,001 whites and 16,551 nonwhites, a total of 24,552. By 1820 the figures were 19,244 whites (an increase of 140 percent), 22,107 nonwhites (an increase of 33.3 percent), a total of 41,351.

3. See the accompanying Bibliographic Note for works containing statistical information.

4. George C. D. Odell, *Annals of the New York Stage* (New York: Columbia University Press, 1931) 5: 230.

5. Ibid., p. 181.

6. An example: When William Gilmore Simms's play *Michael Bonham* was staged for the first time it ran for three nights, March 26, 27, 28, 1855, in his home city of Charleston. Simms was elated and was prepared to "take a benefit" if it was offered (apparently it was not). Congratulations poured in, and one Charleston newspaper commented that the writer of a successful play should be regarded as a "public benefactor." Charles S. Watson, *Antebellum Charleston Dramatists* (University, Ala.: University of Alabama Press, 1976), pp. 122–25.

7. Slaves and free persons of color enjoyed Shakespeare. "The play-going portion of our negro population," the *Daily Picayune* reported on Mar. 14, 1844, "feel more interest in, and go in greater numbers to see, the plays of Shakespeare represented on the stage, than any other class of dramatic performance."

8. *Daily Picayune,* Jan. 22, 1846; Feb. 1, 1848; Jan. 28, 1851. On the latter date the *Picayune* remarked on the brothers' similarity in "figure and form" and voice.

9. Ibid., Mar. 2, 1854.

10. Ibid., Feb. 19 and 22, and Mar. 4, 1854.

11. Nevertheless, a near-excellent performance was rare enough to elicit comment. Commenting on the production of *As You Like It,* the *Daily Picayune* critic said on Apr. 20, 1854, "We had the rare pleasure, last evening, of hearing a play of Shakespeare performed throughout by the *dramatis personae,* without any interposition by the prompter. . . . There was no hesitancy, nor any lack of the words; everything went off smoothly, as such poetry should go off, 'trippingly upon the tongue.' It was as near a perfect Shakespearean performance as we expect ever to have the pleasure of witnessing."

12. *G.A.G., or The Starring System* was performed at the St. Charles Theatre on Feb. 20, 1841, and was published in the *Daily Picayune* on Feb. 24, 1841. On Dec. 10, 1860, the *New Orleans Bee* complained that "The startling, novel, surprising, and attractive rank the most able or artistic productions of the past. Hamlet falls into the

shade by the dashing display of Dan Rice, and 'She Stoops to Conquer' is perfectly conquered by flibflabs of Duvernay. Such is popular judgment. It is folly to run counter to it; then submit."

BIBLIOGRAPHIC NOTE

Play totals and other statistics in this paper are derived from tabulation of all Shakespearean plays mentioned or listed in the following works:

Smither, Nelle. *A History of the English Theatre at New Orleans 1806–1842. Louisiana Historical Quarterly* 28 (Jan., 1945): 84 276; (Apr., 1945): 361–572.

Roppolo, Joseph Patrick. "A History of the American Stage in New Orleans, 1842 to 1845." M.A. thesis, Tulane, 1948.

———. "A History of the English Language Theatre in New Orleans, 1848 to 1861." Ph.D. diss., Tulane, 1950.

———. "A History of The English Language Theatre in New Orleans During the Civil War." Unpublished.

First American performances (and other comparisons) were checked against the following works:

Brown, T. Allston. *History of the American Stage.* New York, 1870.

Carson, William G. B. *The Theatre of the Frontier: The Early Years of the St Louis Stage.* Chicago: University of Chicago Press, 1938.

Hoole, Willian Stanley. *The Ante-Bellum Charleston Theatre.* Tuscaloosa, Ala.: University of Alabama Press, 1946.

Odell, George C. D. *Annals of the New York Stage.* Vols. 1–7. New York: Columbia University Press, 1931.

Wilson, Arthur Herman. *A History of the Philadelphia Theatre, 1835–1855.* Philadelphia: University of Pennsylvania Press, 1935.

Shakespeare in Mobile, 1822–1861

Mary Duggar Toulmin

Early Days

Mobile, Alabama was a community of 2,708 people when two theatrical pioneers presented what was probably the city's first professional performance of a Shakespearean play on June 1, 1822. The play was *The Merchant of Venice;* the producers were Emanuel Judah and James M. Scott, actors who had been with James H. Caldwell's New Orleans company; and the boards were those of the old hospital on Dauphin Street, which had been fitted up "in a very neat and commodious manner."[1]

It is not to be thought that Mobilians had been indifferent to theatrical matters. Their interest is attested by the frequent news of actors and plays appearing in the local press long before there was an active theater. Furthermore, the English-language theater may have been preceded by a French-language theater in the 1790s, although evidence is meager.[2]

By 1822, Mobilians, few in number but cosmopolitan in background and tastes, were no doubt eager for organized entertainment. They had seen important events in recent years: the capture of Mobile by the United States from the Spanish in 1813, the incorporating of Mobile in 1814 and its chartering as a city in 1819, and the admission of Alabama into the Union in 1819. Mobile was beginning to grow and show promise of its coming prominence as a seaport and commercial center. Shoppers, visitors, kinspeople from upriver plantations, tradespeople, and riverboatmen looking for diversion swelled the available theater audience. The time was propitious for the establishment of the drama in the 111-year-old city.

That first presentation of *The Merchant of Venice* was the only Shakespeare play given during the five weeks' season. Emanuel Judah, whose characterizations were said by the local *Commercial*

Register of May 30, 1822, to have "vivacity and confidence," portrayed Shylock. In November, 1822, Judah returned to Mobile to manage a season that ran into June, 1823. On November 22 between the play and the farce the manager recited in character Antony's oration over Caesar's body, standing before a "superb street scene" designed and painted by scenic artist John H. Vos.[3]

February 10, 1823, saw the first recorded production in Mobile of *The Taming of the Shrew*. This was the David Garrick version in three acts, played under the title *Catherine and Petruchio*. The *Commercial Register* reported that the performance gave "general satisfaction to the numerous and respectable audience" and that a greater number of ladies than usual attended—a circumstance that made for a less boisterous and more decorous audience.

In the fall of 1824 actor-manager Noah M. Ludlow completed an unfinished theater building and established what he called the "first regular company that played in the City of Mobile."[4] His capable troupe may have presented a few Shakespearean productions, but newspaper accounts are missing, and Ludlow devotes more attention in his memoirs to the amenities of social life in Mobile that year than to details of dramatic activity.

Soon after Ludlow launched his 1825–1826 season, *Richard III* was given its first recorded Mobile presentation. Abraham Wilton Jackson (playing under the name Wilton), later manager of the Bowery Theatre in New York, was the stock company member who played the lead. The *Commercial Register* advertisement (December 27, 1825) felt it necessary to note that in the last act there would be a "grand combat" between Richard and Richmond. *Macbeth* made its Mobile debut at the benefit performance for the orchestra leader, who was responsible for the inclusion of "the original music of the Witches, which has been some time in rehearsal."[5]

When the fall of 1826 brought Ludlow back to Mobile with a seasoned cadre of players, a new era in Mobile theatrical history began. Although local stock companies continued to perform Shakespeare occasionally, the star system was soon instituted, and visiting luminaries preempted the leads in both Shakespearean tragedies and comedies and gradually monopolized their presentation. Stock

The theater building found by Noah M. Ludlow in an unfinished state and completed by him in 1824.
Courtesy University of South Alabama and the Local History Division of the Mobile Public Library

players assumed the lesser parts unless their contracts permitted them to refuse any but leading roles.

Because they offered stars "meatier" roles, tragedies led the popularity polls in Mobile during the antebellum period. *Richard III* was performed forty-eight times; selections from it were given six times and two burlesque renditions were presented. *Hamlet* and *Macbeth* were each given forty-two times, in addition to two partial presentations of the former and four of the latter. *Othello* was staged forty-one times with one travesty, *Romeo and Juliet* reached thirty-three productions, and *King Lear* trailed with fifteen. Of the comedies, *The Merchant of Venice* led with thirty-three regular presentations, one travesty, and two selections from the play. *Much Ado About Nothing* was second with twenty-five productions, followed by *Catherine and Petruchio* with twenty-two. The fifteen performances of *1 Henry IV* and the nine of *The Merry Wives of Windsor* were almost completely the province of James H. Hackett in his role of Falstaff. Other Shakespearean plays were presented a few times.[6]

Shakespeare play texts differed widely. Although plays other than *The Taming of the Shrew* retained their original title, managers and actors frequently reduced them to three acts and changed dialogue to suit their tastes and abilities.

Shakespearean productions constituted only a small minority of the entertainments given in the theater. The number of visiting stars who included Shakespeare in their repertoire was quite limited. There were far more light comedians, Yankee, Irish, and "Jim Crow" impersonators, dancers, gymnasts, vocalists, elastic cord performers, living-picture posers, and equestrian groups than there were classical actors. The actors who did play Shakespearean roles usually alternated them with parts in standard and contemporary comedy, melodrama, and tragedy. A Shakespeare drama never made up the entire evening's program. Playbills were lengthy; sometimes a dance, an orchestral selection or a recitation, and two, three, and occasionally even four plays were presented. Performances began early—usually at 6:30 or 7:00 P.M.—and lasted until very late. Mobile audiences never had reason to complain of scanty programming.

Beginnings of the Star System

Ludlow's Mobile season of 1826–1827 came to a climax in April with the appearance of the eminent tragedian Thomas Abthorpe Cooper, the first genuine "star" to visit the city. During a ten nights' stay he appeared successfully as Macbeth, Richard III, Hamlet, and Petruchio.[7] This engagement gave Mobilians a taste of what was to come in later years, but the shower of stars came slowly. Indeed, during the 1827–1828 season conducted by Ludlow, it was only the stock company that presented several Shakespeare plays: *Othello, Catherine and Petruchio, The Merchant of Venice,* and *Henry IV.*

An editorial in the *Commercial Register* of February 9, 1829,

heartily welcomed Cooper's return to Mobile and quoted the laudatory remarks of the attorney general of the United States on the
actor's performance of the dagger scene in *Macbeth*. The writer
acknowledged that Cooper's powers were said to be on the wane but
maintained that his ability was still outstanding. The star performed
only principal scenes from two Shakespeare plays—*Julius Caesar*
and *Macbeth,* playing the roles of Mark Antony and Macbeth.

Following a disastrous fire which totally destroyed the Mobile
theater in March, 1829, Ludlow chose to manage and play elsewhere
for two years; and it was not until March, 1832, that Mobilians once
more saw Shakespeare on the stage. J. Purdy Brown, eccentric
young theater manager and circus entrepreneur, who had erected a
new theater on St. Emanuel Street, engaged Cooper for a one-night
stand. The actor played the title role in *Othello,* with Edward (Ned)
Raymond of the stock company as Iago. Raymond then secured
Cooper's services for his benefit, the star playing Mark Antony and
the beneficiary Brutus in the second and third acts of *Julius Caesar.*

Now Mobile was treated to its first sight of a child wonder in
Shakespearean roles—Master Joseph Burke, who was about thir-
teen years old and famous as both a dramatic and musical prodigy.
His varied repertoire included Richard III and Shylock. The *Com-
mercial Register* of April 4, 1832, declared him "an actor, and the
skill with which he overcomes the physical disadvantages of the
Boy, entitles him to the distinction of a great actor." The evening
Burke appeared in *Richard III* he also rendered the "Overture to the
Caliph of Baghdad" on the violin between play and farce, and assumed the part of Crack and sang two songs in *Turnpike Gate.*

Manager Brown, driven from Cincinnati, Louisville, and St.
Louis by cholera, was in Mobile in December, 1832, and ready for
the arrival of the young American tragedian William C. Forbes and
the highly popular southern and western actress Mrs. Alexander
Drake. Forbes acted Hamlet, and then he and Mrs. Drake teamed in
Romeo and Juliet. Close on their heels came Mrs. Mary Duff and
John H. Barton. Mrs. Duff, generally acclaimed the greatest tragic
actress of her time, was now, at the age of thirty-nine, probably at
her peak. Barton, a British provincial actor, was to make many

appearances in Mobile in the years to come. They opened on January 8 in *Macbeth*, followed by a full chorus singing "Ye Sons of Freedom," an actor in blackface reciting "Massa George Washington and Gineral La-Fa-Yet" in commemoration of the anniversary of the Battle of New Orleans, and the farce *Nature and Philosophy*. When Barton took a benefit, Mobile saw its first *King Lear*, the actor playing the title role and Mrs. Duff appearing as Cordelia.

Mrs. Drake, reengaged in January, enacted Beatrice in *Much Ado About Nothing* at her benefit. One newspaper correspondent found Mrs. Drake's interpretation too hoydenish; another praised the production and the acting of Charles Webb as Benedick and Mary Vos as Hero. William McCafferty was "altogether unsuccessful," reported the *Commercial Register and Patriot* of February 2, 1833, principally because he looked at the audience rather than at the person to whom he was speaking. Following custom, McCafferty had been hired as a scenic artist but was frequently called on to double as a second low comedian.

Actor-manager Sol Smith claimed in his book of reminiscences that J. Purdy Brown had an abiding faith in horses, for they never deceived him as his joke-playing actors were prone to do. "Whenever he perceived that a play—be it tragedy, comedy, or melodrama—appeared to 'drag' . . . he ordered out his whole stud of horses and circus riders, and sent them on to 'end the piece.' "[8] In February, Brown inserted in the theater a circle for equestrian performances. It is fascinating to consider that when his acting troupe gave *Richard III* in March, the tragedy doubtlessly served as a vehicle for the on-stage display of eight handsome horses.

The last Shakespearean performance of this season was that of the renowned James W. Wallack as Richard III. One wonders at the assignment of William Heyl of the stock company to support Wallack as Richmond. Heyl's chief experience seems to have been as an entre-act singer and a clown in Brown's circus.

Beginning with the season 1833–1834 and the arrival of increasing numbers of stars, Shakespearean productions become too numerous to be discussed singly, and emphasis must be put on the engagements of the famous. Mr. and Mrs. George H. Barrett appeared as

Mercutio and Juliet, Petruchio and Catherine, and Benedick and Beatrice. Later there were three stars on the boards, sometimes playing together, sometimes alternately. Mrs. Elizabeth Austin and James Thorne introduced and repeated several times *The Tempest,* billed as a fairy opera. She was a lovely Ariel and he a real rather than a burlesque character as Caliban, according to a letter to the editor (*Commercial Register and Patriot,* March 21, 1834). Thorne played Dogberry to the Beatrice of the charming visitor Clara Fisher, and then Miss Fisher repeated Beatrice to newly arrived Thomas Abthorpe Cooper's Benedick.

Cooper returned to Mobile for what was to be his final appearance in the city. He had been given public benefits in New York, Philadelphia, and New Orleans; Mobile, too, decided to honor him. The occasion attracted a large crowd; no one charged for his services; and the receipts of $1,502 (with tickets averaging a dollar) were put into an education fund for his children. The program included the second and third acts of *Julius Caesar,* with Cooper as Antony, and *Catherine and Petruchio,* with Cooper as Petruchio and his daughter Priscilla as Catherine.

J. Purdy Brown died unexpectedly the day after his theatrical season came to a close, and Noah M. Ludlow took over the Mobile management for the 1834–1835 season. Shakespearean plays were presented by minor stars Mrs. Pritchard, John Jay Adams, Charles Mason, and Mrs. Sharpe. The most interesting visitor was Joseph M. Field, who was to play a principal role in Mobile's theatrical history as a star, stock company member, and manager. A letter from Field to Sol Smith discloses that Shakespeare was frequently not financially rewarding. Field's Hamlet attracted a $130 house, Richard III $250, and Romeo $230.[9]

Management of Ludlow and Smith

The season of 1835–1836 marked the inauguration of the Noah M. Ludlow and Sol Smith theatrical partnership, which was to endure for eighteen years in spite of fires, epidemics, misunderstandings, financial depressions, and the incompatible nature and personalities of the two.

The first stars of the season stopped in Mobile on their way to become regular members of Caldwell's new St. Charles Theatre in New Orleans. J. H. Barton offered *King Lear;* James E. Murdoch, the young American soon to achieve great acclaim as a light comedian, opened as Romeo. The British couple Mr. and Mrs. Ternan included five Shakespearean plays in their December repertoire: *Richard III, Much Ado About Nothing, As You Like It, The Merchant of Venice,* and *Macbeth.* The *Commercial Register and Patriot* of January 5, 1836, found Mrs. Ternan a graceful, ladylike, and tasteful actress, more successful in higher comedy characters than in tragedy. Mr. Ternan was said to be respectable in all things, in nothing very excellent. They tried hard but lacked "the necessary energy" for *Macbeth,* concluded the reviewer.

Lydia Phillips appeared as Juliet, Desdemona, and Lady Macbeth, drawing particular praise for her interpretation of the latter role although her houses were not large. William C. Forbes played Hamlet after participating in a benefit for the relief of Americans suffering as a result of the Texas Revolution. Little Miss Meadows, eight years old, was Catherine to Ludlow's Petruchio. The actor-manager could not decide whether to stoop down to her height or lift her up to his.[10]

During the 1836 1837 season Mrs. Alexander Drake was seen in *Catherine and Petruchio;* James W. Wallack played Hamlet and Benedick to sizable audiences; beautiful Annette Nelson (also known as Mrs. C. C. Hodges), of whom the *Commercial Register and Patriot* (April 29, 1837) impudently wrote "is no *actress* except in form," opened as Rosalind in *As You Like It;* and Little Miss Meadows returned with *Catherine and Petruchio,* but Ludlow, in St. Louis, escaped playing opposite her. The last visitor, Augustus A. Addams, often compared to Edwin Forrest in ability, performed Othello and King Lear.

Mrs. Henry (Sarah) Lewis, known for her male impersonations, opened Ludlow and Smith's 1837–1838 season with a spirited interpretation of Richard III. There soon followed Mobile's first recorded sight of *The Comedy of Errors,* with James H. Hackett as the Dromio of Ephesus. January brought a real treat for theatergoers.

The enchanting Ellen Tree charmed large audiences with *Much Ado About Nothing, Macbeth,* and *As You Like It.* The *Commercial Register* editor (February 5, 1838) pronounced her the second best actress he had ever seen (failing to tell his readers who was the best).

A celebrity of another sort was Master St. Luke, eleven-year-old violinist whose father requested Ludlow to bill him as "the youthful Paganini."[11] When the prodigy took a benefit he displayed his dramatic versatility in one act of *Richard III* and as Kentucky Harry in the regional piece, *Yankee Tar.* The last visitor, Mrs. Edward (Eliza) Shaw, the beautiful and accomplished English actress later known as Mrs. Thomas S. Hamblin, played Juliet to the Romeo of Joseph M. Field and the Mercutio of Ludlow. Unfortunately, the theater was out of public favor because of internal dissension which had become public knowledge, and attendance was poor during Mrs. Shaw's engagement.

As if one theater did not have enough of a struggle to survive, there had been a rival theater in Mobile during the latter part of the previous season and a large part of the present season. Louis V. Ferry's theater succeeded in luring away several of Ludlow and Smith's stock members and in booking some stars. During the engagement at Ferry's of Mr. and Mrs. John Barnes and daughter Charlotte, the ladies appeared in *Othello,* the mother as Emilia and the daughter as Desdemona. Augustus A. Addams and his wife, the former Mary Duff (daughter of Mrs. Mary Duff, a Mobile star in 1833) were at the new theater for performances of *Richard III, Hamlet, The Merchant of Venice,* and scenes from *Macbeth.* Mrs. Shaw, swapping allegiances, played Juliet, and a correspondent (*Commercial Register,* May 19, 1838) proclaimed that she far out-shone Ellen Tree as a tragedian.

Within the space of a month during the 1838–1839 season Ludlow and Smith presented the three biggest theatrical names of the era. Ellen Tree battled inclement weather but managed to earn $2,229 for herself and $3,729 for the theater during her twelve nights' engagement.[12] Her selections this year included *As You Like It* twice and *Twelfth Night.* The *Mercantile Advertiser* (February 16, 1839) opined that Rosalind was her best role. Because of the great demand for choice seats during Miss Tree's visit, private boxes in the dress circle and the best parquette seats were auctioned to the highest bidder.

Immediately upon Miss Tree's departure Edwin Forrest arrived by steamboat from New Orleans. He began as Othello, with the support of Field as Iago, Mrs. Field (formerly Eliza Riddle) as Desdemona, and Mrs. Lewis (last year's visiting Richard III and now a member of the stock company) as Emilia. A crowded and fashionable house welcomed America's foremost actor on his initial visit to Mobile. *King Lear, Hamlet,* and *Richard III* were his other Shakespeare offerings. Forrest's demand for half of the nightly receipts with no deductions was met with protests by Ludlow and Smith. They compromised on a division after a $100 deduction.[13] Perhaps Forrest's kind words about the Mobile stock company later provided consolation. Smith wrote Ludlow from St. Louis when Forrest was appearing there that the star had told New Orleans impresario James H. Caldwell "the Ludlow-Smith company at Mobile *could play his pieces*—and the company at the St. Charles could not!"[14]

Forrest was followed the night after his leave-taking by the third of the splendid triumvirate, Junius Brutus Booth. The editor of the *Mercantile Advertiser* (March 7, 1839) anticipated observing Booth's histrionics, but "would remark, en passant, that while our citizens are ever ready to render the meed of homage to genuine talent, which Booth possesses, no community would be less likely than ours, to tolerate . . . those foibles which have, at times, marked the course of that gentleman in other cities."

How he conducted himself in Mobile is open to question. Ludlow, whose recollections contain many inaccuracies, and who might have confused this engagement with one in St. Louis in 1846 when there is definite proof of Booth's drunkenness, claims that "he got into one of his insane or drunken frolics" in Mobile and had only two full houses. In his book Sol Smith makes no mention of misbehavior on Booth's part, saying that receipts were very poor and that only *Richard III* brought out a good house—$690. The newspaper was silent on the subject of ill conduct and praised his Hamlet as the best the critic had ever seen: "he *looked* and *acted* the character."[15]

In April a prodigy new to Mobile bowed as Richard with the first,

fourth, and fifth acts of *Richard III*. This was Jean Margaret Davenport, twelve-year-old English actress, who with her parents were
reputedly the original of the Crummles family in *Nicholas Nickleby*.
She soon followed the male role with another, an interpretation of
Shylock. The managers lost money on her, Ludlow attributing the
failure to the fact she was "too large to have her efforts considered
wonderful as a child . . . not sufficiently developed to be considered
a woman."[16]

Ludlow and Smith's part of the 1839–1840 season was a financial
disaster. The terrible fire that destroyed a great deal of the city,
including the theater, forced them to convert an unattractive building in an inconvenient location into a temporary theater. Hard times
were upon Mobile, the weather was bad, the company had to be
pared down to save expenses, and a rival theater was established.
The only Shakespearean performance by a star was that of Charles
Mason as Petruchio. One night Sol Smith, in desperation for actors,
featured two amateurs in *Othello;* they drew a $13 house.[17]

The Chapman family, famous for their floating theater but now
based on land, presented a short Mobile season that had performances of *Romeo and Juliet* by Mr. and Mrs. Joseph M. Field and by
the Barnes family.

Caldwell's Regime

In the early part of the 1840–1841 season the Chapmans gave
several Shakespeare plays with their stock company and Mary Vos
(now Mrs. Stuart); but Mobilians, as usual in the fall, were slow
getting back into the theatergoing habit. Even a visiting star, Fitz-
gerald Tasistro, appearing in *Othello* and *Merchant of Venice* attracted little attention.

James H. Caldwell supplanted the firm of Ludlow and Smith as
the dominant theater manager in Mobile during the 1840–1841 season. With the assistance of a public stock subscription, Caldwell
was able to build the most spacious theater yet seen in Mobile.
Tasistro, who had scored poorly with the Chapmans, was the first
Shakespearean actor at Caldwell's. He opened as Hamlet and repeated Shylock and Othello. Charles Eaton was seen in *Richard III,*

Othello, scenes from *Hamlet,* and in imitations of Junius Brutus Booth and John Philip Kemble in Shakespearean roles. The *Advertiser and Chronicle* of February 18, 1841, called Eaton a good tragedian and chided theatergoers who thought that only actors associated with Drury Lane were worth seeing.

Caldwell's second season in Mobile brought many stars and novelties but few Shakespearean actors. James H. Hackett came with his oft-repeated Falstaff in *Henry IV* and *The Merry Wives of Windsor.* Samuel Butler, English member of the Jefferson acting family, played to a full and fashionable house as Hamlet. The Ophelia was his kinswoman, Elizabeth Jefferson Richardson, a new member of the stock company. After playing Shylock for the benefit of the theater treasurer, Butler at his own benefit presented a lecture on the drama with illustrations of Shakespeare.

By the season of 1842–1843 Caldwell, perhaps tiring of theatrical enterprise and busy with other more lucrative affairs such as his gas lighting company franchises, leased the Mobile theater to Jules Dumas, operator of a tavern across the street from the theater. The first visitors of the season were Edmund S. Conner and Mrs. William Sefton (Ann Duff Waring). Sharp-tongued Joe Cowell, a member of the stock company, denigrated Conner as a "very gentleman-like specimen of well-dressed mediocrity" but thought highly of Mrs. Sefton, "the very best general actress on the continent."[18] The pair's first Shakespeare offering was *Romeo and Juliet,* with the lady as Romeo and Conner as Mercutio. They were greeted by a "respectable and fashionable audience," (*Advertiser and Chronicle,* January 5, 1843) and repeated the drama later in the engagement. Their repertoire also included *Richard III* and the first and second acts of *Macbeth.* The *Advertiser and Chronicle* of January 9 praised Mrs. Sefton's reading and action as excellent and Conner's voice and costumes as good.

James H. Hackett returned in January with his usual round of characters, including Falstaff. His first night in *Henry IV* attracted a house of only $353, although the newspaper found him superb. On January 23 Hackett made a point "to strengthen my physical energies to their utmost and pen up my spirits all day" in preparation for his enactment of the difficult role of Richard III for the first time in Mobile.[19] Unfortunately, he had not selected a propitious night for appearing in this serious part. Mobilians had other things on their minds. They felt that their favorite actress, Mary Vos Stuart, had been slighted by the management in assigning many of her roles to Mrs. Richardson and Mrs. Hodges, and her adherents were determined to show their wrath, as they had done in similar circumstances seven years earlier. Now their darling was a widow with two small children to support and more deserving than ever of their partisanship. Cowell relates that a huge crowd rushed into the theater without paying, "made a prodigious noise, broke some benches and gas fixings, and demanded a *free benefit* for Mrs. Stuart, and *the whole of her salary be paid for ten weeks,* the period of her engagement—all of which Dumas was *obliged* to agree to. The mayor made a speech, and the row was over. . . ."[20] Hackett's evening, however, was spoiled beyond redemption. He wrote Sol Smith that although "the cause was removed in a quarter of an hour, so had been *all* the *ladies* and the house was noisy above stairs and generally indifferent or disaffected towards the stage."[21]

The disaffection of Mrs. Stuart's friends with the management was also responsible for the failure of George Vandenhoff's engagement, which began the day after the Stuart benefit. Vandenhoff opened as Hamlet, a role in which the *Advertiser and Chronicle* (January 30, 1843) applauded him as "an actor of extraordinary merit, is effortless, uses no stage tricks." He also played Macbeth, but audiences remained rough and rowdy. In his reminiscenses Vandenhoff writes: "I next played six nights at Mobile, of which I need only remark that the company was shockingly bad; and the manager having got into a snarl with the public by discharging a popular favorite, Mrs. Stuart, I had to suffer the penalty of his obstinacy; there being a very general league of absence from the theatre till she should be restored."[22]

Happily, February brought a diversion in the way of a benefit for Protestant and Catholic orphans, which Henry Clay attended. On the program was *The Tempest,* one of its five productions this season by the stock company. Since special expensive scenery was required for *The Tempest,* it had to be used many times, not only in the drama for which it was devised but in others to which it could be adapted. Then J. Hudson Kirby came over from New Orleans to give Mobilians a taste of his stentorian and ranting style. His sole Shakespearean role was Richard III, with a death scene famous for the sheer terror it inspired. In May he was back in Mobile at the same theater, then under the management of Mrs. Richardson rather than Dumas. He assumed the title part in *King Lear* with the new manager as Cordelia.

In April a shortlived theater housed in a large room over the Corinthian Hall sprang up. Cowell says that its first manager, J. S. Haskell, an amateur, "indulged himself by giving *his conception* of Richard III, and got hissed so heartily that he advertised his retirement from dramatic life at the end of the week."[23]

Return of Ludlow and Smith

Ludlow and Smith were at the managerial helm in Mobile for the 1843–1844 season after an absence, except for occasional presentations, of four years. They accepted Caldwell's offer of the lease of his Mobile theater, feeling that the control of three of the leading theaters in the South and West—Mobile, New Orleans, and St. Louis—would greatly enhance their ability to deal with stars and to engage good stock players. It fell to Ludlow to manage the Mobile operation while Smith carried on in New Orleans.

Business started slowly, as usual. Although the *Register and Journal* of November 27, 1843, lauded the stock company as "the most talented and effective that has graced our boards in many years," *Henry IV,* the first Shakespeare effort of the season, combined with a ventriloquist, attracted a house of only $130.[24]

Control of the two southern theaters may have been responsible for the managers' ability to secure Wallack, Hackett, Macready, and Forrest this year. A severe rain storm occurred on January 15, scheduled to be James W. Wallack's opening night in *Hamlet.* Wallack sent Ludlow a note asking to be excused from playing since he thought there would be no one in the theater. Ludlow insisted on his appearance, and the receipts amounted to $243.[25] It is surprising to read in the *Register and Journal* (January 17, 1844) that "the house was full . . . although it rained incessantly." The accuracy of the newspaper's frequent description of a full house is suspect, since the theater could seat at least 900 people and most tickets were priced at either $1 or 75 cents. Wallack's *Macbeth* brought $212, *The Merchant of Venice* $199, and *Richard III* $221, Ludlow recorded in his diary January 17 through 22. The star's benefit as Benedick in *Much Ado About Nothing* pulled "quite a fashionable house" of $402. He was aided by Mrs. Stuart as Beatrice and Mrs. W. H. Smith (sister of Eliza Riddle Field and one of the best-known stock actresses in the East for many decades) as Hero.

The most illustrious actor who had yet appeared in Mobile—William C. Macready—came in March. After the first act curtain fell on his opening night as Hamlet, Macready summoned Ludlow to his dressing room to complain of the actors' inadequacy and their neglect of the business indicated in the marked copy of the script he had furnished. *Hamlet* had been rehearsed three times, and although one rehearsal took place after Macready reached town, the star did not attend, Ludlow noted in his diary of March 3, 1844.

In his own diary entry of March 4, Macready wrote: "Acted Hamlet. I thought I never acted the first scene with the Ghost so well; the audience this night very numerous. Persons going away in some of the steamboats had prevailed on the masters to delay their start until midnight in order to visit the theatre. Many *rowdy* people were there, women of the town—in short it was an audience attracted by sheer curiosity. Perhaps I was not up to my mark, although I strove very resolutely."[26]

The audience was indeed numerous: $833 was in the till—the largest amount of which there is a record this year. *Macbeth* opened the second week of Macready's engagement, the star being assisted by John Ryder, the actor traveling with him, as Macduff, and Mrs. Stuart as Lady Macbeth. Ludlow played Hecate and joked to himself in his diary, "Can't say positively which of us drew the big house." *William Tell* drew only $269, and Ludlow recorded, "People seem to think the Shakespearean characters the only ones worth interpreting—hah!" Receipts climbed back to $424 when *Othello* was played. A disappointing $464 was taken in for Macready's benefit, which the newspaper advertised as *Macbeth* but Macready listed as *Richelieu*.[27] As he was leaving the city, Macready noted in his diary that he liked everything in Mobile except the hotel (the Mansion House, Mobile's best) and the theater.[28]

England's greatest actor was succeeded by America's greatest actor. Edwin Forrest began with *Othello* and followed with *Macbeth* and *King Lear*. These three performances prompted the editor of the *Register and Journal* (March 21, 1844) to write that Forrest "is winning golden opinions from the largest and most fashionable audiences." The week was concluded with *Richard III*. Ludlow's diary (March 18–23, 1844) reports that *Othello* brought $528; *Macbeth* $330, "Bad—bad! bad! for the great American tragedian"; *King Lear* $324; *Metamora* $656; *Damon and Pythias* $319; and *Richard III* $448. This year Forrest, like Macready, demanded a clear half of the receipts.

Ludlow and Smith's 1844–1845 season brought out only one genuine Shakespearean actor and one former stock company regular who essayed Shakespeare. James R. Anderson, young English protégé of Macready, was welcomed by the *Register and Journal* (March 3, 1845) for his youth, force, and energy. During his two weeks' engagement he appeared in *Hamlet, Much Ado About Nothing, Macbeth, The Merchant of Venice, Catherine and Petruchio,* and *Othello*. At his benefit, when he played Petruchio as well as Claude Melnotte in *Lady of Lyons,* the largest audience of the season was present. Toward the end of the season the sterling stock performer of ten years before, Charles Webb, came from the St. Charles Theatre in New Orleans to play Richard III and other roles.

After the prior year's poor showing, it is good to learn that 1845–1846 was probably the most successful year Ludlow and Smith ever had in Mobile. The stock company was excellent and the stars numerous. Junius Brutus Booth, perhaps chastened by the reaction to his drunken behavior in New Orleans, performed in Mobile in December with credit to himself and with admirable effect, according to Ludlow. His Shakespearean repertoire included *Othello, Richard III, King Lear,* and *Hamlet*. From editorial comment, it seems that Mobilians were being permitted to watch the sudden, last flowering of an artist's genuis.

Clara Ellis, promising young English actress who the *Register and Journal* predicted would become the Siddons of her time but who never reached that eminence, played one Shakespearean part—that of Portia to Edmund S. Conner's Shylock. Brothers Henry and Thomas Placide gave three performances of the Dromios in *The Comedy of Errors*. James H. Hackett starred as Falstaff in *Henry IV* with a cast that included Joseph M. Field, Edmund S. Conner, George Skerrett, Charles Webb, Noah Ludlow, J. B. Roberts, "Rowley" Marks, Mary Vos Stuart, Mrs. Richard Russell, Sr., and Miss Sylvia. Probably no theater operating in the United States at the time could have gathered a cast of better quality. The newspaper recognized this fact, pronouncing it the best troupe ever assembled in Mobile.

The most exciting event of the year was the arrival of England's premiere actress, Ellen Tree, accompanied this time by her famous husband, Charles Kean. *Macbeth,* the Keans' first Shakespeare play, produced receipts of $535, while *Much Ado About Nothing* brought $353. The second week began with *As You Like It* to a $456 house. *Hamlet,* announced as Ludlow's benefit, attracted $368.[29] Editorial judgment on the theater, scarce in newspapers this year, acknowledged the Keans to be excellent in *As You Like It* as Jaques and Rosalind. Charles Webb as the senior Duke appealed to the intelligence of the audience, Thomas Placide's Touchstone was fine, Robert's Orlando showed him to be a young man of merit and high promise, and the performance of several others was "very creditable."[30]

The first advertised stars of Ludlow and Smith's 1846–1847 season, James W. Wallack, Jr., and his wife, the former Mrs. Ann Sefton, had actually been engaged as stock company personnel to alternate between New Orleans and Mobile. The pair performed in *Romeo and Juliet* (she as Romeo and he as Mercutio, as usual), *The Merchant of Venice, Richard III,* and *Macbeth*. James E. Murdoch, who had visited Mobile eleven years earlier, presented *Hamlet* during a six nights' engagement. Mrs. Anna Cora Mowatt, accompanied by E. L. Davenport, played *Romeo and Juliet* and *Much Ado About Nothing*. Later in the season, after the arrival of the elder James W. Wallack, the three Wallacks played *Hamlet, Othello, The Merchant of Venice,* and *Much Ado About Nothing*. Sol Smith wrote in his diary that "the engagement of *all* the Wallacks has been peculiarly unfortunate for *us*—a dead loss of about $4,000!—that sum actually thrown away. I do not believe they have attracted a dollar to either Theatre [New Orleans and Mobile] this season."[31]

James R. Anderson came for an eight nights' visit in March and opened in *Hamlet* with the support of the popular Mrs. Charles J. B. Fisher (formerly Elizabeth Jefferson Richardson) as Ophelia. Sol Smith, in town to confer with Ludlow, recorded in his diary of March 4, 1847, that the evening's program brought in only $105. "What is Mobile coming to?" he agonized.

Mobile was coming to the end of the Ludlow and Smith era. The partners decided to concentrate their efforts in the South in New Orleans, where they now had a coalition with a second theater, to engage only two companies for the 1847–1848 season, and to rely on detachments from these companies for the Mobile theater.[32] The theater was to be operated intermittently, as it had been under their aegis in 1840–1841. No Shakespearean performances were given during the season that ran from mid-December to March.

Managements of Deering and Place

William Deering, an obscure actor who had been with Ludlow and Smith in Mobile during the 1846–1847 season and who had played occasionally in minor New York theaters, took over the management of the Mobile theater for the 1848–1849 season. Only three Shakespearean performers were featured under his charge. George Jamieson starred in *Macbeth, Richard III,* and *Othello;* Charles Dibdin Pitt presented *Hamlet, Richard III,* and *The Taming of the Shrew;* and Junius Brutus Booth played unspecified roles in January.

The season of 1849–1850 was conducted by Robert L. Place, a former livery stable clerk who had had a month-long stint as a manager in Mobile. The first star was lovely eighteen-year-old Julia

Dean. She played Juliet to the Romeo of George Jamieson. In January Junius Brutus Booth paid what was destined to be his last visit to Mobile before his death. Mary Vos Stuart came from New Orleans to assist him. Crowded houses were attracted to *The Merchant of Venice* and *Richard III*. The *Daily Register* (January 28, 1850) reported that his benefit in the latter drama was attended by a "perfect jam." When George Jamieson returned during Booth's second week, Booth played his usual role of Iago one night, and then he and Jamieson reversed parts on a subsequent evening. The editor was very complimentary of the cast's rendering of *King Lear,* with Booth in the title role, Jamieson as Edgar, and Mrs. Stuart as Cordelia.

Climaxing the season was the engagement of Charlotte Cushman, now at the pinnacle of her acclaim. She was accompanied by the English actor Charles W. Couldock, and one of Mobile's long-time favorite stock actresses, Eliza Petrie Place, wife of the manager, was brought from New Orleans to assist. Miss Cushman opened to a full house as Lady Macbeth. The *Daily Register* (March 20, 1850) reviewer thought her portrayal superior to anything he had ever witnessed and felt that "she ought to have been a man"—a somewhat left-handed compliment, it would seem, to her forcefulness. Couldock, however, mistakenly interpreted Macbeth as a coward and also "murdered the King's English in regular Cockney style." Another observer thought Miss Cushman's Lady Macbeth was her worst character. She made her "a fury—a demon—athirst for blood—a fiend without heart and without sympathy—a real live devil without one redeeming trait in her character. . . ."[33]

As Rosalind in *As You Like It,* Miss Cushman, who started her career as a singer, interpolated a popular song. For her benefit at the conclusion of the week, the actress repeated *Macbeth*. During the second week her plays included *Much Ado About Nothing* and *Henry VIII*. As far as is known, this is the first representation of the latter-named drama in Mobile. Miss Cushman assumed the role of Katherine, while Couldock did Cardinal Wolsey. The visitors stayed an extra night, announced as the last of the season, repeating *As You Like It* for the benefit of manager Place.

Management of Joseph M. Field

Joseph M. Field, who had withdrawn from the theater several years earlier to edit a newspaper in St. Louis, in 1850 returned to Mobile as lessee and manager of the theater, still owned by James H. Caldwell. The building underwent renovation, the dress boxes and parquette being connected and the parquette raised in order to improve the audience's view. The position of the orchestra was now below the sightline of the nearest spectator. A range of private boxes was fitted up in the center of the house, and the whole of the first circle was supplied with newly cushioned and backed chairs. The theater offered a more comfortable arrangement than earlier players and patrons endured.

The season's first stars were the Bateman sisters, Kate, seven, and Ellen, five, daughters of Sidney Cowell and H. L. Bateman, and grandchildren of Joe Cowell. They appeared as Shylock and Portia, the Macbeths, and Richard and Richmond in *Richard III*, as well as in other roles better suited to their years. In January Mrs. Stuart, who was with Ludlow and Smith in New Orleans, and McKean Buchanan presented *Othello, Hamlet, King Lear*, and the fourth act of *The Merchant of Venice*.

February was noteworthy for the return of Charlotte Cushman. Tickets for the best seats went up from 75 cents to $1 for her visit. She opened as Lady Macbeth; Field, capable of playing almost any role, appeared as Macbeth. Miss Cushman's only other Shakespeare character was Romeo. During the coming summer the *Mobile Daily Register* (June 18, 1851) reported that she had played Hamlet in Cincinnati and that the newspaper of that city called her "*the* Hamlet of the age." The editor ruminated that it was a pity she had not undertaken the parts of King Lear and Grandfather Whitehead (in the popular play of that name). Could it be that Miss Cushman's "breeches" roles were not appreciated in Mobile?

Eliza Logan played a starring engagement with her father Cornelius A. Logan under Field's management in December, 1851. The *Daily Advertiser* of December 4 called her debut as Juliet successful but then candidly stated she was not pretty, was too short for proper stage effect, and had an unpleasing countenance when depicting anger or grief. Her enunciation was clear and her voice had good volume and quality, but she lacked expression in reading. Although encountering formidable obstacles in her stage career because of her appearance, Miss Logan finally achieved a substantial position. Her father wrote Sol Smith that she was not of the "milk and water style of acting—'a rabbit boiled without sauce or salt.' "[34]

Comedienne and songstress Mrs. Howard, née Rosina Shaw, and her husband Charles Howard opened Field's third Mobile season in November, 1852. *Twelfth Night* turned out a large crowd and brought encomiums for all the cast. Mrs. Howard as Viola and W. H. Chippendale as Sir Toby were admirable, Mrs. Stuart as Olivia and Field as Malvolio were perfect, J. B. Fuller as the clown was excellent, Mrs. Fisher as Maria was very good, and even an obscure Morrison was better than passable, according to the *Daily Advertiser* of November 30, 1852.

December saw the return of Eliza and Cornelius A. Logan. Only a small assembly was present for *Much Ado About Nothing,* but the *Daily Advertiser* commended Miss Logan's flair for comedy roles such as Beatrice. Julia Dean, accompanied by her father Edwin Dean, also played Beatrice in addition to Juliet. She drew good houses during a long engagement. The contrast between the beautiful Miss Dean and the plain Miss Logan could hardly have escaped attention. The *Daily Advertiser* (January 22, 27, 1853) heaped praise on Field, calling him "the very manager of all managers" and maintaining that stars pronounced his stock company the best in the nation.

The theater's reopening, scheduled for October, 1853, was deferred to its usual November date because of a yellow fever epidemic. J. A. J. Neafie as Hamlet was Field's first star. Later in the engagement Neafie played Macbeth, King Lear, and Richard III.

Eliza Logan appeared in *Much Ado About Nothing* in December. She wrote Sol Smith that her nights were poorly attended even though she shared the stage with two attractive dancers. The weather was bad, the river was low, business generally had not begun, and she had competition from a circus and a minstrel show.[35]

The Bateman children returned with their usual numbers but this year added the first act of *Hamlet*. Ellen Bateman impersonated the Dane while stock company actress Anna Cruise was Ophelia.

Julia Dean, accompanied by George Jamieson, reached Mobile in February. The *Daily Advertiser* critic (January 26, 28, 1854) was not as kind to her as he had been in previous years: "possessing hardly sufficient power for the delineation of the stronger passions, she is very effective in representing the softer emotions. . . ." And again, "In many plays she is hardly equal to all the requirements of the parts she sustains. . . ." The critic must have had her roles as Lady Macbeth and Juliet in mind. Field was able at this time to pay off several small debts to Ludlow and Smith,[36] so the Dean engagement must have been remunerative in spite of the newspaper's carping.

Making his first Mobile visit in seven years, James R. Anderson began in *Hamlet* in March. He followed this with *Richard III, Macbeth,* and *Catherine and Petruchio.* The newspaper noted that Anderson was not accorded the crowded houses he deserved, and Field wrote to Sol Smith that the engagement was a losing proposition.

The young English couple Louisa Howard and Henry Farren made a joint appearance at Field's theater just before Christmas, 1854, in *As You Like It*. The *Evening News* reviewer found Miss Howard a lovely heroine as Rosalind and Farren very versatile as Jaques. The afterpiece on the program was *Anthony and Cleopatra,* probably a farcical version seen often at this time. During the engagement of these stars the *Evening News* (December 27, 1854) noticed an improvement in both the number and character of the audiences at the theater.

James H. Hackett, absent for several years, opened in December, 1855, with *Henry IV* to what the *Evening News* called an immense house. Charles W. Couldock, Charlotte Cushman's one-time leading man, came to Mobile this year as a solo performer, playing Richard III, Petruchio, Hamlet, and Macbeth. The *Evening News* (December 20, 26, 1855) was particularly harsh in its judgment of Couldock's Richard. He made of it "a farce . . . and a devilish broad farce at that." He had the English style of accenting the last word of a sentence—unimportant though it might be. His voice drawled and his enunciation was imperfect. Couldock's best trait, the critic admitted, was his repudiation of ranting, "a considerable merit in these days of theatrical buffoonery and mediocrity." Shakespeare was beyond his reach; he should stick to melodrama, concluded the writer.

The day after Christmas the young American sister team of Susan and Kate Denim began an engagement to a crowded house. Their Shakespeare presentation was *Romeo and Juliet,* Susan as Romeo and Kate as Juliet. Susan had native ability but needed improvement, advised the *Evening News.*

Now tragedy struck. Joseph M. Field, in poor health for several years, overworked and harassed by misfortunes at his St. Louis theater, died on January 28, 1856, leaving his widow to carry on the theater management. Eliza Field sent for family friend and relative Noah Ludlow, who assisted her during the remainder of the season. The theater was closed only two days in observance of Field's death.

E. L. Davenport, who, like Couldock, had first visited Mobile with a better-known actress, returned after nine years to star by himself. His roles included Richard III, Benedick, and Hamlet. The *Evening News* (February 29, 1856) called him a "superb, finished" actor. The newspaper critic was now berating the stock company and deploring the physical condition of the theater at every opportunity. It was no doubt true that the theater had become run down, and personnel problems began to surface. On February 27, 1856, the *Evening News* contended that Mobile was the "best theatrical city in America of its size—this fact is perfectly notorious, and yet its citizens have more humbugs thrust down their throats—bear more and suffer more than any people *in* America."

The season wore on, and upon the departure of Davenport came another outstanding American actor, James E. Murdoch, who had last visited Mobile in 1847. The *Evening News* (March 3, 1856) urged its readers to see him but, in a roaring blast at the stock company, charged that Murdoch would have no support except for former dancer Sallie St. Clair as leading lady. After his first performance as Hamlet, Murdoch's acting was praised as natural and impulsive and he was declared a superior player.

Duffield's Management

Samuel B. Duffield, Benedict De Bar's acting manager at the St. Charles Theatre in New Orleans and in St. Louis, signed a five-year lease in 1856 for the Mobile theater soon after Mrs. Field relinquished the building.

Mrs. George P. Farren (née Mary Ann Russell) inaugurated Duffield's administration with popular dramas of the day and two evenings as Lady Macbeth. The role should have been suitable for what was described as her "ranting" style, which the *Daily Advertiser* of December 9, 1856, said her audience seemed to like.

Hamlet and Iago were offered in December by J. B. Conway; James H. Hackett returned as Falstaff; and Mr. and Mrs. George Pauncefort of the stock company played *Romeo and Juliet* at a benefit for the purpose of putting an iron rail around the public square. In February, J. A. J. Neafie starred as Macbeth, Othello, Richard III, Hamlet, and Brutus in *Julius Caesar*. This seems to be the only time in our chronicle that *Julius Caesar* was presented in its entirety.

March, 1857, was a memorable occasion in Mobile's theatrical annals, for it marked the debut of Edwin Booth, "young American tragedian," and son of Junius Brutus Booth. Young Booth had had eight years of stage experience, the previous five in California and Australia. The father was now dead, and the son was preparing to assume the tragic mantle. Although Booth had not yet returned to New York, where even then reputations were made or broken, his fame was in the ascendancy, and audiences realized they were seeing something out of the ordinary. He was not yet the Booth of ten years later, but he was slowly approaching the peak of his art. Because of bad weather there were small crowds for Booth's first and second nights in *Richard III* and *King Lear*. The audiences were very appreciative, however. The *Advertiser* (March 11, 13, 1857) remarked on the striking resemblance between Edwin Booth and his father and praised his clear enunciation and excellent reading. March 11 brought *Othello* with Booth as Iago, and after playing several other pieces, he wound up the engagement with *Richard III*. The *Advertiser* glowed that the young man had produced the most favorable impression of any actor this season. Booth returned in April for a few days, giving *King Lear* to a great ovation and *Hamlet* at a "complimentary" benefit.

In January, 1858, Mr. and Mrs. James W. Wallack, Jr. were engaged for their first visit to Mobile since their contract had been bought off by Ludlow and Smith eleven years before. They attracted a large and very grand assemblage to *Macbeth*. The January 20, 1858, *Advertiser* complained that Wallack mouthed his words and overacted but conceded that the pit audience seemed to enjoy his interpretation. Mrs. Wallack, although better than her husband, could have been much improved. Only stock player McWilliams drew praise as Macduff. The Wallacks also gave *Othello, Romeo and Juliet, Richard III,* and two evenings of *Winter's Tale*— probably its first showing in Mobile.

The most prestigious engagement of the season took place with the arrival of Charlotte Cushman in March. As usual, her first Shakespearean role was Lady Macbeth. When she was announced for *Romeo and Juliet,* the *Advertiser* (March 3, 1858) said she was acknowledged to be the best Romeo on the stage. She was Katherine in *Henry VIII* and then Rosalind in *As You Like It,* which she combined with an afterpiece. This was for her mid-engagment benefit, when most stars, no matter how important, felt obliged to give the audience its money's worth by playing in at least two pieces, if not more.

After having skipped a year, Edwin Booth returned in February, appearing first as Hamlet. An odd bit of casting found seventeen-year-old Alice Mann listed as the Queen and Mrs. Hattie Bernard, engaged to play soubrettes, slated as Ophelia. Booth continued with *Othello* (the star as Iago), *Richard III, The Merchant of Venice, Catherine and Petruchio,* and *Macbeth*—all to large houses.

Jane Coombs made her Mobile debut as Juliet in late March to a very slim audience. The *Advertiser* (March 30, 31, 1859) attributed this partly to the foul weather and partly to the "miserable piece selected—*Romeo and Juliet. . .* which should now be excluded from Shakespeare's acting plays. . . ." However, the critic had considerable praise for the actress, who was still but a novice, having not yet appeared on the stage for four consecutive weeks.

The season concluded with a week's engagement of the Marsh children, a group of about thirty-five juveniles who had visited Mobile several times. This year they added *Macbeth* and *The Merchant of Venice* to their varied repertoire. The troupe was excellent and several members were "finished actors," according to the *Advertiser* of June 5, 1859.

Ignoring the advice of the *Advertiser* critic, Jane Coombs brought out *Romeo and Juliet* again in December, 1859, near the beginning of Duffield's fourth Mobile season. Later in the month the distinguished tragedian Barry Sullivan was welcomed in *Hamlet*. He also performed *Macbeth, Much Ado About Nothing, Richard III, Othello,* and *King Lear* to "full and fashionable houses and with a very fair degree of satisfaction to his auditors," reported the *Advertiser* of December 23, 1859. James R. Anderson joined with Agnes Elsworthy to present *Macbeth* to a "crowded house" and "thunders of applause." This was followed by *Hamlet* twice (said to be one of Anderson's best roles) and *Richard III*. At his benefit as Falstaff in *The Merry Wives of Windsor* (his first attempt at this part) all the standing room in the theater was taken.[37]

Edwin Booth, engaged for two weeks, gave *Hamlet* and *Richard III* twice, *Othello* (once in the title role and once as Iago), *King Lear, Macbeth, Catherine and Petruchio,* and *Romeo and Juliet.* The *Advertiser* (February 4, 1860) thought his Iago one of the truly great stage interpretations. Mobile audiences showed their enthusiasm by turning out the largest house of the season.

Wilmarth and Emma Waller were seen in *Othello,* he as the Moor and she as Iago. Their other Shakespeare role assignment was more conventional when they played the Macbeths on two occasions. The Wallers were the last stars to tread the boards of the old Royal Street Theatre. On March 13, 1860, the building was destroyed by the largest fire Mobile had seen in many years. Duffield immediately rented the amphitheater on the corner of Royal and Conti streets and wound up the season with gymnasts, opera, and minstrels. No time was lost in converting the amphitheater into a legitimate theater to be ready for the coming fall season.

The first Shakespearean performance in the new house took place in December, 1860, with Kate Bateman, now an attractive young

woman, as Juliet. Edward Brown quotes the mixed review of the
Daily Advertiser of December 21: "Miss B's Juliet had its merits and
its defects, the latter pertaining to the tender passages, the former to
those where more force was required. . . . She raved slightly in some
places but generally kept herself under excellent control. Her voice
lacks the softness requisite to give effect to the gentler emotions, but
that endures the audience against being wearied by the milk and
waterishness which is the characteristic of most Juliets. . . ."[38]

Mr. and Mrs. James W. Wallack, Jr. made the unusual selection
of *Othello* for Christmas Eve and *Macbeth* for Christmas night, and
again the *Daily Advertiser* withheld wholehearted endorsement of
their conceptions of their roles. The last Shakespearean representation was that of Edward Eddy, who played Hamlet and closed
as Othello on March 1, 1861.

With the coming of the Civil War in April, 1861, we bring to an
end the story of Shakespeare in antebellum Mobile. The Bard had
been played by the famous and the obscure, the native and the
foreign, the juvenile and the elderly, to slim and overflowing audiences seated on rough benches and plush chairs, in ballrooms and
elaborate theaters, in heat and rain, and with great and little success.

Cultivated Mobilians knew and appreciated Shakespeare; they
had seen the dramas during their visits to New Orleans, Charleston,
and New York. The riverboatmen had patronized Shakespearean
performances in river ports such as Cincinnati and Pittsburgh; their
appetite for the robust may have influenced the frequency of the
production of *Richard III* and *Macbeth*. The quadroons had seen
Shakespeare in New Orleans. Many spectators followed the text of
the plays line by line and enjoyed comparing the relative merits of
stars in their interpretation of the same role. Although most audiences gave the nod to standard and contemporary melodramas, "do-
mestic" dramas, and light comedies and farces, no season was
considered complete without a full quota of Shakespearean comedies and tragedies.

Mobile, in 1860 a city of 28,559 whites and 12,571 blacks, had
supported a theater that offered outstanding legitimate drama for
almost forty years. Along with New Orleans, Charleston, and St.

Louis, Mobile could hold its own as to players and programs with New York, Philadelphia, and Boston. The professional theater would continue during the war, would see a resurgence after hostilities ceased, but would gradually fade away. After 1868 there was no resident stock company; and although touring stars such as Hackett, Forrest, Booth, Mr. and Mrs. Charles Kean, Adelaide Ristori, and Lawrence Barrett brought Shakespeare and other plays for several more decades, the presentations were sporadic. Mobile's days of glory as a theatrical capital and a home for Shakespearean drama were past.

NOTES

1. *Mobile Commercial Register*, May 2–30, 1822.

2. See Erwin Craighead, *Mobile: Fact and Fiction* (Mobile, Ala., 1930), p. 172, and Frances Margaret Bailey, "A History of the Stage in Mobile, Alabama from 1824–1850" (M.A. thesis, State University of Iowa, 1934), p. 16.

3. *Mobile Commercial Register*, Nov. 18, 1822.

4. Noah M. Ludlow, *Dramatic Life As I Found It* (St. Louis: G. I. Jones, 1880), p. 264.

5. *Mobile Commercial Register*, Apr. 21, 1826.

6. This tally is only approximately accurate. Information is lacking or incomplete on several seasons, and programs advertised in the newspapers, from which the information is largely derived, were subject to last minute changes.

7. Ludlow, p. 289.

8. Sol Smith, *Theatrical Management in the West and South for Thirty Years* (New York: Harper, 1868), p. 85.

9. Joseph M. Field to Sol Smith, Mar. 21, 1835, Smith Collection, Missouri Historical Society, St. Louis.

10. Ludlow, pp. 452–53.

11. John St. Luke to Ludlow and Smith, Mar. 29, 1838, Smith Collection.

12. Smith, p. 135.

13. Ludlow and Smith Letter Book, Sept. 29, 1838, Smith Collection.

14. Sol Smith to Noah M. Ludlow, May 5, 1839, ibid.

15. Ludlow, p. 509; Smith p. 135; *Mobile Mercantile Advertiser*, Mar. 14, 1839.

16. Ludlow, p. 510.

17. Sol Smith to Noah M. Ludlow, Mar. 17, 1840, Smith Collection.

18. Joe Cowell, *Thirty Years Passed Among the Actors and Actresses of England and America* (New York: Harper, 1844), p. 97.

19. James H. Hackett to Ludlow and Smith, Jan. 23, 29, 1843, Smith Collection.

20. Cowell, p. 98.

21. James H. Hackett to Ludlow and Smith, Jan. 29, 1843, Smith Collection.

22. George Vandenhoff, *Leaves from an Actor's Notebook* (New York: Appleton, 1860), p. 213.

23. Cowell, p. 102.

24. Diary of Noah M. Ludlow, Nov. 28, 1843, Ludlow, Maury, Field Collection, Missouri Historical Society, St. Louis.

25. Ibid, Jan. 14, 1844.

26. *Macready's Reminiscences and Selections from His Diaries and Letters*, ed. Sir Frederick Pollock (New York: Harper, 1875), p. 552.

27. Diary of Noah M. Ludlow, Mar. 4, 11, 12, 13, 1844, Ludlow Collection.

28. *Macready's Reminiscences*, p. 553.

29. Memorandum Book of Sol Smith, Smith Collection.

30. *Mobile Register and Journal*, Apr. 1, 1846.

31. Diary of Sol Smith, Mar. 7, 1847, Smith Collection.

32. Record of the Proceedings of the Board of Directors of the St. Charles, American, and Mobile Theatres, New Orleans, May 1, 2, 1847, Smith Collection.

33. Bernard A. Reynolds, *Sketches of Mobile* (1869; reprint from typed transcript, Bossier City, La.: Tipton Printing & Pub. Co.) 1971, p. 41.

34. Cornelius A. Logan to Sol Smith, Mar. 15, 1852, Smith Collection.

35. Eliza Logan to Sol Smith, Dec. 19, 1853, ibid.

36. Diary of Noah M. Ludlow, Jan. 14, 28, 1854, Ludlow Collection.

37. *Mobile Daily Advertiser*, Jan. 11, 1860.

38. Edward Devereaux Brown, "A History of Theatrical Activities at the Mobile Theatre, Mobile, Alabama, from 1860–1875" (M. A. thesis, Michigan State College, 1952), p. 54.

BIBLIOGRAPHIC NOTE

All newspapers in the files of the *Mobile Press Register* (now on microfilm in the Mobile Public Library) covering the period 1821 to 1861 were consulted in the compilation of this material. Unless indicated by footnotes to other sources, the names of plays and players were taken from newspapers contemporaneous with the events. Much of the material for this article was taken from the author's thesis, Mary Morgan Duggar, "The Theatre in Mobile 1822–1860" (M. A. thesis, University of Alabama, 1941). Letters, playbills, diaries, and other documents of the Smith Collection and the Ludlow, Maury, Field Collection were consulted at the Missouri Historical Society, Jefferson Memorial Building, St. Louis, Missouri.

Shakespeare in Mississippi, 1814–1980

Linwood E. Orange

Mississippi may with reasonable justification claim three theatrical firsts. To begin with, eleven years before statehood was granted, there was performed in the Natchez City Tavern *The Provoked Husband* (Sir John Vanbrugh's unfinished play completed by Colley Cibber). This dramatic event is said to have been "the earliest known professional theatrical performance ever to be given in English west of the Alleghenies."[1] Eight years later, the following notice in the *Mississippi Republican* announced Shakespeare's stage arrival: "On Friday evening the 15th of April [1814], will be attempted the performance of 'OTHELLO THE MOORE OF VENICE,' to which will be added, that diverting Afterpiece, 'THE LIAR.'" The notice added a plea to parents who might not be able to find babysitters: "Those bringing young persons are requested to keep them under their own eye to prevent the noise sometimes experienced, from too great an assemblage of youth on one seat."[2] This was apparently the first of Shakespeare's plays to be performed in English west of the Alleghenies. Third, there is evidence that the first performance to take place on a showboat occurred in Mississippi on the evening of December 10, 1817, when Noah Ludlow and his company, having floated down the Mississippi on a keelboat christened *Noah's Ark*, landed at Natchez-under-the-Hill and presented on deck *Catherine and Petruchio*, Garrick's popular adaptation of *The Taming of the Shrew*.[3]

Yet, despite such a promising beginning, it was a number of years before Shakespearean performances gained appreciable popularity. For one thing, early audiences also had a taste for the works of Kotzebue, Sheridan, Goldsmith, George Colman the Younger, Vanbrugh, and such lesser lights as William Dimond, as well as for sundry acrobats, jugglers, and bird callers; for another, progress was all too often impeded by ill-timed misfortunes.

The 1814 *Othello* was performed by local actors, the Natchez

Theatrical Association. They performed in the first Natchez building designed to be a public playhouse, erected in 1812 or early 1813 and large enough to accommodate about five hundred people.[4] The next performance, in 1818, was by the first of many professional acting companies to visit Natchez. Included in their repertoire were *The Taming of the Shrew* and *Romeo and Juliet.* [5] Doubtless, Shakespeare would have been well launched in Mississippi at that point had there not occurred in rapid succession two major disasters. The first was a yellow fever epidemic that lasted until 1821, with ruinous effect on theater life.[6] There were, nevertheless, two plays of Shakespeare performed during that period, both in 1820: *1 Henry IV* and *The Taming of the Shrew*. The second disaster was a fire in 1821 that reduced the frame theater building to ashes.

During the next seven years, only two of Shakespeare's plays were presented, *The Merchant of Venice* and *Othello,* both in 1823 by James H. Caldwell's company from New Orleans and both staged in the ballroom of a local hotel, Traveler's Hall. But, at last, thanks to the perseverance of Caldwell himself, a new theater said to be large enough to seat nearly seven hundred people was completed on Main Street in 1828.[7] That same year *The Comedy of Errors* and *The Merchant of Venice* were staged and, according to actor Sol Smith, so was a *Hamlet* that was uniquely affected by its Mississippi setting.

Caldwell's theater was constructed on the site of what had been a graveyard. Distressingly, the former occupants had not all been removed from the premises when the first actors arrived. This fact was brought sharply to Sol Smith's attention when the lamplighter, in a hurry and lacking a proper receptacle, stuck two candles in the eye sockets of a skull and set it on the actor's dressing table. Says Smith, "Human bones were strewn about in every direction. . . . In digging the grave of Hamlet, I experienced no difficulty in finding bones and skulls to "play at loggats with.""[8]

In 1829 *King Lear, The Merchant of Venice, Hamlet* (twice), *Othello,* and *Richard III* (three times) were presented. More significantly, in that year two of the greatest actors of the nineteenth century made their first of many visits to Natchez, Junius Brutus

Booth and Edwin Forrest, leading the way for a long list of famous actors and actresses who followed. The future was promising indeed for Shakespeare in Mississippi, but once again there was a severe setback. Caldwell, who can be chiefly credited with this progress, sold his interest in the Natchez theater to Richard Russell and James S. Rowe. This managerial transition, inexplicably, caused a cessation of theatrical entertainment in Natchez for the next two years.

Providence, however, at last shifted in favor of the thespians. Sixty miles up the river, veteran actor James S. "Long Tom Coffin" Scott resolved that Vicksburg should have a theater. By 1836, when Russell was finishing plans for his 1836–1837 season, Scott, in partnership with English actor-singer "Jemmy" Thorne, completed construction of the Citizens Theatre. The two groups got under way almost simultaneously and, aided by an unprecedented period of financial prosperity in the river region, ushered in a veritable golden age for the stage in Mississippi, especially for lovers of Shakespeare.

The number of people in these two river cities who supported the theaters in the late 1830s was not at all large. Although Natchez and Vicksburg nearly doubled in size between 1830 and 1840, they were still relatively small, totaling 4,800 and 3,100 respectively in 1840. At least one-third of these were slaves, and many of the whites were children too young to attend. Actually, neither town could muster more than two thousand whites of theatergoing age from the immediate vicinity, and of those not all were financially able to sustain the burden of regular attendance. Tickets were not cheap for the time. Admission was usually $1.00 for a white adult (though choice seats sometimes cost $1.50) plus 50 cents for each child. Any accompanying slaves sat in the gallery at an additional cost of 50 cents each.[9] Since the season lasted from January to May and performances averaged five nights per week, the cost for a family man who frequently attended quickly mounted. Nevertheless, records show that over a period of 128 nights in Vicksburg, receipts averaged $232, and frequently when stars such as Booth, Forrest, and Ellen Tree arrived, there were sell-outs grossing over six hundred dollars.[10] One can conclude only that a very large percentage of the more affluent local residents were the most loyal of patrons.

As an audience, however, this small and loyal group frequently was an interesting challenge even for veteran actors. It was capable on the one hand of utterly disgusting etiquette and on the other of expressions of genuine affection. Theater historian Joseph Miller Free comments,

> Theatre audiences during the 1830s were not noted for their decorous behavior. Despite the posting of notices and policemen, Natchez and Vicksburg audiences often became boisterous and ill-mannered, spitting tobacco-juice, chatting loudly, hooting and cat-calling, moving about and making themselves a nuisance generally. On some benefit occasions, however, demonstrations of a special sort were warmly welcomed. Flowers and money, often in substantial amounts, were thrown at the feet of the charming performer with an enthusiasm which must have gone far toward obliterating any ill feelings aroused on previous evenings.[11]

It is evident that there were far more performances than extant documentation supports, for available records are woefully incomplete; but at least of the following we can be certain: four plays of Shakespeare were staged in Natchez and nine in Vicksburg during the 1836–1837 season, eight in Natchez and nine in Vicksburg during the 1837–1838 season, and eighteen in Natchez, ten in Vicksburg, and three in Jackson during the 1838–1839 season, for a minimum of sixty-one performances. Better than 40 percent of all of the performances of Shakespeare's plays in Mississippi prior to 1860 were enacted in the brilliant three-season span.

J. W. T. Scott's manuscript notes on the Vicksburg theater operated by his father are quite enlightening regarding the scheduling of the plays. He itemizes the following from January 7 through January 22, 1839:

> January 7, 1839. Mr. [Charles H.] Eaton's first appearance. "Richard III."
> January 8, 1839. Mr. Eaton in "The Iron Chest."
> January 9, 1839. Mr. Eaton in "A New Way to Pay Old Debts."
> January 10, 1839. C. H. Eaton.
> January 11, 1839. Mr. Eaton in "Damon and Pythias."
> January 12, 1839. Mr. Eaton's Benefit. "Julius Caesar" and "Sylvester Daggerwood," in which Mr. Eaton gave imitations of Forrest, Booth, Keene, Kemble, Vandenhoff, A. Adams, Mr. Pelby, Mr. Macready and Daddy Rice.
> January 14, 1839. "Macbeth"; C. H. Eaton.

January 15, 1839. C. H. Eaton.
January 17, 1839. First night of Booth as "Richard III."
January 18, 1839. Second night of Mr. Booth. "A New Way to Pay Old
    Debts."
January 19, 1839.
January 21, 1839. "The Apostate"; Benefit of J. B. Booth. Booth as
    Pescara.
January 22, 1839. The elder Booth in "The Iron Chest."[12]

First, these entries (and the point is supported by the written comments of Scott and by newspaper accounts) indicate that far more plays than those of Shakespeare were performed and that plays were given five (occasionally six) nights per week during the season. As Free observes, "for both quantity and quality the winter of 1838–1839 is one long to be remembered in the theatrical annals of both cities."[13]

Next, on the seventh, eighth, and ninth of January, Charles H. Eaton appeared in three plays in which Junius Brutus Booth was also to appear the following week: *Richard III, The Iron Chest,* and *A New Way to Pay Old Debts.* Such curious repetition occurred mainly as a result of the star system, which, reaching its peak in America at this time, brought to Natchez and Vicksburg (as well as to Jackson on a few occasions) a parade of famous British and American actors, names such as Tyrone Power (great-grandfather of the twentieth-century movie idol), James Wallack, Sr., Charles Kean (son of the famous Edmund), James H. Hackett, Clara Fisher, and Ellen Tree, in addition to Junius Brutus Booth and Edwin Forrest. These stars were not escorted by their own companies; they performed with local stock companies and were fortunate if they had an opportunity to rehearse even once before opening. As in the above case, arrangements were made for more than one star to make use of plays the local company had prepared.

Scott's listing, finally, documents the burden that these itinerant professionals shouldered. Booth, Forrest, and the others were not only prepared to appear in a number of plays in addition to those of Shakespeare, but they willingly subjected themselves to exhausting schedules. Booth's Vicksburg-Natchez tour during the latter part of January, 1839, is a case in point. He opened in Vicksburg on Thursday evening, January 17, with a performance of *Richard III*. The next night he played Sir Giles Overreach in Philip Massinger's *A New Way to Pay Old Debts*. After resting the weekend, he performed in *The Apostate* on Monday evening, January 21, and in *The Iron Chest* on Tuesday evening. On Thursday, January 24, he acted the title role in *Macbeth*. Having spent the next day on a riverboat, he opened in Natchez on Saturday evening, January 26, with his famous interpretation of Hamlet. After another welcome weekend, he offered *Richard III* (the only repeated play in this run) on Monday evening and then closed with *King Lear* Wednesday, January 30. In summary, within a space of two weeks he performed seven different principal roles, four of them the most demanding in all drama. To top it all, he enjoyed "rave" reviews before the season eventually got the best of him. For his opening night performance in Natchez, Booth received this accolade:

> On Saturday evening our theatre was crowded to witness Booth's first night in Natchez. It was a masterly performance—that same Hamlet, as performed by Booth. We were particularly pleased to see that the wing of the eagle was not broken though the plumage may have been ruffled by the tempests of passion that have swept across the daring flight of this great master of tragedy. Booth has deep and unfathomable feelings; that's certain—or else how could he so well depict them, and thrill an audience with them. The forlorn, the lone, the stormy, the vindictive, the relentless or the sublime are familiar passions to Booth; he sketches them with the hand of a master.[14]

Nor was the schedule of Edwin Forrest, Booth's American competitor, any less demanding. In addition to appearing in less noteworthy plays as *The Lady of Lyons, Damon and Pythias, Metamora,* and *The Gladiator,* he took the title roles in *Othello, Richard III, Macbeth,* and *King Lear*. An unusually appreciative reviewer described his opening night Othello on Saturday, March 16, 1839.

> Mr. Edwin Forrest appeared on Saturday evening in the character of Othello. It has been many years since this gentleman visited Natchez; his long absence and deserved fame, had raised the expectation of a dramatic public to the heights of the Pyrenees. The house was crowded in every part—the audience consisting of the elite and ton of the city; of the man of letters and of as an intelligent mechanic population as any city, of our number can boast of.

'Twas the *first* time we ever saw Othello performed, although we have seen it twenty times before attempted. The form of Mr. F. suits the character precisely—then the coloring he gave to his face, made him the Moor before you. The black speck under the eye, his beautiful white teeth, the dress, the beads, and in fact every thing calculated to make one look the Moorish character, Mr. F. possessed. The voice, harsh and distinct, and the step, filled up the whole character of Othello. The passions, the love, the jealousy, and the out-bursting agony of Othello was before us, during the performance of the five long acts. It is useless to say which scene we liked best—*all* parts were best.[15]

Seven days later, having witnessed Forrest's portrayals of Damon ("in our opinion his best character"),[16] Sparticus, and, on successive nights, Richard III and Macbeth, the reviewer summed up the week's triumph: "During the past week, Mr. Forrest has appeared in several characters, the representation of which not only gave entire satisfaction to the audience but they showed every mark of approbation, by plaudits and cheering. We cannot add to Mr. F's fame, and it will therefore be unnecessary to give our opinion. Suffice it to say, that all the critics of the north and south, have not flattered him in the least, as he well deserves the name of the American Talma."[17]

Ten years Booth's junior, robust and in his prime, Forrest apparently thrived on the strenuous tour routine. His last recorded performance that season in the role of Lear was praised as lavishly as were any of his previous ones. "Last night Mr. Forrest played Lear to a crowded house, and the representation of the heart-broken old King was powerful in the extreme. When he heaped the mountain of scathing curses on his heartless, ungrateful and unnatural daughter, the scene was terrifically sublime; and the rapturous applause which burst forth as if by an explosive impulse from the assembled crowd, proved that Mr. Forrest had reached the depths of human passion."[18] Not so with Booth. Aging rapidly at forty-three, he took increasingly to heavy drinking for support, a habit which doubtless inspired the eccentric behavior described by Mrs. John Drew, grandmother of the well-known twentieth-century actors John, Lionel, and Ethel Barrymore.

We were playing "Hamlet" one night in Natchez, and during Ophelia's mad scene a cock began to crow lustily. When the curtain fell upon that fourth act this crowing became more constant; and when the manager could not find Mr. Booth to commence the next act he looked up and saw him perched on the top of the ladder, which was the only way to reach the "flies" in that primitive theatre. The manager ascended the ladder and had quite a lengthy discussion with Mr. Booth, who at last consented to come down on condition that he should resume his high position after the play, and remain there until Jackson was re-elected President.[19]

A Jackson critic thus described Booth at the end of his tour: "Mr. Booth seemed not to feel what he said or did, and in fact took no real interest in the part, but hustled through it with almost a stoic indifference. . . . We have seen Mr. Booth at least ten times in the character of Richard and never do we remember to have seen him so entirely lost, but once, as on this occasion."[20]

As mentioned earlier, there were also female stars in Natchez, and it is of particular interest that they sometimes played breeches roles. The first such impersonator was ten-year-old Louisa Lane, who later became Mrs. John Drew, in the role of Richard III on March 21, 1829, in Natchez, obviously played for laughs.[21] But in late 1836 Mrs. Henry Lewis took the role seriously and earned the following glowing tribute:

> Not having examined the dramatic notices in the northern papers, we were surprised to find Mrs. Lewis announced for Richard on Saturday last, and concluded it was intended as a burlesque—a kind of *serio comico* affair—it never having entered our head that a *woman* could play that character *well*. We must confess that we were taken wholly by surprise to find such a character as that of the "crook'd back tyrant" so truly delineated by a female. Her readings were remarkably good; the "wooing scene" with Lady Anne, so often made but mockery, was admirably done; her conception was so perfect that not a gesture or a syllable was lost, so well did each action and cadence suit the word. She also did herself great credit by the manner in which she pronounced the soliloquy—"Now is the winter of our discontent," etc. It is a common fault with actors to address this to the audience, and make their gestures and distort their countenances accordingly; but Mrs. Lewis was *alone* in this soliloquy, and every gesture, word, smile or frown was the free action of an unobserved villain—it was truly conceived and well pronounced. Mrs. Lewis is possessed of great physical power, and sustained the character well, difficult as it is, to the end. We do hope that it may be repeated.[22]

Her Vicksburg attempt in April, however, received a shower of abuse. "During the past week we have had some delightful entertainment, but then we have been bored with a great deal of intolerable trash—that is, in our humble opinion. Mrs. Lewis murdered Richard the Third . . . after stabbing some other royal personages. . . . She is a lady of great histrionic talents, but it is impossible for us to sympathize in the characters to which she devotes her attention."[23]

The famous and very popular Ellen Tree also tried male roles. When she was to act Juliet on February 5, 1839, the reviewer for the *Natchez Free Trader* wrote, "Would there could be found a suitable Romeo for such a Juliet."[24] As if to answer his prayer, she took the role herself a month later. The reviewer ungratefully conceded only grudging praise. "On Saturday evening [March 9, 1839], Miss Tree left off the actress, and appeared as Romeo, Mrs. Hunt as Juliet; but we are sorry to say, that she was not, could not, be the *lover* Romeo—the ardent, enthusiastic Montague. She is a lady—and an accomplished one she is too. Romeo was a *man;* with the robust voice, proud and stately step of a man; with all the passions, actions and conduct of a man. How can woman know those masculine traits? . . . This much, however, we will say, that Romeo was performed better than any other *lady* could do."[25] Pluckily, two weeks later she tried again in Vicksburg, but with even less success: "On Saturday last Miss Tree played Romeo to a full house. She gave, we believe, general satisfaction, though we would say, that neither the play nor the performance suited our taste. Miss Tree ought to es chew the pantaloons. As a lady of high intellect, cultivated taste, temper and feeling, she is inimitable; but she is not at home in the breeches. We have seen inferior actors play Romeo with more effect than she did."[26] There is no record that she again attempted a male role in Mississippi.

For Shakespeare in Mississippi, the late 1830s were the best of times, but they soon gave way to the worst. The reasons are not difficult to find. To begin with, the star system which brought such talent as Booth and Forrest to Mississippi was a heavy financial burden and, despite full houses, the management received only meager profit. Of course, adjustments could have been made to alleviate that difficlty had not other problems followed. Mississippi's unprecedented financial prosperity, which had contributed to full houses, came abruptly to an end, curtailing sharply the patronage.

As a result, Vicksburg's Citizens Theatre closed in January of 1840, and the company moved to Natchez for the remainder of the 1839–1840 season. Finally, on May 7, 1840, a tornado completely destroyed the Natchez Main Street "graveyard" theater, ending a brilliant moment in American theater history.[27] Free sums up the accomplishments of this period:

> Contemporary newspapers, actor's accounts, a few manuscripts, and a handful of playbills have yielded some record of more than 1650 dramatic performances which entertained the populace of Southwestern Mississippi on more than 1100 nights between 1806 and 1840. A total of thirty-four theatrical campaigns took place during these thirty-four years. . . . The names of more than four hundred actors, managers, treasurers, stage managers, dances, singers, scenic artists, and machinists have been recorded, nearly all of which can be found in the annals of other theatres of the Union. More than four hundred and fifty plays by one hundred and sixty different dramatists were presented, Shakespeare, as ever, leading the vanguard of authors.[28]

Still, Shakespeare continued to be performed in Mississippi, although at a markedly reduced rate. Between 1841 and 1860 there were eight more performances in Natchez and thirty-nine in Vicksburg. Then the last great disaster, the war between the states, not only closed all theaters for the duration but caused a cessation in Shakespearean dramatic performances for nearly four decades.

In the postwar years acting companies returned to the state to perform in makeshift theaters, but clearly public theatrical taste had been one of the casualties of the conflict. Shakespeare was replaced by more novel and less profound forms of entertainment, such as the *Mazeppa* of one Miss Hudson, who shared billing with her "highly trained steed Black Bess,"[29] the increasingly popular traveling circuses, and, in the early twentieth century, the movies. Albeit slowly, interest did revive, however, thanks not to public theaters but rather to state institutions of higher learning, where heavy emphasis on Shakespeare in the academic curricula inspired first a few and then a steady stream of productions, some by the students themselves and some, as in the heady antebellum days of Natchez and Vicksburg, by visiting Shakespearean troupes. Even from the first, the members of the nonacademic community formed a large part of the audiences.

The earliest collegiate performances of Shakespeare seem to have occurred in the last decade of the nineteenth century at the University of Mississippi. Under the direction of Miss Sarah McGehee Isom, *Romeo and Juliet, Macbeth,* and *Hamlet* were performed, as well as an "Al Fresco Shakespearean Festival" as part of the "Semi-Centennial Celebration" of the university. The latter, titled "Under the Greenwood Tree" and including scenes from *As You Like It* and *The Taming of the Shrew,* took place June 20, 1899. A local reviewer described the manner of presentation: "The Open Air Shakespearian Festival on the University campus Tuesday evening, by the students of elocution, under Miss Ison's [*sic*] management, was one of the most artistic and beautiful entertainments that could be dreamed of by painter or poet. . . . The stage was erected under the spreading branches of a group of live oak trees, with green boughs and rustic garnishments, the only scenery."[30]

The performance is especially significant not only because it is the first to be well documented but also because two of the participants would become well known in the state and another would achieve national literary prominence. Alfred Hume, a young mathematics professor who assisted Miss Isom in directing the show and whose wife sang solos between acts, was later to hold several high administrative positions at the university, including that of chancellor. Lemuel Augustus Smith, who played the roles of Duke Senior and Hortensio, was to serve from 1945 to 1950 as a Mississippi Supreme Court justice. And Stark Young, who portrayed Oliver and Nathaniel, went on from these modest roles to make an important contribution to American letters, writing over thirty plays, directing for Provincetown Playhouse and the Theatre Guild, serving on the editorial staff of *Theatre Arts Magazine,* and functioning as drama critic for *New Republic* and the *New York Times* (although, ironically, he is now best remembered for a nondramatic work, his Civil War novel *So Red the Rose*).

Young's participation in a collegiate Shakespearean production comes as no surprise, of course, to those familiar with his work, which constantly reveals an intense admiration for and an intimate knowledge of Shakespeare's plays. His letters are replete with quotations from them, references to them, and observations regarding them approaching Bardolatry. "Shakespeare," he once wrote to Allen Tate, "when he is good overpowers me with brilliance and finality."[31] And his reviews of John Barrymore's Hamlet, David Warfield's Shylock, Maurice Evans's Hamlet, Laurence Olivier's Hotspur, Ralph Richardson's Falstaff, and Margaret Webster productions of *Othello* and *The Tempest*—to cite only a few—display a textual familiarity that could have been wrought only by the closest reading; even when Young was reviewing plays by other authors, both ancient and modern, Shakespeare remained his touchstone. Quite fittingly, then, "Under the Greenwood Tree" provided the undergraduate Young not only with an opportunity to play two roles created by his beloved author but also to write perhaps his earliest published drama review, much in the graceful, poetic style that was to characterize his later professional work.

> In among the leafage of the liveoak and the palm, rose and fell the music of the orchestra like the waters of a fountain diffusing with the myriad colored eerie starlights of the stage; came the music drifting on the night air; all aquiver with the passion of that night of June, over-weighted with odors, oversated with moonlight, came stealing out to wake the audience to the realization of their dreams, came to lead them through Titanialand, Arden, and the realms of Ariel.
>
> The broad and deep stage was in nature's own simplicity, a wilderness of ferns and flowers with boughs and fallen trees and interlacing vines. "Who loves to lie with me, under the greenwood tree?" rose the words of that beautiful song and the audience was alive to the beauty and poetry, to the music and grandeur of the great Shakespeare's words, the jewels of his wit, the fascination of his sentiment. Never before had Oxford been brought so near to the master, so near to his loftiness, so near to his sympathy as by those lines of the play delivered without affectation, but dropping like pearls clear and rounded without background of tinsel and gaudy stage fitting, but framed in the witchery of the lisping leaves and the fancy of the hearer.[32]

Not long thereafter, in the southern section of the state, interest began to stir at Mississippi Normal College and Mississippi Woman's College in Hattiesburg. On February 17, 1914, the Shakespeare Club was formed at Normal, thanks to the efforts of Anne H. Augustus, an English literature instructor. An item in the yearbook, *Neka Camon,* states that the members read *Othello, The Tempest,* and *Midsummer Night's Dream* and planned "to read during the session several more." The readings were evidently dramatic, but there seem to have been no performances outside of the room in which the club met. A few years later, a speech instructor at Mississippi Woman's College, Kate Downs P'Pool, decided to give Hattiesburg its first taste of Shakespeare on stage. But there were two major problems: first, male roles predominate in Shakespeare's plays and Mississippi Woman's College had no male students; and second, the college's rules strictly forbade dressing a female in male attire for whatever purpose. Undaunted, Mrs. P'Pool found a simple solution to both problems. She wrote her own Shakespearean play. Entitled *The Women of Shakespeare's Plays,* it featured the best known of the great playwright's ladies: Juliet and her Nurse, Petruchio's Catherine, Rosalind, Portia, Ophelia, Lady Macbeth (complete with a heavy Scottish dialect), and Desdemona. Having come together "to take the waters" at a fashionable resort, they also took turns cutting one another and revealing hitherto unreleased information about their husbands, liberally quoting and half-quoting familiar Shakespearean passages.[33]

It was not until the second half of the century, however, that colleges and universities began to be active in producing Shakespeare's plays on stage. At Mississippi Southern College (now the University of Southern Mississippi), under the direction of John Mullin of the speech department, members of the Alpha Psi Omega fraternity presented during a chapel program on January 15, 1954, scenes from *Julius Caesar, Macbeth,* and *The Taming of the Shrew.* The attempt was well received, and the students repeated the performance at several south Mississippi high schools, including those of Petal, Perkinston, Biloxi, and Moss Point. It was said that they became so professional in their work that they were able to strike their set and pack it in thirty minutes.[34]

In April of 1956 Mississippi College for Women performed an all-female *Midsummer Night's Dream,* and, perhaps encouraged by the interest aroused by the Alpha Psi Omega venture, the administration of Mississippi Southern College that same year brought in Players, Incorporated, a touring company, to stage *Richard III.* Audience response having been good, Touring Players, Incorporated, was invited in 1957 to do *Henry IV*. The time was obviously ripe for the theater department to attempt the college's own first full-length Shakespearean play, and it did so in April, 1959. Directed by Robert Treser, *Julius Caesar* was acted in three-quarter round on five successive nights to packed houses. Critical comment, though candid, was nevertheless encouraging. "Generally, the merits of the production outweighed the defects, which were mainly due to blocking, timing, and inexperienced actors. By taking a familiar Shakespearean play packed with such actions as murder, suicides, ghosts, and battles, the Theatre Department proved itself competent to carry Shakespeare. The enthusiastic response from the first nighters confirmed Shakespeare's own idea that 'the play's the thing.' "[35]

The 1960s saw a continuation of the staging of Shakespeare by Mississippi colleges and universities. *1 Henry IV* was performed at the University of Mississippi in the spring of 1966, *The Taming of the Shrew* at Mississippi College and *The Tempest* at the University of Southern Mississippi in January of 1968, and *The Comedy of Errors* at the University of Mississippi in December, 1969. Of these, *The Tempest* appears to have been the most unusual in that the director employed instead of a curtain a fogging device to shroud the stage for scene changes and to contribute an appropriately mysterious effect.

In 1971 the University of Southern Mississippi presented a *Twelfth Night* that was said by one reviewer to be "a monumental success" and "a theatre experience which provided the opening night audience with beauty, humor, and sheer entertainment of a type that made the two-hour-and-twenty-minute production pass too quickly."[36] *Macbeth* was performed by Delta State University's Delta Playhouse in 1972 and by the University of Mississippi in 1980, and *A Midsummer Night's Dream* made several appearances: in 1973 at Mississippi College for Women (this time men were recruited for the male roles), in 1974 at the University of Misisippi, and in 1975 at Mississippi State University. *The Taming of the Shrew*—the favorite Shakespearean comedy for this state in both the nineteenth and the twentieth centuries—continued to appear, once at the University of Southern Mississippi in 1976 and once each at the University of Mississippi and Mississippi College in 1979.

The *Shrew* of 1976 at the University of Southern Mississippi is worthy of special note. Appropriately, since 160 years earlier a presentation of it at Natchez was probably the first of all showboat performances, the play was on this occasion given a Mississippi showboat setting. Directed by I. Blaine Quarnstrom, chairman of the Department of Theater Arts, it was the most elaborately staged, the most colorful, and certainly the most innovative Shakespearean production ever to be given in the state.

The stage, as shown, presented to the audience a 35-foot replica, rear view, of an 1840s Mississippi showboat (the audience sat in the imaginary "deck" area). There were three levels, approximating remarkably the generally accepted design of the Elizabethan stage. Two large double-hung doors were centered at the first level, flanked by stairways to the second and third levels. At the second level was a balcony acting area between a decorative ballustrade and the rooms (cabins), and on the third level, the top deck, Christopher Sly reclined to view the play in the manner of *A Shrew*. Costumes were antebellum, frock coats and hoop skirts. For his freakish wedding costume, Petruchio wore a "Davy Crockett" outfit complete with leather fringes and coonskin cap. In keeping with the setting and period, local names were substituted for Padua, Verona, Mantua, and Pisa.

Striking as these departures from traditional Shakespeare were, there was no evidence of audience disapproval. Said one reviewer, "None of the Shakespearean humor was lost, and the effervescent humor of the South added an unexpected level to the play. . . . If you missed 'Shrew,' you missed a fantastic play. Seldom does a chance come to see a Shakespearean play so successfuly updated and so expertly executed."[37] Another remarked, "Although the locale and costumes were Southern, the director and cast were remarkably faithful to Shakespeare's text. . . . Staging *The Taming of the Shrew* on a Mississippi showboat may indeed have made theatrical history. . . . it remained faithful to Shakespeare's dialogue and tried to reproduce the general shape of his stage while still placing both in a Southern scene."[38]

Finally, the 1970s witnessed a renewal of Shakespearean activity on the part of community "little theatre" groups. Jackson's New

The Taming of the Shrew production at the University of Southern Mississippi, 1976
Courtesy I. Blaine Quarnstrom

Stage company, directed by Ivan Rider, acted *The Taming of the
Shrew* in 1972, *A Midsummer Night's Dream* in 1973, and *Twelfth
Night* in 1975. David Kemp directed Pas-Point Little Theatre's *A
Midsummer Night's Dream* in 1976, and Norman Maxwell directed
The Walter Anderson Players' *A Midsummer Night's Dream* in 1978
and the Coast Classics Theatre's *Much Ado About Nothing* in 1979,
both in Biloxi. Thus, the wheel has come full circle. After a period of
Shakespearean inactivity in the wake of the Civil War and a gradual
resurgence of interest, for which the state's colleges and universities
must be given much credit, local acting groups, like those who were
responsible for introducing staged Shakespeare to Mississippi in
1814 and who gave way to the more professional stars and traveling
troupes, have once again begun to put his plays on the boards.

    To conclude, documentation is sparse, playbills rare, and old newspaper files broken, but one thing is clear: Mississippians have held Shakespeare dear for nearly 170 years—longer than they have enjoyed statehood, and have to their credit not only some important theatrical firsts but also one incredibly bright peak of Shakespearean dramatic activity—that of the Natchez-Vicksburg region in the late 1830s—the like of which few if any other urban areas of similar size can claim to equal or even hope to approach.

NOTES

1. Joseph Miller Free, "The Ante-Bellum Theatre of the Old Natchez Region," *Journal of Mississippi History* 5 (1943): 14.

2. *Natchez Mississippi Republican*, Apr. 13, 1814.

3. Philip Graham, *Showboats: The History of an American Institution* (Austin: University of Texas Press, 1951), pp. 5–7.

4. Free, pp. 15–16. Prior to the opening of this theater, the association had acted in an old Spanish hospital that had been renovated for their purposes.

5. Free, p. 17. The dates of the performances of Shakespeare's plays are those cited by William Bryan Gates, "Performances of Shakespeare in Ante-Bellum Mississippi," *Journal of Mississippi History* 5 (1943): 28–37, plus those listed by Graham and in J. W. T. Scott's manuscript notebooks on the Natchez and Vicksburg theaters entitled "Vicksburg Ante-Bellum Theatricals" in the Mississippi State Department of Archives and History.

6. Free, pp. 19–20.

7. Ibid.

8. Solomon Franklin Smith, *Theatrical Management in the West and South for Thirty Years*, ed. Arthur Thomas Tees (New York, 1868; Rpt. New York: Benjamin Blom, 1968), p. 52.

9. Free, p. 20n.

10. Scott. The manuscript pages are unnumbered.

11. Free, p. 21. For a further account of the frontier atmosphere by traveling actors in the nineteenth century, see Esther Cloudman Dunn, *Shakespeare in America* (New York: Macmillan, 1939), pp. 175–79.

12. Scott. Minor editorial liberties have been taken for the sake of simplicity.

13. Free, p. 25.

14. *Natchez Mississippi Free Trader*, Jan. 28, 1839.

15. Ibid., Mar. 18, 1839.

16. Ibid., March 25, 1839.

17. Ibid.

18. *Vicksburg Daily Sentinel*, Apr. 26, 1839.

19. Mrs. John Drew, *Autobiographical Sketch of Mrs. John Drew* (New York: Charles Scribner's Sons, 1899), pp. 49–50.

20. *The Mississippian*, (Jackson) Apr. 19, 1839, as quoted in Gates, p. 35.

21. *Natchez Southern Galaxy*, Mar. 19, 1829; Gates, p. 35.

22. Natchez Mississippi Free Trader, Dec. 27, 1836.
23. *Vicksburg Daily Sentinel*, Apr. 11, 1837.
24. *Natchez Mississippi Free Trader*, Feb. 5, 1839; Gates, p. 31.
25. *Natchez Mississippi Free Trader*, Mar. 11, 1839.
26. *Vicksburg Daily Sentinel*, Mar. 25, 1839.
27. Free, pp. 25–26.
28. Ibid., p. 27.
29. *Jackson Clarion Ledger*, Apr. 20, 1869.
30. *Oxford Eagle*, June 22, 1899.
31. John Pilkington, ed., *Stark Young: A Life in the Arts: Letters, 1900–1962*, vol. I (Baton Rouge: Louisiana State University Press, 1975), p. 397.
32. *Ole Miss* (1901), p. 96.
33. A copy of the manuscript has been preserved by Miss Virginia Scott, granddaughter of Mrs. P'Pool.
34. *The Student Printz* (USM), Feb. 26, 1954.
35. *Hattiesburg American*, Apr. 14, 1959.
36. Ibid., May 5, 1971.
37. *TheStudent Printz*, Feb. 3, 1976.
38. Philip C. Kolin, "*The Taming of the Shrew*—Southern Style," *Shakespeare Newsletter* 26 (May, 1976): 23.

The Reception of Shakespeare in Houston, 1839–1980

Waldo F. McNeir

The megapolis of today's Houston started as an ugly village of log cabins, shanties, and tents on the muddy banks of Buffalo Bayou, almost before the smoke at the Battle of San Jacinto on April 21, 1836, had settled over the surrounding swamp. As the first capital of the infant Republic of Texas, Houston yearned for the cachet of culture. From the beginning it attested the myth of a paradise on the frontier, not the double-edged Renaissance view of the New World upheld by Shakespeare in *The Tempest,* but the notion that "westward the course of empire takes its way," its civilizing way. Along with this was the older vision of "That unfallen, western world," as Melville wrote in *Moby Dick,* "which in the eyes of the old trappers and hunters revived the glories of those primeval times when Adam walked majestic as a god." Both ideas lurked in the collective unconscious of the new trappers, hunters, and land-hungry colonists who settled Texas. They had no transcendental illusions, however, that "The noblest ministry of nature is to stand as the apparition of God," as Emerson said in his pedantic piety.

Before Houston was a year old, culture appeared while the Young Men's Society was debating "Have theaters an immoral tendency?"[1] when John Carlos, merchant, built a "house designed for a Theater" (40 feet by 100 feet) on Congress Avenue between Milam and Travis streets.[2] The first production on June 11, 1838, was Sheridan Knowles' popular comedy *The Hunchback,* followed by a farce, *The Dumb Belle, or I'm Perfection.*[3] A reviewer opined that "the actors have exceeded the expectations of their most sanguine friends. It must be exceedingly gratifying to every true friend of the drama, to behold its infancy in our country attended by such favorable auspices." True friends of the drama were not consistently gratified, for one of the earliest offerings was so bad that John Carlos was hanged in effigy from the limb of a pine tree in front of his theater. *The School for Scandal* should have fared better, but when it was rumored that one of the actors had been bitten by a mad dog, the *Morning Star* acidly suggested that the company could produce *Hamlet, King Lear,* or *Othello* and give the actor a chance to display his new ability in madness.[4]

For the 1839 season, the Market Square theater was remodeled. Henry Corri, a British ballet dancer and "veteran actor," brought his troupe from New Orleans and took over as manager. The *Morning Star* gave Corri frank advice. "He should now be careful to suffer none of the vulgar low comedies . . . that are so frequently served up to the mortification of the boxes and the uproarious applause of the galleries. And above all he should prevent the uproar occasioned by low ruffians who by their boisterous and unmannerly conduct have driven ladies from the theatre disgusted with everything they saw or heard and dreading to return." Corri abolished the galleries and offered uplifting attractions such as *My Sister Dear.* Police were hired to enforce decorum. Parquet seats were $2; private boxes, $3.[5] Shakespeare was about to hit Houston.

On February 12, 1839, Mr. Lewellen starred in *Othello.* He had scored the year before in Saint Louis doing an equestrian melo-drama with his spendid horse Mazeppa,[6] an act presumed to be sufficient preparation for his appearance in Houston as the noble Moor. In March, J. R. Scott played *Othello,* and in May he played *Richard III.* An actor of the Forrest school, Scott perhaps played both roles rantingly,[7] a style calculated to catch the buckskinned buckaroos of a frontier settlement. H. L. Waldron said farewell to the stage at Corri's in *Romeo and Juliet,* emphasizing the fights, then did an encore in *Macbeth,* again emphasizing the fights.[8]

To paraphrase Boileau, "enfin Shakespeare vint," but the arrival heralded little change. The showman Henry Corri in 1840 offered "three excellent comedies," *A Loan of a Lover, The Rival Pages,* and *The Irish Tutor,* with reserved box seats free for the ladies if they would brave the "inclement weather" to wade through the heavy mud that was thick everywhere.[9] The population of about two thousand counted many floaters as well as some transient redskins, whose occasional bouts of intoxication caused no inconvenience to hard-drinking Texans; luckily, the cannibalistic Karankawas encountered on the Texas coast by Cabeza de Vaca had gone out of business.

In 1840, at the behest of President Mirabeau B. Lamar and over the objections of former President Sam Houston, the capital of the republic was removed to Austin. President Lamar, a poet and man of letters,[10] may have been influenced by the *Morning Star*'s complaint of "rowdies and black legs who make life intolerable by their carouses and fights." The drama languished in the former capital. Amateurs of the Thespian Society did some scenes from Shakespeare. A farcical *Richard III* was presented in 1845 when a strolling company of players that included young Joe Jefferson, down on its luck, let the retired actor Pudding Stanley play his pet role.[11] The Republic of Texas, scarcely credible as an independent nation, except as part of a "Third World" and in dire need of loans from a "World Bank," came to an end in 1845 with its annexation as the twenty-eighth state of the Union, over the bitter opposition of anti-slavery forces.

The first real theater, built in 1854 by one James Thompson, burned in 1859.[12] Perkins' Hall was built in the 1850s and in its long life served many theatrical figures, but records of early Shakespearean performers are scant.[13] In 1861 at the outbreak of the Civil War, Clark's Dramatic Troupe, which had some Shakespearean pieces in its repertoire, played to large audiences at Perkins' Hall.[14] Ironically, when Texas joined the Confederacy it seceded from the Union it had joined only fifteen years before. The Civil War caused a virtual suspension of entertainment in the Confederate states, a cease of theater analogous to the break caused by the Civil War in England two hundred years earlier.

Long pent feelings burst forth in 1866 when a ludicrous "Shakespearean reading," a one-man show, was given at Perkins' Hall. Mrs. Bates in *Camille* left the reporter for the *Daily Telegraph* speechless with admiration, *Love's Sacrifice* and *The Widow's Victim* were well received, and *East Lynn* filled the aisles. John Brougham, an actor of some consequence, paid a two-day visit in

1869 and found the town appreciative of his efforts in *Much Ado About A Merchant of Venice,* which was probably a burlesque, since this actor had had training and experience in such shows with Madame Vestris at the Olympic Theatre in London. Before the year was out audiences had seen Brougham in serious productions of *Romeo and Juliet* and *Macbeth.* [15]

In the 1870s it was realized that Perkins' Hall had a stage that was definitely outmoded, so low and shallow that many actors refused to act on it. The Houston Opera House (Gray's) had been built in 1874 and offered more adequate facilities. Edwin Forrest, on his last tour in 1871–1872 at the age of sixty-six, did not disdain to play Lear, his greatest role, in a one-night stand at Perkins'.[16] Such notable actors as Charles Fechter and Edwin Davenport did "tread aloft in bus-kin fine," but not so high as to bump their heads, on the creaking boards at Perkins' in *Hamlet,* while lesser performers appeared in *Macbeth,* twice in that rousing Houston favorite *Richard III,* and twice in *Romeo and Juliet.* On September 28, 1873, Sophie Miles acted the Prince in *Hamlet* at Perkins', continuing a tradition of actresses in breeches roles that was apparently not familiar in Texas, for Miss Miles was received with little enthusiasm. As the decade ended, Texas was ready for Shakespearean comedy when Fanny Davenport brought *As You Like It* to Galveston, Denton, Dallas, Austin, and Brenham, as well as to Houston, where the audience was her favorite.[17] At Gray's Opera House in the mid-1870s the town saw *Macbeth, Hamlet* twice, and *Othello.* To relieve this diet of tragedy, it saw Ben De Bar, who was recognized as the best Falstaff in America, in *1 Henry IV* and *The Merry Wives of Windsor.*

Erected in the late 1870s, Pillot's Opera House was a handsome four-story building with the largest auditorium in Houston. It was able to bring some favorites of the stage, including "Mrs. Langtry, the Jersey Lily . . . at $2,000 a night" in 1882.[18] The two opera houses, Gray's and Pillot's, offered competing attractions that included some Shakespeare to the growing city (50,000 by 1890), until Pillot's Opera House was destroyed by a fire that burned it to the ground on May 3, 1888. The season of 1889–1890 opened at Gray's, but it was torn down and Sweeney and Coom's Opera House took its place for the season of 1891–1892.

In the 1880s Houston welcomed Frederick Warde's *Hamlet* and *Romeo and Juliet*. The *Post* said, "Had nature . . . endowed Mr. Warde with a more imposing presence and a strong voice, he would be inaccessible to all rivals in histrionic fame." Mercutio's "fine voice and elocutionary force" were more impressive than Warde's Romeo. Lawrence Barrett in his production of *Julius Caesar* appeared as Cassius, Louis James as Brutus, Otis Skinner as Caesar. "Scholarly" was the *Post* critic's accolade for the "polished schooling" of Barrett, who later treated his local audience to *The Merchant of Venice*.[19]

Helena Modjeska, whose Polish accent was noticeable only when she talked very fast, and Maurice Barrymore in *Twelfth Night* delighted a large matinee crowd. Rose Eytinge brought *The Winter's Tale;* she gave a strong portrayal of Hermione. Just at the beginning of his career, young Thomas Keene played the Prince in *Hamlet*, about which the *Journal* complained that he spoiled his quiet scenes by "mouthings, which his worshippers call facial expressions." Undeterred, he did *Richard III*, which restored him to favor, *Macbeth*, and *Othello*.

Frederick Warde and Tom Keene returned season after season. On one of his visits, Warde appeared in something called "Jack Cade," an otherwise unknown play probably derived from *2 Henry VI*, thus providing splendid opportunities for chilling cruelty. In the season of 1885–1886, Adelaide Moore at Pillot's Opera House acted Rosalind in *As You Like It* and Capulet's daughter in *Romeo and Juliet*. She was better as Juliet than as Rosalind, being more ingenuous than ingenious. On his first visit to Houston on January 23, 1886, the great Edwin Booth's *Hamlet* played to a packed house at Pillot's.[20]

Stuart Robson and William Crane arrived in February of 1887 with a company of forty-five artists and several railway cars of special scenery. The *Post*'s review of *The Comedy of Errors*, Shakespeare's rollicking farce, noted that "nearly all the seats were taken at Pillot's. There were camp stools in the aisles. The attention of the chief of the fire department is called as the place is a veritable fire-trap." This warning was evidently not enough. The same company put on *The Merry Wives of Windsor,* showing off more of the special scenery, and relying on the self-defeating tricks of Falstaff to amuse.[21]

Edwin Booth's return in 1887, eagerly awaited, was a sell-out. The celebrated actor, who was now fifty-six, arrived in his private car "David Garrick," with Lawrence Barrett and others of his company.[22] Ticket scalping was vicious, seats going for as much as $18 or $20. Booth's Hamlet was forceful, yet thoughtful and melancholy, with no excess motion. He was not stately like Forrest, but spare of frame.[23] Although his acting of Hamlet constantly changed, he had developed his mature conception of the role in his much-discussed performances at the Booth Theater in New York beginning on January 3, 1870. Critics almost unanimously agreed on the grace, dignity, and naturalness of his interpretation. His low-pitched voice easily carried to all parts of the house. His audiences felt that his splendid dark eyes and black, disheveled hair, his whole bearing, produced "a remarkably well-studied and harmonious piece of acting."[24] The generation of Americans who saw Booth in *Hamlet* believed they had lived with the Prince, had seen him as Shakespeare conceived him.

Booth's triumph in Houston continued with a matinee of *Julius Caesar,* in which his sad face as Brutus held the audience until his death at Philippi. His dignity paralyzed the wrath of Cassius (Lawrence Barrett) in the great quarrel scene, and his silence at his realization of Portia's death was eloquent.[25] He was masterly as Iago that evening. The *Post* reported his "cold-blooded villainy . . . sardonic deviltry . . . abominable hypocrisy . . . unrelenting malice." And yet "there is the inimitable grace of it all—he brings out the fascinating quality of the rogue—playing in a kind of lurid light through the malignity which steeps his soul." One may hear in this an echo of Coleridge's "motiveless malignity." It was the last time that Texas saw Edwin Booth.

The Ladies Reading Club had been established in 1885. In preparation for the advent of Edwin Booth, they studied *Hamlet.* When the Ladies Shakespeare Club was organized in 1890, the credo of the club had two articles: (1) Shakespeare's plays were written by William Shakespeare and not by Bacon, Marlowe, or anybody else (*pace* Delia Bacon); (2) Shakespeare is the crown and chief glory of English literature.[26]

Houston having recovered from the pains of Reconstruction, in the Gilded Age Sweeney and Coom's Opera House satisfied local playgoers during a period marked by the decline of the actor-manager system and its replacement by an economy-minded, New York-based syndicate.[27] In the 1890s the opera house sheltered many Shakespearean productions, both old and new, it got a new interior, and the acoustics were excellent. In 1891 electric street cars replaced mule-drawn conveyances. Some of the streets were paved with macadam or oyster shells. Prosperity was just over the horizon as Houston began to develop its hustler image.

Early on Tom Keene returned with *Richard III* and *Hamlet,* with *Romeo and Juliet* and *Julius Caesar,* a versatile reportoire. Louis James brought *Othello.* Marie Wainwright drew generous praise for her Viola in *Twelfth Night.* The *Post*'s reviewer was a proper Victorian and a southern gentleman.

> Even old theatregoers found her a veritable revelation. Never has one of the lighter creations been presented in Houston with more fidelity or better effect. Viola is one of Shakespeare's strongest pictures of noble womanhood, in which audacity and modest reserve, witchery and earnest truth, gayety light as air and passion strong as death are harmoniously blended, but Miss Wainwright surpasses all preconceived ideas. Unlike most actresses who attempt the role, she does not overdo nature for the sake of effect, but follows reverently in the footsteps of the great author.[28]

Genteel enough, but the largest turn-out Houston ever had was for three appearances by John L. Sullivan.

At the end of 1891 when Patti Rosa played to a half-full house and even her great winking song fell flat, the *Post* deplored this indifference as a sign of cultural lag, saying that only a "tank drama" was sure to please the oafs in the gallery. The paper vented its disgust with lovers of aquatic drama in lines of verse on a versatile actor who "had played with Booth and Forrest / Knew Shakespeare all by heart / It seemed a shame to him / To have to throw a part / Up because he couldn't swim."

Warde & Bowers did *Henry VIII*, new to Houston, as a gaudy pageant in the manner of Henry Irving, and had to hire local spear carriers. Later the same combination, as a joint stock company was called, gave *Henry VIII* again, *Julius Caesar, 1 Henry IV*, and *Romeo and Juliet*. The combination of McLean & Prescott did the balcony scene from *Romeo and Juliet* as part of a larger bill, perhaps vaudeville. Bella McLeod Smith performed Ophelia's mad scenes from *Hamlet*, and Clay Clement and then Crestin Clark offered *Hamlet* in a full version. Effie Ellsler won favor as Rosalind in *As You Like It*, Hortense Rhea was well received as Portia in *The Merchant of Venice*, and rather remarkably, since *Cymbeline* was not often produced anywhere, Margaret Mather was well liked for her portrayal of Imogen. The Bayou City enjoyed a procession of Shakespeare's plays.

The favorite actress was undoubtedly Marie Wainwright, as she proved when she returned to star in *As You Like It*. She was tender and womanly, but youthfully impulsive as Rosalind. Despite her buxomness as Ganymede, her performance impressed the reviewer, "generous nature having given her curves that should be perpetuated on canvas or on [*sic*] marble." At the final curtain she was presented with a large bouquet of magnolias.

In 1898 when Modjeska & Haworth came to give *Macbeth*, a great crowd turned out. Helena Modjeska, Countess Bozente, was remembered from her visit of some years earlier. Her voice seemed weaker than formerly (she was now fifty-four years old), but it was allowed that Madame understood Lady Macbeth as well as any other actress in the great role, including Charlotte Cushman, who in 1835 had begun playing Lady Macbeth, the part in which she was said to be unequalled. In the sleep-walking scene, the Countess acted with tragic intensity, and with no trace of her Polish accent. At the end of the performance a bust of Kosciusko was presented to her by the Poles of the city.

In the last season of the nineteenth century, the James-Kidder-Hanford combination offered three plays, *The Winter's Tale, The School for Scandal*, and *Macbeth*. The first was the most refreshing.

Hanford's Leontes was the best part he had done on the Houston stage, Louis James's Autolycus "was as pleasing as could be expected," and Katherine Kidder as Perdita was at her best in the rural feast in act 4 in "her love scene" with Norman Hackett's Florizel. Louis James, who had often appeared here, "understood" Macbeth; but fifteen-year-old Bessie Barriscale was said, somewhat ambiguously, to have "got all out of her part as Fleance"[29]—milked it, or forgot her two lines?

It is difficult a century and more later to feel the social value to Houston of its makeshift or substantial, temporary or long-lasting, poorly equipped or well-designed theaters and opera houses, which served as forums for lecturers on literature, art, and politics, and as community centers. They were reasonably democratic: all classes of white society came together to see "players and plays . . . sue alike for pardon or for praise," as Byron said in his *Address* spoken at the opening of the Drury Lane Theatre in London in 1812. In the latter part of the century in Houston the theater developed as a civic institution. Earlier, Houston could not challenge its rival Galveston, which by 1871 had the $150,000 Tremont Theater,[30] modeled after Edwin Booth's sumptuous theater in New York.

The Ladies Reading Club (1885) and the Ladies Shakespeare Club (1890) joined the City Federation of Women's Clubs in 1900, and the number of such organizations was increased by the South End Shakespeare Club in 1904 and by the Houston Pen Women in 1906. Self-improvement activities were afoot. None of the semi-professional theater groups in the area was founded before 1930. Vaudeville, circuses, and rodeos were popular kinds of entertainment. Between 1910 and 1935, when the regular stage sank to melodrama and extravagant romances, and movies were beginning to replace road companies and small-town theaters, dozens of little theaters, community, and regional theaters sprang up in the South, notably in Chapel Hill, Charleston, New Orleans, and Shreveport. Considerable ballyhoo attended these developments,[31] but Houston was slow to take heed. After the Houston Little Theater had sprouted, it attempted nothing more significant than *Dinner at Eight* and considered *R. U. R.* "very ambitious."[32]

The Rice Dramatic Club, organized in 1917,[33] at first contented itself with programs of one-act plays at Autry House, with faculty members as actors and also directing student casts. In 1925 the club put on *Shakespeare,* in five "episodes" by H. F. Rubenstein and Clifford Box (pseudonymous or mythical?) at the Scottish Rite Cathedral, which had a good stage but vile acoustics. For a brief period under the unsure guidance of a young English instructor, the club became almost professional in the quality of its productions, and at the same time it became notorious.[34] Soon thereafter, in 1933, it settled comfortably into Clemence Dane's *Will Shakespeare.* Then the club became embroiled in controversy with the United Daughters of the Confederacy,[35] after which it emerged briefly to present *Twelfth Night.*[36] Then it disappeared but came to life again in the early 1950s as the Rice Players.

Meanwhile, Houston audiences responded enthusiastically when Fritz Leiber[37] came on New Year's Eve, 1928, to give a brilliant performance in *Hamlet,* and in the first week of 1929 he won minds and hearts with his powerful acting in *Romeo and Juliet, Julius Caesar,* again in *Hamlet* at a matinee and in *Macbeth* that evening, in *The Merchant of Venice,* and as the wastrel Sly and the masterful Petruchio in *The Taming of the Shrew.*

For once the actor had a critic worthy of him. Stockton Axson had been a brilliant lecturer on Shakespeare of the old school, a combination of scholar and rhetorician, at Vermont (1894–1896), Adelphi (1896–1899), and Princeton (1899–1913) before he joined the original faculty of Rice Institute, and a visiting lecturer at Oregon (1914), Colorado (1916), and California at Berkeley (1915, 1917, 1920). He was a noble personality in whom one could sense "the free interplay of intellect and feeling, a simple courtesy that was also a magnificent courtliness."[38] The Axson Club was founded in 1917; he lectured on Shakespeare to the members. In the spring of 1929 he delivered a series of lectures at Rice that was remarkable for depth of humanistic learning, as well as surprising for modernity in a multi-faceted approach to Shakespeare.[39]

The two long reviews by Axson of Fritz Leiber's Houston repertoire revealed the virtue of the reviewer and the virtuosity of the reviewed.[40] Axson was qualified to praise or blame. Even Booth, he wrote, "the incarnate Hamlet, lacked (and he knew it) the gaiety which Hamlet mingles with his profundity and sadness; Sothern's Hamlet lacked the lofty intellectuality of the original; Forbes Robertson's lacked the simplicity; Walter Hamden's the warmth; John Barrymore's—everything except the personal charm of Barrymore." Leiber impressed Axson by his "total lack of affectation, mannerism, self-exploitation." He was an actor's Hamlet, "not any of the many different kinds of philosophical Hamlets which have emerged from scholars' lucubrations."

Leiber was forthright, "obedient to the text (George Nathan's phrase), takes the lines at their face value," and Axson thought "he was nothing less than great in the rapid fire dialogues which follow the Murder of Gonzago, this chameleon scene (the greatest of its kind in drama, excepting some of Cleopatra's scenes) where Hamlet changes from mood to mood, almost from personality to personality before our eyes. Mr. Leiber encompassed all of it with unsurpassable virtuosity." At the same time, Axson faulted the too rapid pace of Hamlet's scenes with Ophelia and Horatio, and the lack of ensemble playing. He commended Virginia Bronson as Gertrude, had qualified praise for Philip Quin as Polonius, who "lacked unction," found John Burke as Claudius "earnest but frequently inarticulate."

Fritz Leiber and Virginia Bronson (Mrs. Leiber) stayed at the Rice Hotel, where Stockton Axson lived all his years in Houston. The old Shakespearean critic and the young Shakespearean actors enjoyed each other. In his second review, Axson thought the matinee performance of *Hamlet* was "immensely better than the opening night, although there were weak spots—on Ruskin's principle that no truly great thing can be really perfect." After the performance, Leiber talked about the character of Hamlet.

"He spoke of Hamlet's ascent or descent through the play—whichever it is. He does not assume that he has plucked out the heart of the mystery, although he's lived with the character for many years. I know he is highly intellectual, but, after all, his reactions are purely human. Some say that Hamlet vacillates. I can not see it. He is bewildered as any human being would be in such a situation, but that doesn't mean he hesitates or delays. So I don't want to emphasize his 'antic disposition.' I think that would be a mistake."

Axson saw in Leiber the virtue of humility. "Not mawkish, self-conscious, self-depreciation (often only inverted vanity), but the deep humility of a proud soul, lofty enough to discover something loftier than itself and sufficiently devoted to endeavor to make that greater thing prevail. In Leiber's case, that greater thing is the art of Shakespeare."

January 4, 1929, the evening for *The Merchant of Venice,* brought a great storm, and on such a night Leiber said he would not have gone voluntarily to see anybody act anything. But there the audience was, so dense that extra chairs were needed in the aisles, an overflow audience tense, receptive, responsive. In the reviewer's opinion, the best production of the week was *The Merchant of Venice.* "Leiber's Jew is one of the great Shylocks of stage history. He has the defiance and despair, the choked subservience, wheedling, wiliness, and mechanical yet very human responses that the role demands. The business was effective, sometimes inspired in the production. The Prince of Aragon (Jack Forest) minces about the caskets with an affectation which carries the prideful conceit of a Spanish grandee, overlaid by the conceited pride of an Elizabethan fop."

To Axson, the least satisfactory play was *Macbeth.* He wrote that he "had heard two distinguished actors, Henry Irving and Leiber, talk greatly about Macbeth and seen each play the role inadequately." The performance of *Romeo and Juliet* was moving, but some members of the cast did not grasp the poetry. "Miss Russell was a gracious Juliet, but one wishes for more poetry in her balcony speeches, a keener sense of word values in 'Oh, comfortable friar,' and 'Oh, churl' in her last speech to her dead husband. Miss Russell might profit from E. E. Stoll's comment on the magic of 'churl' in this speech."

The Taming of the Shrew came last. Both Axson and Leiber were sensitive to the complexities of women's liberation, a movement which of course had begun long before, and one that fifty years ago seemed to strain no feverish allegiances. Axson: "Who started the myth that women lack a sense of humor? They laughed as heartily as the men, who laughed perhaps mingling with their laughter a hidden wish that they could do what Petruchio did." Leiber in a brief curtain speech: "Let the men understand that this works on the stage, but. . . ."

In summing up the tremendous impression made by this unprecedented Shakespearean week, Axson wrote that Leiber, with high intelligence and great physical assets, "yet achieves subjection of himself to Shakespeare's magic." Nobody in America was then presenting Shakespeare so consistently as Leiber. "The brilliant John Barrymore turns away periodically from motion picture clap-trap for a dip into Shakespeare—an incident in a varied theatrical career. Walter Hamden specializes at intervals in Hamlet. David Warfield and George Arliss play Shakespeare amid a number of unrelated things. Robert Mantell is dead. Frederick Warde is retired, and so is Edward Sothern. While others play at Shakespeare from time to time, Mr. Leiber plays him all the time. He is wholly dedicated to Shakespeare. Can an actor have a higher mission?" Fritz Leiber was the last of the fine Shakespearean actors in America who toured with their own companies and who brought high dramatic art to the South.

The Great Depression was about to enter at stage center. One hopeful branch of the Works Progress Administration (WPA) was the Federal Theater Project, which operated from 1936 to 1939. The failure of the Federal Theater Project in Houston was perhaps made inevitable by the orneryness of Texas politicians, who have resisted many programs that originated in Washington. When the Federal Theater Project failed here, Margot Jones took a job with the Recreation Department to direct children's plays in the city parks. As soon as she could wangle a building that nobody else wanted, she announced the Houston Community Players. In 1936 she put on some plays, such as *The Importance of Being Earnest* and *Hedda Gabler*, that compelled attention. She directed *Macbeth, The Master Builder, The Taming of the Shrew, Uncle Vanya, The Comedy of Errors*, and *As You Like It*. These classics were hot at the box office, playing to SRO, demonstrating the short-sightedness of community theater directors who insist on a permanent fare of modern light comedies or musicals. She had produced more than sixty plays by

the time World War II came along and dried up the supply of actors.[41] Margot Jones was a dynamo, in love with the theater, highly
talented, and almost infinitely ingenious, but she had to bide her
time.

Another dynamic lady, Nina Vance, was to become Houston's
most famous theatrical impresario. In 1937, when Margot Jones and
the Community Players were doing plays in a sample room at the
Lamar Hotel, and in a room on the mezzanine at the Rice Hotel, as
well as in other unlikely places, Nina Vance was Margot Jones's
girl-Friday.[42] She, too, was stage-struck, and a very strong-willed
person. The Alley Theater began its fabled years in a dance studio at
3617 Main Street, then moved to a former fan factory at 709 Berry
Avenue, where it remained from February, 1949, until March,
1968.[43] In 1952, after a power struggle with her board of directors,
Nina Vance obtained complete control of the business and artistic
affairs of the theater.

Although she was sympathetic to modern playwrights, whose
plays not infrequently flopped, and put her stamp on the premiers of
a number of new and experimental plays, she was hesitant about
Shakespeare. A firm pragmatist, she insisted that her choice of plays
was based on no philosophical principle. After *Six Characters in
Search of an Author* had failed at the box office, she said, "The
standard theory that improving the product will automatically increase its acceptance just does not seem to be true in the theater."
Whose theory did she have in mind? What was the quality, in the
first place, of the product to be improved?

The Alley's first flirtation with Shakespeare came with *Julius
Caesar* in 1958. Although brought in with fanfare, it was a disaster.
Three years passed before the next venture into classic drama with
Volpone in 1961, which was such a smash that it had to be revived
later that season. *Hamlet* in 1962, starring one Chris Wiggins, was
called by a reviewer, with admirable restraint, "under powered." In
the next season, *The Taming of the Shrew* was attended mainly by
high school and college students, set no box office records, and was
therefore not successful by Alley standards. Nina Vance concluded
that culture was not yet popular (i.e., profitable) in Houston.[44]

The new Alley Theater's opening in 1968 in its eye-popping, modernistic fortress was greeted with ruffles and flourishes.[45] The Alley was already internationally respected for its resident and professional company and its productions that occasionally equalled Broadway and London's West End. Yet the same policy of play selection continued. In 1972 one critic asked, "Why is the Alley not striking out with new plays of social importance or of theatrical significance? What about *King Lear,* never seen here in the memory of serious theater watchers?"[46] In 1975–1976 Nina Vance staged *Twelfth Night,* but she jazzed it so as to display the diminutive talent of a diminutive black actor as Feste, who trilled like a canary while perched in a swing.

Miss Vance had confessed many years before that she valued her commercial successes more than her artistic ones.[47] She had many of both kinds. In thirty-three years as an important director and producer, a person of wit and charm who always wanted to be at the theatrical center of things, if there was money in it, she tackled only four of Shakespeare's plays, two tragedies and two comedies. With these she achieved neither the commercial success that she prized nor the artistic success that with her was secondary. The obituaries praised her work and said that "her heart and her developed moral sense were as important as her head."[48] Several months later a slightly different assessment hailed "the moves apparently afoot to bring the long-simmering Alley to a boil again. These would revive the spirit . . . that marked the 33-year-old company's early, more dynamic, lower-overhead years. Most of the fresh-minted plays presented at the Alley in the last several years have been . . . sure-fire, Broadway-tested comedies, beamish musical revues, sanitized versions of comparatively astringent Broadway dramas *(The Shadow Box)* or even a criticism-proof, one-man recitation of a book from the world's all-time best seller . . . the Bible."[49]

When commercial and professional theaters concentrate on what is either safe or trivial, university theaters in the area sometimes try harder. In the decade 1950–1960, the Rice Players offered a series of plays that were imaginatively staged in natural settings around the campus.[50] Commendable daring, if not overweening confidence, was needed to produce Milton's *Samson Agonistes* in 1953. *As You Like It* appears to have been more conventional, as well as scenes from *Richard II* "to convey the single essential impression of his character which is central to the play." A Shakespeare Festival each spring was planned. Scenes from *Othello, Henry V, Macbeth,* and *The Taming of the Shrew* were presented "on the steps of the Chemistry Lecture Hall." The ghost scenes of *Hamlet* sounded aloft from "the battlements of the Physics Building," act 5, scene 1 of *Macbeth* "on the steps of the Chemistry Building," the balcony scene of *Romeo and Juliet* on "the balcony of the Chemistry Building," the tedious brief interlude of Pyramus and Thisbe from *A Midsummer Night's Dream* "in the court of the Chemistry Building." One spring, *1 Henry IV* was staged "on the lawn beside Lovett Hall;" another spring, *The Merchant of Venice* was staged "by the Physics Building;" the next year, *Macbeth* "on the Rice campus by Lovett Hall"; and finally, for the seventh annual Shakespeare Festival, *Twelfth Night* "by the Chemistry Building."

These programs showed the latitude possible in Shakespearean staging. Shakespeare's plays are seen out of doors "in natural settings" fairly often, but not usually in juxtaposition with permanent university buildings. The eclectic architecture at Rice, Lombard Romanesque with an overlay of Byzantine and Moorish features, probably invited these experiments. Thereafter the Rice Players went back inside to the 500-seat auditorium in Hamman Hall for *A Midsummer Night's Dream,* with bully Bottom rampant; *Much Ado About Nothing,* with the subplot inevitably taking precedence;[51] and *Othello,* with the Moor outmaneuvered by the Ensign. Another indoors *As You Like It* would have sparkled "on the lawn beside Lovett Hall," or in any other pastoral setting.[52]

Rice University became involved in 1964 with Shakespeare's quadricentennial. Eugene Waith, Clifford Leech, Willard Farnham, and "Virgin" Whitaker (as he was called in one announcement) came for lectures. Another event was six performances of *The Taming of the Shrew,* of which a program note said, "The harlequinesque styling of the comedia [*sic*] dell' arte has been included in the Elizabethan framework presenting a modern statement." Coincidentally, Neil Havens, well educated in theater, became faculty adviser of the Players.

Havens directed a polished production of *The Winter's Tale,* in which John Velz, now a well-known Shakespearean scholar at the University of Texas in Austin, played the Bear. Later in 1965 Havens mounted a satisfactory *Richard III* for the Houston Shakespeare Society. He followed with a well-conceived *Julius Caesar.* Feeling that a little self-congratulation was in order, the Rice Players in one program note bragged, "The Players continue to provide amateur drama that in most respects meets and occasionally surpasses professional standards of excellence."

In 1967 their pallid *Hamlet,* however, neither met nor surpassed any standards. It aped David Warner's "weak" Hamlet, the atrophied Hamlet of the previous summer at the Royal Shakespeare Theatre in Stratford, in contrast to the "strong" Hamlet of Alan Howard, which had also been seen at Stratford. A few years hence, college Hamlets will be imitating the flamboyantly neurotic Hamlet of Derek Jacobi, offered in the third season of the BBC Shakespeare, and repeated in the fourth season. David Warner's "weak" Hamlet, which the Rice Players chose as a model, had outdone the Hamlet of Laurence Olivier, "who couldn't make up his mind" by having no mind to make up. For their foolishness, they got a bad review.⁵³ Academic tolerance in 1973, a holdover from the eccentricities of the 1960s, permitted Charles Marovitz's travesty, "A Macbeth."

Several years earlier the drama at Rice had headed toward decentralization with the arrival of "College Theater," analogous to "states' rights" in outmoded political lingo. Weiss College had its venturesome Tabletop Theater, which had done *Antigone, Doctor Faustus,* and *The Alchemist;* Brown College was committed to a couple of morality plays each year; Baker College had theater-in-the-round in its commons room,⁵⁴ where students have staged homemade productions of *1 Henry IV, Love's Labor's Lost, The Winter's Tale,* and *As You Like It.* The Rice Players continue to draw from all the colleges when they perform in Hamman Hall. Recently, *A Midsummer Night's Dream* there used an awkward, all-purpose set of low platforms and ramps, put everybody into unattractive, oversimplified costumes, and in my opinion was a retreat from Shakespeare.

Other colleges in the area have cheerful theater programs, but they seldom look at the classics.[55] The University of Saint Thomas could, if it chose, think of Shakespeare as an Old Catholic; Texas Southern University might take a look at Joseph Papp's Black Ensemble. The University of Houston at Clear Lake has a 500-seat auditorium in the Bayou Building and a director from Minneapolis who is surprised that so few classics are staged in Houston. In Texas City, the College of the Mainland draws most of its audience from Houston, fifty miles away; the drama teacher there says, "We have some former Alley subscribers who say they've given up on the Alley." In a coastal metropolitan area such as Houston, aficionados of almost anything—sail boating, swimming, fishing, sea food, or theater—seem willing to drive a hundred miles to enjoy it. I can recommend the Upper Deck Theater of Galveston College, with its neat arena stage, where I saw an uncluttered production of *The Merry Wives of Windsor* that featured a wickedly roly-poly Falstaff who needed no padding.

The University of Houston Central Campus has an intrepid drama department under Sidney Berger. Before Berger arrived in 1969, the department was willing to take risks: *King Lear, The Tempest, Romeo and Juliet,* and *The Merchant of Venice,* none of them easy, held up fairly well. An earlier venture with *Hamlet* failed all up and down the line.[56] When Berger was first testing the ground, he was not a sure-handed director of *Richard III*, probably because of a set design that looked vaguely Egyptian.

Sidney Berger, founder and producing director of the Houston Shakespeare Festival, presenting two plays free during a two-week period each summer at the Miller Theater in Hermann Park for heterogeneous audiences, holds the main hopes for Shakespeare in this area. He is a professional who feels comfortable with Shakespeare, likes to "think Elizabethan," would like to produce the history plays for the Houston Festival, or even *Pericles* (perhaps by 1990), but first he wants to build an audience with the more familiar

Houston Shakespeare Festival production of *King Lear,* 1980
Courtesy Houston Shakespeare Festival

Sidney Berger, producer and director of the Houston Shakespeare Festival
Courtesy Houston Shakespeare Festival

plays before surprising them, not too rudely.[57] In collaboration with a Parks and Recreation Department no longer as feeble as it was when Margot Jones came in like a lion nearly fifty years ago, the Houston Shakespeare Festival has already created "a new blooming of the Town and Gown tradition." One day it may rank with the major Shakespeare festivals, such as those at Ashland (Oregon), San Diego and Los Angeles, New York, and Stratford (Ontario), or at least the lesser Stratford (Connecticut). It has already in its brief life advanced to a high level.

The productions of 1975 made a prudent beginning, although that of *A Midsummer Night's Dream* took the risk, now fairly common, of doubling Theseus and Oberon, Hippolyta and Titania, Philostrate and Puck. *The Taming of the Shrew* dispensed with Christopher Sly and got down to the business of Petruchio's rough lesson in How to Know a Good Wife from a Bad, using "Kate the curst" as Exhibit A. The disciplined pellmell of Sidney Berger's direction set the right pace for such a romp. In 1976 nothing seemed right in *The Tempest,* few things seemed right in *Romeo and Juliet,* and the sets were absurd. In 1977 *Hamlet* and *The Comedy of Errors* made an extraordinary pair, high tragedy and low farce. Hamlet was a melancholic wit, a meditative athlete, a sensuous moralist, and finally an active fatalist. Such oxymorons dissolved in the other play's uproar, a tumult that threatened to rock the enormous stage of the Miller Theater off its foundations. In 1978 *Macbeth* and *The Merry Wives of Windsor* again linked dark and bright, a tortured hero in the one and a fat scalawag in the other. In 1979 *Much Ado About Nothing* and *Twelfth Night* (with some commedia dell' arte touches) brought together two different kinds of romantic comedy and showed that in Shakespeare's hands they were not so far apart.[58] For its seventh season in 1980, its most ambitious and most successful, the festival returned to an earlier practice of matching unmatchables with *As You Like It* and *King Lear.*[59] A smart Rosalind and a stalwart but dense Orlando enlivened the comedy. Dan O'Herlihy as a formidable Lear, three admirably cast actresses as his two detestable daughters and his one loving and loyal daughter, a poignant Fool, and well-trained principals in other roles—all of them made *King Lear* a wrenching tragedy. *As You Like It* was a surpassingly clever comedy of character; *King Lear* reached the heights of man's humanity and the depths of his animality. The Houston Shakespeare Festival seems able to maintain the high standard it has set for itself, and it will continue to provide enlightened entertainment for a diversified audience that comes from all parts of a diversified city.

Let me draw to a semi-oracular conclusion. In retrospect, Shakespeare's fortunes in Houston contravene the law of probability and confirm the principle of uncertainty. So did the fortunes of Elizabeth Tudor and the first James Stuart, the sovereigns under whom Shakespeare lived and wrote. The futurologists in the plays—the Soothsayers in *Julius Caesar* and *Antony and Cleopatra*, Owen Glendower in *1 Henry IV*, Margaret Jourdain in *2 Henry VI*, Time as Chorus in *The Winter's Tale* and old Gower in *Pericles*—could not have foretold the squalid frontier village of yesterday or the affluent Houston of today, six times more populous than Shakespeare's London. No one could foresee—not even Dr. John Dee—that Shakespeare would be as much alive four centuries later as he was when he lived. Nor can the sophisticated computers of high technology tell how Shakespeare and his plays will fare in the time to come. But perhaps I can. The plays survived the discontinuities in the historical and artistic evolution of Houston, some primitive and some praiseworthy presentations of them in the nineteenth century, careless neglect and belated rediscovery of them in the present century. Shakespeare's universal appeal and the sheer theatricality of his plays are now recognized as vital parts of the local environment, parts that cultural conservationists will try to preserve. They are likely to succeed, because his plays—comedies, histories, and tragedies—illustrate piercingly the ironic balance between human happiness and human vulnerability. For nearly a hundred and fifty years in Houston, Shakespeare has had bad times and good times. The best times for him probably lie ahead.

NOTES

I am grateful for the generous assistance of the librarians of the Texas and Local History room at the Houston Public Library; and those of the Woodson Research Center of the Fondren Library, Rice University.

1. Writer's Program of the WPA, *Houston: A History and Guide,* American Guide Series (Houston, 1942), pp. 49, 193.

2. "Dim Pages of Pioneer Newspapers," *Houston Chronicle,* Jan. 24, 1937; Houston Public Library, Houston Scrapbooks, vol. 27, "Houston History," p. 174. Hereafter cited as HPL Scrapbooks.

3. "City's 'First Night' in 1838," *Chronicle,* Aug. 30, 1936; HPL Scrapbooks, vol. 34, "Theaters."

4. Benajah H. Carroll, *Standard History of Houston, Texas* (Houston, ca. 1911), pp. 46–47.

5. *Houston: A History,* pp. 193–94.

6. Joseph Gallegly, *Footlights on the Border: The Galveston and Houston Stage before 1900* (Mouton, 1962), pp. 27–28.

7. Forrest was known for ranting. William R. Alger, *Life of Edwin Forrest: the American Tragedian,* 2 vols. (Philadelphia, 1877; rept. 1972), defends the acting style of Forrest, the first national idol of the American theater.

8. Gallegly, p. 32.

9. HPL Scrapbooks, vol. 27, p. 175.

10. "Houston's Boom Days," *Houston Post,* Apr. 21, 1936; HPL Scrapbooks, vol. 34. Lamar had traveled with a theatrical company in Georgia before coming to Texas. Sam Houston had acted in Home's tragedy of *Douglas* given by an amateur club in Nashville in 1818. One hopes he played the part of the hero Young Norval, not the villain Glenalvon.

11. Joseph Jefferson, *Autobiography,* 3 vols. (New York, 1889; rept. 1964), 3: 65.

12. Carroll, pp. 429–30.

13. HPL Scrapbooks, vol. 27, p. 1; Gallegly, pp. 72–89.

14. *Houston: A History,* pp. 72, 195.

15. Gallegly, pp. 89–112.

16. Alger, 2: 810.

17. Gallegly, pp. 124–25.

18. *Houston: A History,* p. 196.

19. An excellent romantic actor, Lawrence Barrett (1838–1891) was a devoted friend of Edwin Booth, became his manager, and they toured together for several seasons.

20. *Houston: A History,* p. 95.

21. Gallegly, pp. 114–25, 195–207.

22. Katherine Goodale (Kitty Malony), *Behind the Scenes with Edwin Booth* (Boston, 1931), p. 137.

23. When Stephen Orgel saw Booth's costume for Richard III on display in the Folger Shakespeare Library's traveling exhibition, "Shakespeare: The Globe and the World," ("Shakespeare Observed," *SQ* 31 [Summer, 1980]: 139), he confessed that Booth "was smaller than I'd imagined." A renowned actor always gets a little taller in the imagination of later generations.

24. Charles H. Shattuck, *The Hamlet of Edwin Booth* (Urbana, 1969), pp. 67–69, 90–91.

25. Booth and Barrett had a wide repertoire. Booth acted Brutus, Hamlet, Macbeth, Lear, and Shylock. Barrett acted Cassius, Laertes, Macduff, Edgar, and Bas-

sanio. William Winter, *Life and Art of Edwin Booth* (New York, 1893; rept. 1968), pp. 124–26.

26. Carroll, p. 298.

27. Ben Iden Payne, *A Life in a Wooden O: Memories of the Theatre* (New Haven, 1977), pp. 37–40, points out that Richard Mansfield (1854–1907) in England and Edwin Booth (1833–1893) were almost the last and certainly the greatest actor-managers. The failure of the system was not the excesses of egoistic actors, or lack of loyal audiences, or even a dearth of good plays, but almost wholly economic.

28. Gallegly, pp. 156, 211.

29. Ibid., pp. 158, 159–67, 211–17.

30. Consequently, Galveston saw more Shakespeare and other classics. As early as 1867 it had *The Duchess of Malfi;* in 1875 Booth played Overreach in *A New Way to Pay Old Debts.*

31. *Theatre Arts Magazine* (1916) and *Theatre Arts Monthly* (1924) regularly carried news of developments in the United States and abroad.

32. HPL Scrapbooks, vol. 27, p. 118. The *Chronicle* on Dec. 17, 1972, in an informative article on the history of serious theater ventures in Houston, mentioned the Houston Little Theater in the 1930s and 1940s, the Playhouse Theatre built in 1951, the Rivoli Theater on Capital Avenue and Louisiana Street, Theatre, Inc., and Nina Vance's Alley Theatre as "longtime houses," and Margot Jones of the Houston Community Players, 1936–1940; HPL, fiche 1–6.

33. *Rice Thresher,* Mar. 1, 1917. A file folder labeled "Rice Dramatic Club" is kept in a file box in the Woodson Research Center of the Fondren Library, Rice University. The folder contains newspaper clippings and other materials.

34. It presented at the Palace Theater downtown *The Royal Family, The Queen's Husband, Outward Bound, The Dover Road,* and without permission to do so gave John Drinkwater's *Bird in Hand* its American premier. For this malfeasance it was assessed the royalty due, whereupon it tried to get out of the hole by sponsoring an antiquated and distinctly inferior Shakespearean company known as the Ben Greet Players.

35. The club announced a major production of George Aiken's dramatization of *Uncle Tom's Cabin,* had cast the play, made all the costumes, and rehearsed, when the state president of the UDC publicly declared the play "an insult to the South," said she would rather have her ears cut off than attend a play that defamed southern honor, denounced the Rice thespians for selecting it, and declared that she intended, with the aid of 10,000 like-minded ladies, to stop it. The club graciously withdrew *Uncle Tom's Cabin* and gave instead *Rose of Roseland; or, The Spirit of Robert E. Lee,* for which it used the same cast and costumes but had to discard the bloodhounds.

36. *Rice Thresher,* Dec. 3, 1937.

37. For nearly ten years, Leiber was the leading man of his mentor Robert Mantell (1854–1928), who was admired in the United States, and in England before he came to this country about 1874, as a romantic interpreter of Shakespeare's tragedies. On a barnstorming tour he played *Hamlet* in Houston about 1925, in modern dress.

38. Alan D. McKillop, "Stockton Axson, 1867–1935," *Rice Institute Pamphlet* 34 (Jan., 1937): 1–30. McKillop, the eminent eighteenth-century scholar, who had known him as a colleague for more than twenty years, succeeded him as head of the English Department.

39. "Shakespeare: Thinker, Showman, and Artist," *Rice Institute Pamphlet* 17 (Jan., 1930): 1–94.

40. "Portrayal of Hamlet by Leiber is Most Sincere Since Booth," *Chronicle,* Jan.

1, 1929, p. 11; "Week of Shakespeare Heartening, Satisfying," *Chronicle,* Jan. 7, 1929, p. 22.

41. Margot Jones, *Theater-in-the-Round* (New York, 1951), pp. 44–48. The Margot Jones Theater is on the campus of Southern Methodist University.

42. Robert M. Treser, "Houston's Alley Theatre" (Ph.D. diss., Tulane University, 1967), pp. 12–14.

43. Hubert Roussel, "It Started with a Nook on Main: How It Grew," *Tempo* 1, 47 (Nov. 24, 1968): 26–31.

44. Treser, pp. 116–36, 141–42.

45. William Beeson, ed., *Thresholds: The Story of Nina Vance's Alley Theatre, Inaugural Season, 1968–69* (Houston, 1968). Hubert Roussel, for many years the *Post*'s knowledgeable dramatic critic, wrote "Rising Brightly" for this Festschrift.

46. Ann Holmes, "The Spotlight," *Chronicle,* Feb. 27, 1972.

47. Victor Junger, "Nina Vance's Path to Success, " *Post,* Mar. 24, 1957.

48. Ann Holmes, "End of a Golden Era, *Chronicle,* Feb. 27, 1980.

49. William Albright, *Post,* June 22, 1980.

50. Two file boxes in the Woodson Research Center of the Fondren Library, Rice University, contain play programs and other materials related to the Rice Players.

51. Bill Byers, "Shakespeare Returns," *Post,* Apr. 16, 1961, observed that Shakespeare had been "conspicuously absent" in Houston. He described the Rice Players' *Much Ado* as "a romp, so broad that it seems out of focus and without real wit." What he called "the spry staging with curtain boys, heralds, and a chamber music ensemble" may have reflected the outdoor performances of recent years.

52. The BBC production of *As You Like It* in its first season, staged and filmed at Glamis Castle, made wonderfully effective use of the sylvan setting; Maurice Charney, "Shakespearean Anglophilia: The BBC-TV Series and American Audiences," *SQ* 31 (Summer, 1980): 289.

53. D. J. Hobdy, "Colorful *Hamlet* is Raced Through by Rice Players," *Chronicle,* Apr. 25, 1967. One thousand lines had been cut, leaving a not over-long play, so it did not need to be raced through.

54. *Rice Thresher,* "Drama at Rice—A Special Report," Apr. 13, 1967.

55. Everett Evans, "The University Play Scene," *Chronicle,* Sept. 16, 1979, is a useful survey of the situation.

56. Bill Byers, in the review cited in n. 51, wrote that the play's "penetrating magic was lost in its heavy direction, on the set of dark, unattractive platforms, and by the student performers. Hamlet was not a credible prince, Gertrude was a sweet-voiced little matron, Claudius was too obviously a villain, Polonius too obviously a fool."

57. Personal interviews with Sidney Berger, July 29, 1980, and with Miriam Strane, of the Drama Department at the University of Houston Central Campus, July 31, 1980.

58. See my "Shakespeare in Texas," *SQ* 30 (Spring, 1979): 225–26; 31 (Summer, 1980): 245–47.

59. The question asked by Ann Holmes in 1972, "What about *King Lear*?" (see n. 46) was answered eight years later.

Othello as Black on Southern Stages, Then and Now

Charles B. Lower

The history of the South has been bound up with racial issues, with the status of blacks. One might therefore reasonably expect the southern production history of Shakespeare's *Othello* to be skimpy or traumatic, for the tragedy demands that an audience care about the love of the "sooty" Othello and the "fair" Desdemona.[1] Yet such sociological expectations do not hold up in today's South of civil rights and equal opportunity or with the yesterdays of the stage history of *Othello* in the antebellum South. A 1979 Atlanta production received enthusiastic applause and a record-breaking box office. And theater historians minimized the record of the tremendous popularity of *Othello* on the stages of the slaveholding antebellum South and have grasped desperately at wrong straws to explain that popularity.

James Dormon's *Theater in the Ante Bellum South* fairly reflects the current views of theater history. Dormon speaks of merely a southern "tolerance" of the play, explicable in part because *Othello* "was commonly viewed as an anti-miscegenation play." He cites only an early claim that "The great moral lesson of the tragedy of *Othello* is, that black and white blood cannot be intermingled in marriage without a gross outrage upon the law of Nature."[2] That writer had found Desdemona "false to the purity and delicacy of her sex and condition when she married" and had found her "fondling with Othello . . . disgusting." The view is unequivocally anti-miscegenation, but that writer was a Yankee, John Quincy Adams.[3] Adams is hardly representative, but some fear of a "gross outrage upon the law of Nature" did infect the frequent nineteenth-century expressions of sensitivity about Othello's racial identity. Coleridge is probably the most familiar and the mildest: "Can we suppose [Shakespeare] so utterly ignorant as to make a barbarous negro plead royal birth—at a time, too, when negroes were not known but as slaves. . . . To conceive this beautiful Venetian girl falling in love with a veritable negro . . . would argue a disproportionateness, a want of balance, in Desdemona, which Shakespeare does not appear to have in the least contemplated."[4] Critics through the nineteenth century found increasingly elaborate means of arguing that Othello was a Moor of Arabian ancestry rather than African and black.[5] In effect, they sought to show that Shakespeare had intended no "gross outrage." Yet adding this Bardolatry to the rarer and more explicit opposition to miscegenation of Adams, one confronts a considerable chasm to be bridged before concluding that such views, even analogously, reflect how antebellum southern audiences experienced *Othello*. For these views all come from "the study" and are the precious literary concerns of brahmin (and, rather frequently, Abolitionist) taste.

But even proponents of a black Othello became queasy at the thought of *seeing* what they defended. For example, A. C. Bradley was "nearly certain" that Shakespeare "imagined Othello as a black man," but he added a footnote recommending that Othello not be played black: "as Lamb observes, to imagine is one thing and to see is another. Perhaps if we saw Othello coal-black with the bodily eye, the aversion of our blood, an aversion which comes as near to being merely physical as anything human can, would overcome our imagination and sink us below . . . Shakespeare."[6] Did a tawny stage Moor eliminate repugnance? Here enters the historians' second claim explaining the play's appearance on antebellum southern stages. Dormon asserts:

> But as the slavery controversy grew ever more heated and the Southern defense of the institution more militant, Othello became a more objectionable figure in the South. Strolling player Harry Watkins was told in Macon, Georgia, in 1852, that the play was "very displeasing to many citizens" and that they would "not permit his being played dark" under any circumstances. In order "to avoid a row," Watkins wrote, "I played him nearly white." Finally, on December 24, 1860, Noah Ludlow noted in his diary that in a Mobile production of the play, star James Wallack, Jr., flatly refused to perform the lead. He was, according to Ludlow, "afraid of the negro part." Wallack's refusal is understandable. The Alabama

Secession Convention convened on December 24. So by the end of the antebellum period, Othello had to be played as near-white, or not at all.[7]

Such a view badly distorts the surviving historical evidence. *Othello* was performed frequently on all southern stages up to the Civil War, its popularity being only slightly less than that of *Richard III, Macbeth,* and *Hamlet.* For example, Charleston stages had sixty-three *Othello* performances from the earliest in 1809 through one late in March, 1860, including at least sixteen during the 1850s. It was performed in Memphis twenty times between 1837 and 1858, forty-one times in Mobile from March, 1832, until fire destroyed the theater in 1860, and twenty-two times from 1846 through 1860 in Louisville. In New Orleans it averaged more than one and a half performances annually through 1860.[8] Obviously the character Othello was hardly an "objectionable figure" on antebellum southern stages.

I will argue, quite counter to received theater history, that by and large southern audiences in the pit, the boxes, and the galleries enjoyed *Othello,* recognized Iago as its villain and not as the scourge of abhorrent miscegenation, and sympathized with a tragic *blackamoor* Othello. I begin with a newspaper review:

> Thursday night "Othello" was the attraction at the theatre, and its announcement drew a full house. Mr. Ralton as the "Moor" did himself great credit, notwithstanding he seemed to be laboring under the effects of a cold, which lent an unpleasant hoarseness to his voice and interfered much with cleanness of speech.
>
> The wily, smooth spoken, insinuating "Iago" was most happily delineated by Mr. [Edwin] Booth. The general expression of countenance and changes of expression from that of smooth, cool villainy, to the malignancy of crafty hate were inimitable. In a word, Booth was Iago's self for the time.
>
> "How do you like Booth's 'Iago,'" said we to a friend. "Like it? I like it amazingly well. Don't you?" "Yes, very much, but think him much more admirable in 'Richard,' or some other tragedy, it suits his talent and genius better." "In Richard? of course, he plays that to perfection, but d——m it he plays everything to perfection; one has not the enjoyment of cavil if one desired it." Our friend and we agreed, and, as friends will, when of the same mind and dry withal, we adjourned and took something.

This reviewer found no issue in Othello's color and had no revulsion at the interracial marriage. His concerns were the timeless ones of good theatre—how skillful and impressive the performances, how pleasurable the evening.

That review comes from the *Mobile* (Alabama) *Register* for February 4, 1860. The front page of that issue included, "The highest court in the Union has affirmed its principles, and decreed that negroes are not citizens, but property." *Othello* and the slavery controversy could coexist.

But was the performance unobjectionable because its protagonist was "near-white"? The Mobile reviewer made no mention of Ralton's makeup; for most antebellum southern performances, no explicit evidence about Othello's makeup survives. Can one justifiably assume that the camouflage trick of "near-white" makeup explains the absence of discomfort with or complaint about the play's subject? I believe that such a view of southern productions and southern audiences is quite wrong. Such Othellos as Thomas A. Cooper, Junius Brutus Booth, William Charles Macready, Edwin Forrest, and Edwin Booth likely played no differently when on southern stages, for the system in which a visiting star joined with a resident company in repertoire performances permitted only the briefest rehearsing, and had the star "do his thing" without concern for an ensemble effect.[9] Altering the makeup would, of course, hardly force the actor to alter his customary delivery or business. But we have even more promising cause to look beyond the South itself. "Near-white" is really hypothesis, presumably to meet more urgent social conditions in the South, a hypothesis built out of a nearly clichéd explanation in theater history: Edmund Kean's innovation of a *tawny* Othello was "generally followed" through the rest of the nineteenth century in Britain and America, prevailing because it served to whitewash the awkwardness of the play's "sooty" and "thick lipped" protagonist.[10] Thus, we may learn much by reexamining this larger context: were nearly all nineteenth-century Othellos tawny, not black? And would, or could, such altered makeup make acceptable a character otherwise offensive to audiences?

Concluding that nineteenth-century Othellos were nearly always tawny or bronzed is, I believe, facile and unwarranted. It exaggerates the relevance of social and literary attitudes, and it depends upon too selective a use of theatrical evidence.

Abundant in its evidence of racial prejudice, the social history of Britain and the United States in the nineteenth century almost irresistibly lures a theater historian into abuses of the rules of evidence.

The romantics . . . rebelled against his skin. There is a good possibility that this sudden shift in taste was influenced by new political and social attitudes. . . . Othello, if he was played as a veritable negro at a time when the country was acutely aware of the negro problem, might run the risk of seeming low and ignoble to his audience.[11]

The Abolition Movement was building up its strength by this date [1787], and people were becoming reluctant to associate Othello with the descriptions of oppressed slaves that were current.[12]

The presence of Negro slaves in the United States made the idea of Desdemona's marriage to a black man seem to many people not only shocking but incomprehensible.[13]

Such critics cite unquestionable facts of social history but fail to show their immediate, direct influence on stage productions. Such claims could be convincing only if the evidence showed that actors avoided black makeup as Othello. If people voiced objection to a black Othello, by staying away from the theater, by rioting, or by responding perversely to the dramatized action, then no actor would have appeared with even a touch of burnt cork. No theater manager endorses empty seats or rioting, and no actor enjoys boos, catcalls, or hurled missiles. Yet, as will be shown, blackfaced Othellos appeared on nineteenth-century stages, including southern antebellum stages, and these facts destroy facile associations of social history and tawny Othellos.[14]

Even more powerfully tempting for the theater historians is literary criticism arguing against a black Othello. Three cautions make any use of this material to explain nineteenth-century stage practices likely suspect and surely slippery. First, the tangible evidence of influence is scarce. Few actors reveal any interest in Othello's racial ancestry. Numerous actors' memoirs refer to *Othello* and cite anecdotes about its performance without alluding to, much less finding an issue in, Othello's exact skin color. Second, the literary rationalizings for a non-negroid Othello come mostly from critics who are disappointed with, even disapprove of, the stage generally. Such literary voices cannot represent theatergoers generally.[15]

Third, theater historians err by failing to appreciate the differing semantics of stage and study. In theater circles and in the recurring apologetics of criticism, the crucial terms "Moor" and "Negro" had quite different semantic contexts. Among critics, "Moor" and "Negro" refer to contrasting choices for Othello's racial identity. They are separate blood lines: "Negro" is synonymous with "black" and "Ethiopian," while tawniness is an invariable attribute of "Moor." On the other hand, in theater talk "the Moor" is merely an equivalent of "Othello," a substitution for the name without any suggestion of some precise ancestry. An actor could conceivably have used black makeup and still have identified his role as "the Moor." And, for actors almost without exception, "Negro" denoted only the racial group, primarily contemporaneous, existing outside Shakespeare's play-world. For example, in 1823 in New York City a theater manager "cajoled" Charles Mathews, a comedian best in farce, into playing Othello. His fellow actor Cowell recorded that Mathews "was actually childish enough to believe he could play it— not in imitation, but in the manner of John Kemble! But no matter whose manner it was intended to convey, he made the Moor the most melancholy, limping Negro I ever beheld."[16] Cowell used "the Moor" as merely identifying the role, whereas his "Negro" referred to the blacks, free and slave, who were Cowell's contemporaries, making "Negro" serve to disparage the quality of Mathews's acting. The makeup itself is not at issue (although this insult would have been apt only if Mathews had used lampblack). If, on the other hand, a literary disciple of Coleridge had said that some actor "made the Moor the most melancholy, limping Negro I ever beheld," he would have been criticizing (makeup) choices within the control of the actor, whatever his talent ("melancholy, limping" mitigating, a not especially barbaric African Othello). We would be at complete odds with Cowell's ridicule of Mathews.

The social and literary materials have encouraged theater historians unwittingly to distort and to restrict the use of evidence from within the theater—makeup instructions, visual illustrations, and descriptions of actors' performances. Evidence about the appearance of nineteenth-century stage Othellos is more complex and ambiguous than current theater history can accommodate because that history *assumes* that, without the sleight-of-hand rescue that tawny makeup provided, Othello would have been an "objectionable figure."

Makeup instructions, memoirs, paintings, and lithographs provide considerable evidence of tawny Othellos. Leman Thomas Rede's *The Road to the Stage* (1827), the "earliest comprehensive account of the use of make-up in the English theatre," stated that "A tawny tinge is now the colour used for the gallant Moor," as distinct from the usual burnt cork overlaid with carmine for Negro roles.[17] Many portraits show actors in the Othello role with little if any visual suggestion of black. Contemporary descriptions of stage Othellos include, for example, Katherine Goodale's "a slightly bronzed son of the desert" for Edwin Booth.[18]

Nevertheless, there were also many Othellos with black makeup. Henry Irving in 1881 and William Charles Macready throughout his career, 1816 through 1851, were black in the role. George Vandenhoff, whose acting career began in 1839, mentions a house manager's walking into his dressing room "as I had just finished my change of dress, and washed off the last tint of Othello's *swarthy* hue."[19] William Winter, the *New York Tribune* reviewer, reports an anecdote that, "having no black stocking," Junius Brutus Booth once "blackened his legs as well as his face and hands."[20] Despite Jim Crow prohibitions that reflect increased racial sensitivities at the times of performance and publication, Frederick Warde in 1920 recalls matter-of-factly Louis James's "dark" Othello of the 1890s.

> When playing Othello, standing by the bedside of Desdemona in the last act, apostrophising her sleeping form, he took some of the dark color of his make-up and marked a moustache and imperial on the face of the sleeping figure. It was unnoticed by the audience, but later, as other actors came upon the scene and saw the face of Desdemona lying on the pillow wreathed in golden hair but disfigured by apparent hirsute tufts over her mouth and chin, they were convulsed with laughter and the effect of a great tragic scene was destroyed.[21]

Hostile reviews of Ira Aldridge's 1833 London performance included such phrases as "fitted by his nativity and complexion to play the part without the aid of art" and "his face being of a natural instead of an acquired tint."[22] Neither phrase implies that the Othello of "art and acquired tint" must be tawny; in fact, both assume Othellos "played dark." Even the pictorial representations of Kean himself in the role do not provide unanimous testimony to his tawniness. In at least one (the first illustration), he looks both rather darkly made up and "African."[23]

This sampling of theater materials suffices, I trust, to show that reconstructing the color of nineteenth-century stage Othellos is murky and ambiguous. But the focus of theater historians on the makeup color itself is not merely despairing of precise results; it is largely a regrettable focus, as it asks an empty question. For, if the choice of tawny or black stage makeup did *not* reflect the literary debate about Othello's ancestry and did *not* evoke the racial feelings of audiences, then the whole matter becomes merely an ephemeral on-stage accidental. Determining what nineteenth-century audiences experienced should be our concern. The question is, I believe, both answerable and significant: however bronzed the makeup or oriental the costuming, those audiences saw an African, a blackamoor Othello. If so, then however "nearly white" the makeup, antebellum southern audiences would have experienced that same Othello, a blackamoor. Three examples must suffice to show that however unreconstructable is the onstage detail of makeup hue, we can nevertheless understand audiences' theater experience.

If residents of Macon in 1852 warned Watkins against an Othello "played dark," the incident shows that they knew the role thus, that a blackamoor was their experience. No makeup could obliterate that experience. Thus Dormon could properly use the incident at most to prove that—in Macon, 1852—burnt cork was "objectionable." But Watkins's successful performance, for so he reports his reception, proves that Othello, known as a "played dark" role, had *not* been an "objectionable figure."

The 1881 production in which Henry Irving and Edwin Booth alternated as Othello and Iago illustrates the paradox more fully. Katherine Goodale's adulation of Booth is highly subjective: "You are the first Othello I have seen, Mr. Booth, whose skin does not make me shudder." Thus her description of him as "a slightly

Figure 1. Edmund Kean as Othello
Courtesy Harvard Theatre Collection

bronzed son of the desert" is not necessarily accurate description of his makeup.[24] Her comments should be balanced against the report by Ellen Terry, the production's Desdemona, that Booth promised her, "I shall never make you black. When I take your hand I shall have a corner of my drapery in my hand. That will protect you."[25] By itself, this use of "black" would not assure us that Booth used burnt cork or its equivalent, for Terry might be complimenting him as being chivalrously gentle. Was Miss Goodale color blind from love? Was Miss Terry intending "black" to mean only "dirty, from (any) makeup"? What color was Booth's Othello? Yet these conflicting testimonies share an understanding of the theater experience of Othello as a blackamoor. If Booth used tawny makeup, he was but one of many, yet Miss Goodale's compliment indicates a norm of communicated blackness—"You are *the first* Othello . . . ." And Booth's drapery could have protected Ellen Terry from brown, red, or tan as well as black makeup without affecting his promise that "I shall never make you black," which reveals at the least Booth's obliviousness to the precious rationales for a non-African Othello.[26]

A comparable maze of primary material exists even with Edmund Kean's 1814 innovation itself. Illustrations of Kean's Othello conflict among themselves about his tawniness. Several reviews and Henry Crabb Robinson's diary, all treating the putatively decisive opening night, fail to mention the innovation in makeup. And one hostile reviewer, William Robson writing pseudonymously, derided Kean's Othello as "a little vixenish black girl in short petticoats." Obviously, Kean had not satisfied Robson's desire for tragic stature. But does the addition of "black" square with the physical appearance of Kean? George Henry Lewes, in *On Actors and the Art of Acting* (1875), insisted that the "very tragedy" depended on recognizing that "Othello is black," yet in memory he singled out Kean's acting of the role as exemplary.[27] The visual disparities, the reviewers' silence, Lewes's comment, and even Robson's term "black" do not call into question Kean's innovation, but they do demonstrate that an onstage detail and audience reception are separable. A tawny Kean could evoke the perception and memory of Othello as a blackamoor.

Theater reminiscences cannot determine for us exactly what makeup was used. Yet they agree on a blackamoor protagonist, and no actor's decision—bronzed makeup, oriental attire, elocutionary or busy style, more gentility or more range in characterization—could subvert this experience or destroy the play's sympathetic treatment of miscegenetic love. Such a boldly simple interpretation of the primary material, including large numbers of antebellum southern performances, is possible if one resists the lures of social history and brahmin critical sensitivities that encourage myopic concentration on makeup. Expecting realism, we have thought that surely turban, burnouse, and sooty makeup must have signified blackamoor, and that other costuming and other makeup must have provided a character identification mutually exclusive of blackamoor. Not so in 1820 or 1855.[28] We are struck by the differences among illustrations of Kean as Othello, but much more significant is what they share over against Kean in such roles as Hamlet and Sir Giles Overreach (Figures 1–4).

Further proof comes from surviving nineteenth-century promptbooks. What did an audience hear and not hear? Most nineteenth-century promptbooks show considerable cutting, as much as 1,000 lines. The nineteenth-century stage preserved its inheritance of cutting to remove faults of decorum. Melodrama, thriving on moral absolutes, on villains without redeeming qualities, on heroes without warts, lice, or halitosis, reinforced and extended the cutting. For example, the whole of act 4, scene 1, was regularly cut, as it had been in the eighteenth century, thus eliminating the "gross" and "ridiculous" behavior of Othello's faint and eavesdropping. And Othello must not slap Desdemona. Concern for sexual propriety meant changing Othello's "What sense had I of their stolen hours of lust" to "stolen hours of unfaithfulness" and cutting Iago's fabrication of Cassio's erotic dream. Even "happiness to their sheets" became "happiness be theirs," and one by one all instances of "whore" were removed, or euphemisms such as "a simple friend" and "a subtle one" were substituted.[29]

The more one knows of the cutting and altering, the more impressive is the survival of references to Othello's blackness. The text

Figure 2. Edmund Kean as Othello
From the Art Collection of the Folger
Shakespeare Library

Figure 3. Edmund Kean as Hamlet
Courtesy Harvard Theatre Collection

Figure 4. Edmund Kean as Sir Giles Overreach
Courtesy Harvard Theatre Collection

was subjected to the most thorough scrutiny, purifying genre, hero, and language. Decorum and sexual reticence were respected, but the racial prejudice of the age was not a comparable influence. Such signals in dialogue of Othello's blackness as Iago's "a measure to the health of black Othello" and Othello's own "Haply for I am black" remain untouched in surviving promptbooks. Brabantio's "To fall in love with what she feared to look on . . . Against all rules of nature" speech was usually retained—as was Brabantio's being answered, silenced, defeated by Othello's explanation of the wooing and by Desdemona's declaration, "But here's my husband." The play's values—the goodness of the love of its blackamoor and a Venetian—remain solidly in nineteenth-century promptbooks. The script preserved Othello as blackamoor. For those in the pit and the galleries, no makeup would obliterate their awareness of that fact.

Decisive testimony of how audiences perceived Othello, irrespective of makeup, even "near-white" makeup, comes from the many parodies of *Othello* written and performed in the nineteenth century.[30] The most popular in the United States, with five editions in the 1870s, *Othello Ethiopian Burlesque,* jests repeatedly about race and racial intermarriage. For example, Othello and Desdemona have a duet, "Dey say dat in the dark all cullers am de same." The playbill for *Rice's Grand Shakespearian Burlesque* described "Otello" as "a Nigger good as a White Man, and a little gooderer" and said that Desdemona "became Mistress Otello in spite of Papa's restrictions—black looks—lucky thing for Otello she hadn't any brother, or he might look both black and blue." The racial humor is commonplace and stale, but its use in these parodies presupposed that the legitimate stage had conveyed, by whatever means, a blackamoor Othello. The parodies presupposed audiences that knew Shakespeare's *Othello* as the story of a miscegenetic love.

Othello was *the* blackamoor in the popular imagination. The Shakespeare text had communicated Othello's nature. The romantic stage aesthetic, oblivious to anomalies in costuming or makeup, kept audiences from letting the visual appearance of a particular Othello mold its own precise character identification. As the parodies demonstrate, a performance of *Othello* did not exist in a vacuum, its protagonist at the outset an unknown. Othello was a blackamoor.

Thus, antebellum southern audiences understood Othello to be a blackamoor. But did they find Othello an "offensive figure"? The four performances usually cited as showing audience objections to *Othello* involve southern cities, Charleston in 1806, Baltimore in 1819, Macon, Georgia, in 1852, and Mobile in 1860. Are they, as theater history finds them, representative of a pervasive southern antipathy, an antipathy that "near-white" makeup could somehow mitigate? How convincing is each?

A British traveler, John Lambert, claimed a prohibition against staging *Othello* in Charleston in 1807.

> I expected to find the Charleston stage well supplied with *sooty negroes,* who would have performed the *African* and *Savage* characters, in the dramatic pieces, to the life; instead of which the delusion was even worse than on our own stage; for so far from employing *real negroes,* the performers would not even condescend to *blacken* their faces, or dress in any manner resembling an African. This I afterwards learnt was occasioned by motives of *policy,* lest the negroes in Charleston should conceive, from being represented on the stage, and having their colour, dress, manners, and customs imitated by the white people, that they were very important personages; and might take improper liberties in consequence of it. For this reason, also, Othello and other plays where a black man is the hero of the piece are not allowed to be performed.[31]

Thomas A. Cooper's 1806 performances initiating the star system in Charleston included eight Shakespeare plays. Does Lambert's "not allowed" explain (partially, for the passive frustrates) the absence of *Othello?* If so, it did not last long, for Cooper performed in *Othello* twice in the 1808–1809 Charleston season, and the play appeared at least annually thereafter through 1819–1820. Even if Lambert reported theater fact rather than street scuttlebutt, his testimony cannot represent southern or even Charlestonian attitudes.

Carlisle, for one, has found the Baltimore incident the key to unlock large doors of performance silence.

> In America the question of Othello's color had become particularly acute. Thus Henry Wallack was considered ill-advised when he selected Othello for his first appearance in this country (during the 1818–19 season in Philadelphia)—"and more so," writes William Wood, "from his persisting to make him a black, in a place where the general practice prevailed of

showing him a tawny man." The presence of Negro slaves in the United States made the idea of Desdemona's marriage to a black man seem to many people not only shocking but incomprehensible, and Garrick's conception of violent passions unrestrained by the time-ingrained habits of civilization would have suggested to Wallack's American audience an immediate threat to society.[32]

But William Wood's remarks, the only surviving comment on Henry Wallack's performance, are a dubious cornerstone for generalizing:

Henry Wallack also first appeared in America during this season as Othello, a part ill chosen, and more so from his persisting to make him a black, in a place where the general practice prevailed of showing him a tawny Moor. This excellent actor, by an injudicious pertinacity in acting Richard or Othello, made an unfavorable impression in Baltimore, which required some little time to efface. His after performances in melodramatic parts as Daran, Roderic, Dhu, Rob Roy, Ethiop, and Don Juan, obtained him the favorable estimate hazarded by his first attempt. At Philadelphia he was persuaded to a more judicious choice on his first appearance. The "Libertine," as produced at Covent Garden, was selected and given with care, H. Wallack as Don Juan. It succeeded well.[33]

Is Wood's "place" a slaveholding and color-sensitive United States? Or is it more likely Baltimore, a city then abounding in feelings against theater and thus unlikely to have had theatrically sophisticated audiences? Is Othello "a part ill chosen" because of the play's subject matter? Wood valued the play highly,[34] and he had recorded without comment receipts from twelve earlier *Othello* performances. Probably more relevant is that Henry Wallack specialized in comedy, becoming best known for his Falstaff. Richard and Othello were beyond his talents. The "general practice" of a tawny Moor cannot antedate Kean's London innovation in 1814. Probably Thomas A. Cooper had performed most of the Baltimore Othellos of the decade before 1819.[35] In the Kemble school, Cooper had played Othello in London in 1804, presumably blackfaced. There is no evidence that mid-career he imitated Kean in the role. And in the memoirs of the tragedian who rivaled Cooper, James Fennell, it is a Baltimorean who during a performance offered "to buy that intelligent Negro."[36] Such considerations circumscribe the import of Wood's "more so from his persisting to make him a black" to the uniqueness of the one actor in the one performance.

Regrettably, nothing exists to supplement Noah Ludlow's diary entry that James Wallack, Jr., refused to play Othello, being "afraid of the negro part," on December 24, 1860, in Mobile. War was imminent. Feelings were undoubtedly running high on the streets and in the bars; possibly, this tension panicked the actor. The phrase "the negro part," not found in theater reminiscences, suggests such a hypothesis. And earlier in 1860 *Othello* had enjoyed a good box office and a favorable review *in Mobile*.[37] Therefore, the report of Wallack's fear will not support the chronological hypothesis that Dormon offers. Rather, it suggests a singular occasion combining heightened social tension with the reaction of a skittish actor.

Nor does an incident in Macon in 1852 permit generalizing about the use of "near-white" makeup or about Othello's having become an "objectionable figure" in the 1850s. Dormon cites the diary in which Harry Watkins recorded being told that *Othello* was "very displeasing to many citizens" (theatergoers?), who would "not permit his being played dark."[38] The immediate diary context displays considerable complexity.

> *Tuesday 21st.* This is the most fastidious town I ever performed in. I am opposed to offensive language on the stage, but it would be impossible to please the people of Macon without expunging all the humor in a play; they deem everything smutty that creates a laugh. *Wednesday 22nd.* Played Othello. The audience called for me but I did not respond. I was told that "Othello" is very displeasing to many citizens. They will not permit his being played dark so, to avoid a row, I played him nearly white. My partners, Myers, Coolidge and Rogers are not the slightest use to me. All the work is on my shoulders. McVicker unwell. Seized with a spasm after the first piece. Compelled to change the farce.

If his performance was indeed a success, that applause complicates our evaluation of the threat he felt before the performance. And the larger context of the diary reveals prejudices about Macon particularly, the South generally, and personal distress that may color the diary enough to undermine its reliability.[39]

But even the most generous weight given to Wallack's fears and Watkins's makeup change is overwhelmed by, say, the sixteen *Othello* performances in Charleston in the 1850s.[40] Wallack and Watkins are specks on the large canvas of box office receipts and newspaper announcements from hundreds of performances on various antebellum southern stages. Actors' apprehensions, production modifications for a southern stage, and theater disturbances should have been grist for the mill of theater anecdotalists; in actuality, theater memoirs offer no hint of such controversy about *Othello*.[41] Reviews, regrettably few, respond appreciatively. In 1849 the *Picayune* reported of the New Orleans performance of William Charles Macready, who unquestionably used black makeup, that "We have never yet seen anything so brilliant; such acting would redeem the vices of the stage, were they tenfold what they are."[42] The reviewer I began with had enjoyed an 1860 performance in Mobile.

And the critic in the *Augusta* (Georgia) *Chronicle* for February 1 and 5, 1821, writes effusive praise of Thomas A. Cooper's Othello. Such a review must be seen in its entirety to appreciate its lack of prejudice against the play's values and central character:

> Mr. COOPER made his appearance on our boards last evening, in the character of *Othello*—and, notwithstanding the inclemency of the weather, he was cordially greeted by a numerous and fashionable auditory. The character we think, was sustained with more energy and spirit, than we have ever before seen him exhibit; and the approbation of the audience was testified by repeated plaudits.
>
> On Wednesday Mr. Cooper made his appearance in *Othello*. The character of Othello is ingenuous, noble and energetic—It requires neither "pomp or circumstance" nor the factitious aid of stage trick, to help it out—it speaks for itself in its own native sublimity. Hence the character is rendered more difficult of personation—and requires a master's hand to delineate its natural, bold, and prominent features— Othello's vindication of himself, before the "grave and reverend seignors" was delivered in a chaste, distinct, and unaffected manner. But in the more interesting and impassioned part of the character, where the insidious policy of *Iago* is too successfully employed, the personation we think was complete. The agonizing uncertainty of *Desdemona's* fidelity— the deep workings of jealousy when he learns that the handkerchief is in the possession of *Cassio*, were managed with so much effect, that for a while we mixed our feelings with the scene, and forgot it was ideal. And when the treachery of *Iago* is discovered, the compunctious visitings of conscience were so forcibly expressed, and with such intensity of feelings, that a long and affecting silence pervaded the audience.—In his amatory scenes, Mr. Cooper is peculiarly happy—the soft cadence of his voice lingers on the ear, in melting sweetness. He never loses sight of his attitudes, and general actions is [*sic*] appropriate, graceful, and dignified—But we have reached the limit prescribed ourselves, and must stop. "More anon."[43]

To have seen it! From such negative evidence especially, a rather different pair of conclusions from Dormon's have merit: Othello was almost never an objectionable figure in antebellum southern playhouses, and playing him as near-white would have been not only unlikely but pointless.

But how could *Othello* have sustained popularity on the stages in the slaveholding South, up to the Civil War? Is there something inexplicable in finding an 1860 Mobile audience, or any antebellum southern audience, being moved to care about the "fair" Desdemona and the "sooty" blackamoor at the same time that southerners, including those very theatergoers, defended slavery, the black as property? Surely not. Theater was separate from the affairs of the day. The nineteenth-century theater in America most prominently offered Art, deliberately distanced from life. Seen in the best historical reconstructions, theater generally in the years before the Civil War was melodramatic, presentational, participatory, democratic, and a theater of "the star."[44] This theater offered "enchantment," something quite other than the mundane and the routine. It was "the show" those in the pit and galleries went to see—and to applaud, to hiss or to compete with, simply to attend, enjoying the occasion.

The circus acrobat may be performing, technically, only the routines of a physical education classroom, but he does not seem thus because of the drumrolled fanfare of tension, the spotlight, the spangles and sequins. Yet the circus is our exceptional mode of experiencing art. We can easily underestimate the theater's being a special world. Our immersion in a realistic aesthetic is more than cinematic costuming and "ah . . . you know" diction. We can confuse the television drama and the commercials, for dramatic art and advertising use the same mode of credibility. And choreographing to musical accompaniment the gymnastics floor exercises blurs what once had been the clear distinction between athletic competition and circus entertainment. Our artistic experiences give us little help to understand an era in which the first Negro minstrel companies performed in blackface, thus declaring the presentationalism of Art.[45]

Antebellum southern audiences regarded theatrical performance as Art, quite distinct from life. That distinction resides within many accounts. I will offer three.

Robert Montgomery Bird's *The Gladiator,* the story of the slave Spartacus rebelling against Rome, had for Bird parallels with the Nat Turner uprising. The play became a staple in the repertoire of Edwin Forrest. In 1838, momentarily caught up in a whirlwind of partisan Yankee politics, Forrest gave a Fourth of July speech to a Republican rally, a speech printed almost immediately. Yet in 1839 *The Gladiator* was a box office success throughout Forrest's tour of southern theaters.[46] It was a superb vehicle for Forrest's voice and muscularity, and it abounded with spectacle from Roman antiquity. It was (only) theatrical entertainment.

The *Nashville Daily Gazette* expressed regret about an 1855 performance of *The Old Plantation,* one of the "replies" to *Uncle Tom's Cabin.* "We have always regarded theatrical representation of negro life as in bad taste, especially so when attempted by a theatrical company. . . . Negro shows and the drama are two very separate and distinct things, each doing very well when kept to itself, but producing a flat and insipid effect when mixed. . . . We strike against all unions that mar beauty and promote discord."[47] Yet the *Othello* performance in Nashville that same year prompted no such objection.

Third, Charles Mason, Thomas Abthorpe Cooper, J. W. Forbes, Junius Brutus Booth, and Edwin Forrest had performed in *Othello* in New Orleans between 1836 and 1839. A touring opera company had given five commercially successful performances of Rossini's *Otello* in New Orleans in 1836. No newspaper objected to play or title character nor suggested any audience objection on any of these occasions. On the other hand, in 1837, when "Old Corn Meal," a familiar New Orleans street vendor, had appeared in the burletta *Life in New Orleans,* a newspaper noted that "some objected to the introduction of a Negro on stage."[48] The topical burletta was at best minimally Art, and "Old Corn Meal" was unmistakably not.

But, in the antebellum South, Shakespeare was consummate Art and thus was part of a city's coming of age culturally. *Othello* suited well an actor's theater in the "age of Melodrama." It was a superb actor's vehicle, its "act 3" being frequently selected for potpourri benefits. *Othello* had a melodramatic villain, sentiment, violent incidents, and a distantly exotic story. "Had any other man but Shakespeare made such . . . an ill assorted match it would have damned him."[49] It was a story (safely) far away and long ago particularly because it *was* "Shakespeare."

Theater as Art kept Othello from being "the negro part" on the stages in the slaveholding South. *Othello* thus could and did flourish on antebellum southern stages, could and did move those audiences.

No antebellum southern audience would have been prepared for the "untheatrical" experience of a black actor as Othello. That became a reality in the twentieth century.

In 1979, in Atlanta, the Alliance management had rejected any Caucasian in the title role. The commitment to *Othello* and the signing of Paul Winfield occurred simultaneously.[50] The tandem of Richard Dreyfuss and Winfield (see Figure 5) generated an impressive box office. The scheduled three-week run sold out immediately; a fourth week was added and sold out. The immediately preceding Alliance production, *Little Foxes,* had drawn 14,443; *Othello* played to 19,247 plus 4,601 high school students in special matinees. Whereas *Little Foxes* had produced $27,000 in single-ticket sales, *Othello* brought in over $66,000. Most remarkably, the entire run had only six unsold seats. Blacks constituted roughly 5 percent of the audience.

Winfield's presence provided the Alliance with the crucial leverage for the (black) city government of Atlanta to fund two free "in the park" performances of *Othello,* drawing over 30,000. From this new rapprochement of the Alliance with City Hall grew not only an expanded "in the park" Shakespeare in spring 1980, but also city funds to support the 1980 Alliance production of *For Colored Girls who have considered Suicide when the Rainbow is Enuf.* Its audiences averaged 17 percent blacks. The Alliance season-ticket sales rose from a record-setting 8,800 in 1978–1979 to over 15,000 in 1979–1980, thanks—as the Alliance management acknowledges—to the reception of the Winfield-Dreyfuss *Othello.* Tangibly, the Alliance gained much from its selection of this production and these stars.

Much in the Othello characterization depended wholly on Winfield's being a black. Like Olivier, Winfield made the decisiveness of his convictions about Desdemona's guilt evident by

Figure 5. Richard Dreyfuss as Iago and Paul Winfield as Othello in the Alliance Theatre production, 1979
Courtesy Alliance Theatre

removing the Christian symbol of neck chain-and-cross. For Winfield's Othello, it was a thoroughly European symbol as well. Whereas Olivier had retreated thereafter into bestialism, Winfield's portrayal sought the fetal protection of his own elemental yet rich racial heritage. It culminated in the ritual chant he chose to substitute for Othello's "trance." In a press interview Winfield volunteered that here the text had "disturbed me a lot."[51] Attired in ritual robes of native Africa, he chanted over a pile of time-whitened bones, squatting to beat the stage floor rhythmically, eventually collapsing from the very intensity of the ceremony. Counter to the text, only then did Iago enter. All of Othello's asides as he watched Cassio and Iago discuss Bianca—immediately after the "trance"—were cut.

In the final scene, as he entered to the sleeping Desdemona, Winfield remained barefoot, wearing a loosely flowing caftan—fully African. With a manservant, he performed in utter silence a slow tribal ritual, seemingly a priestly cleansing. The African pantomime accentuated the calm of the opening of act 5, scene 2, especially as sandwiched between the chaos of act 5, scene 1, the wounding of Cassio and the murdering of Roderigo, and the melee which culminated in Othello's suicidal blow. The suicide shocked. Blood gushed as Winfield slashed his throat. Earlier, Othello's wounding Iago had been an emasculating groin-slash. The unusually swift-paced finale following the pantomime was the culmination of a stunningly powerful portrayal by Winfield.

And in the Alliance production the largest affective movement in the play had worked: an audience found itself gradually forced to abandon its enchantment with Iago, moving to an abhorrence that redoubled tragic regard for Othello. Credit goes to Chappell's sensitivity and control, to Winfield's acting power, and to Dreyfuss—his skill in creating rapport and his unselfishness in permitting an audience to jump ship, to hate him. In the opening scene, audiences (led by the many *Goodbye Girl* fans) responded to his charismatic charm, spontaneity, and need for support and were caught in over-easy assent to the assumption of Caucasian superiority in such slurs as "black ram tupping your white ewe." The reversal of that assumption began with Winfield's commanding presence and his quietly authoritative "Keep up your bright swords" in the second scene. It should have grown in the "senate scene," act 1, scene 3, but, although Desdemona's face and figure might explain Othello's interest, her thin, insipid speaking was especially unconvincing in the crucial "Here's my husband" speech. Her petulant bang on the table accompanying "Let me go with him" had more life, but only as the outburst of a silly adolescent. Such a vapid Desdemona risks our finding Othello doting, not loving. And in this scene, the only time in the play, Winfield seemed to assume the role of "uppity darkie" expecting and receiving Venetian patronizing. He cowered, resentful but silently so. How were we intended to respond to the Venetian racial slurs?

Winfield's and Dorothy Fielding's kissing in the Cyprus scene (or, rather, its rumored occurrence) prompted a handful of hate letters, but the response of the audience in the theater was not that crude or censorious. When Othello and Desdemona first kissed, there were audible gasps, but gasps testifying to the depth of audience involvement. Through the opening sequence of four scenes the blacks attending in numbers beyond Alliance precedent promoted an audience self-consciousness that, with aesthetic appropriateness, electrified the play's presenting and then defeating racial antipathy.

In 1979, in the South, the theater could present *Othello,* with a black as Othello, successfully.

I have reported my own theater experience with the Winfield-Dreyfuss *Othello;* various antebellum *Othello* performances are accessible only from reconstruction of tidbits of primary material, partial and frustrating. And, of course, there are huge contrasts between the two—between Winfield and an Edwin Forrest or Thomas A. Cooper, between the resources of the Alliance and those of the Memphis theater management in 1850, between a 1979 audience and one in 1829 or 1859. Nevertheless, three parallels deserve highlighting.

First, neither antebellum theaters nor the Alliance provided the full dimensions Shakespeare gives his protagonist. The cutting in both included portions of Othello's language and behavior. Junius

Brutus Booth, Edwin Forrest, and Paul Winfield protected their Othellos. But, significantly, "the South" was not the cause. Surviving nineteenth-century promptbooks usually cut most of the fourth act, including Othello's "fit" and his eavesdropping, but the cut text was performed everywhere. The promptbooks do not provide evidence of any additional cuts done especially for southern performance, nothing special to accommodate the play to southern audiences. Mobile, Nashville, and Charleston heard the same script and saw the same performance from the visiting star as did Philadelphia, New York, and London. Yet the Alliance fourth act was only a little more faithful to the Quarto or Folio. Winfield had refused to play the trance, and director Chappell, together with Winfield, had experimented with and finally rejected Othello's asides as he watches Iago talk with Cassio. The pair of decisions preserved this Othello from the severest derision in Shakespeare's text, from becoming first a blithering, frothing vegetable and then a comic butt, absurdly and thus tragically bamboozled. Instead, this Othello had retreated into a ritualized primitivism and then had watched in desperate silence. But neither the southern location nor atmosphere of Atlanta had determined Winfield's decision: he would have refused to perform the fit, would have chosen (his words) "to become blacker" with the tribal chanting if the production had been in Boston or San Francisco. Winfield and Chappell had disliked the asides for technical reasons; in deciding to cut, they gave no thought to any possible "southern" sensitivities in the audience. Paul Robeson was likely correct in saying, about his 1943 New York City *Othello,* "Try playing it in Memphis." But the uniqueness of the South was not evident in 1843, even in 1859, or in 1979.

Second, today, as in the nineteenth century, distortions of the racial dimension of *Othello* occur outside theater buildings. The Alliance production received much critical attention. Major newspapers, suburban newspapers, arty giveaways, radio, and television featured and reviewed it. They shared a silence about the play's interracial nature beyond the epithet "The Moor" and whatever recognition Winfield's name gave. Yet that silence is not distinctly southern. Most recent *Othello* criticism ignores Othello's race and color. Not atypical is the lengthy discussion of Othello's character in the *Times Literary Supplement,* June 20, 1980: its only mention of color was "Time is like Othello's blackness, a factor constantly present but never decisive, never pointedly leant on by the playwright to underpin his case."[52] Such ignoring of Othello's color is merely the flip side of nineteenth-century efforts to argue away Othello's African blackness. For neither tendency understands the import of the play's interracial love, its endorsement and subsequent tragic destruction.

But, third, immune from the critical tempests and silence, both antebellum audiences and Alliance audiences felt those values. Their emotional experiences were aesthetic, not sociological. For *Othello* performances in New Orleans of 1838, Mobile of 1860, and Atlanta of 1979, being "in the South" did not restrict Art. Theater worked; Shakespeare worked.

NOTES

1. The best historical study of Othello's blackness is G. K. Hunter, "Othello and Colour Prejudice," originally a British Academy lecture, in his *Dramatic Identities and Cultural Tradition* (New York: Barnes and Noble, 1978), pp. 31–59. See also Eldred D. Jones, *Othello's Countrymen: The African in English Renaissance Drama* (Oxford: Oxford University Press, 1965); G. K. Hunter, "Elizabethans and Foreigners," in *Shakespeare in His Own Age,* vol. 17 of *Shakespeare Survey,* ed. Allardyce Nicoll (Cambridge: Cambridge University Press, 1965); and Winthrop D. Jordan, *White Over Black: American Attitudes Toward the Negro, 1550–1812* (Chapel Hill: University of North Carolina Press, 1968), esp. chaps. 4 and 6. I am indebted to my colleague Michael Cassity for calling the Jordan study to my attention and for reading, as a historian, a draft of this essay.

2. James H. Dormon, Jr., *Theater in the Ante Bellum South 1815–1861* (Chapel Hill: University of North Carolina Press, 1967). The quotation appears on p. 276.

3. Adams's discussion of *Othello* occurs in a letter and in "The Character of Desdemona" in James Hackett, *Notes, Criticisms & Correspondence Upon Shakespeare's Plays and Actors* (1863; rpt. New York: Benjamin Blom, 1968), pp. 217–49; the passages quoted appear on pp. 224–25.

4. *Coleridge's Shakespearean Criticism,* ed. T. M. Raysor (1930; rpt. London: Everyman's Library, 1960), 1:42. Cf. Lecture IV at Bristol, 1813–14: "Mr C. ridiculed the idea of making Othello a negro. He was a gallant Moor, of royal blood, combining a high sense of Spanish and Italian feeling" (Raysor, 2:228).

5. See, for example, the excerpts in the appendix "Othello's Colour" in *A New Variorum Edition of Shakespeare: Othello,* ed. H. H. Furness (Philadelphia: J. B. Lippincott, 1886), pp. 389–96.

6. A. C. Bradley, *Shakespearean Tragedy* (1904; rpt. London: Macmillan, 1965), p. 165.

7. Dormon, p. 277.

8. My awareness of the frequency of *Othello* performances draws on the many available local theater histories. See the "Selected Bibliography" in David Grimsted, *Melodrama Unveiled: American Theater and Culture 1800–1850* (Chicago: University of Chicago Press, 1968), more extensively annotated in his "A Mirror for Nature" (Ph.D. diss., University of California, Berkeley, 1963). See, for example, William Stanley Hoole, *The Ante-Bellum Charleston Theatre* (Tuscaloosa, Ala.: University of Alabama Press, 1946); Charles C. Ritter, "The Theatre in Memphis, Tennessee, from its Beginnings to 1859" (Ph.D. diss., University of Iowa, 1956); Mary Morgan Duggar, "Theatre in Mobile to 1860" (M.A. thesis, University of Alabama, 1941); John Jacob Weisert, "A Large and Fashionable Audience: A Checklist of Performances at the Louisville Theatre 1846 to 1866" (Ph.D. diss., University of Louisville, 1955); Nelle Smither, *A History of the English Theatre in New Orleans* (New York: Benjamin Blom, 1967; reprinted from *Louisiana Historical Quarterly* 28 [1945]).

9. See Grimsted, *Melodrama Unveiled,* pp. 76–98, for one useful survey of the practical matters of acting and staging plays in the first half of the nineteenth century.

10. See such recent accounts, essentially in accord, as those found in Carol Jones Carlisle, *Shakespeare from the Greenroom* (Chapel Hill: University of North Carolina Press, 1969); Gino Matteo, *Shakespeare's Othello: The Study and the Stage, 1604–1904* (Salzburg: University of Salzburg, 1974); and Ruth Cowhig, "Actors, Black and Tawny, in the Role of Othello,—and their Critics," *Theatre Research International* 4 (1979): 133–46.

11. Matteo, p. 232.

12. Cowhig, p. 134.

13. Carlisle, p. 192. Later, Carlisle adds that "Othello must be set apart from Desdemona and her countrymen, if not by a pronounced color difference, then in some other way. The idea that he is meant to be, not a 'blackamoor,' but a true Moor—a person of mixed Berber and Arab ancestry, with Mauritania as his people's native home and with the conquest of Granada as one of their exploits—met this requirement in a particularly satisfying way since it made him an exotic figure without offending the taste or prejudices of the audience" (p. 194).

14. Evidence for blackfaced Othellos will be provided later in the essay. Stage, audience, and social history together may explain why a particular performance of *Othello* was cancelled or poorly received. But the four performances usually cited look suspicious; they are discussed later.

15. On *Othello,* even the *New York Tribune* theater reviewer William Winter is a literary voice. He insisted that "Othello is not a Negro and he should not be represented as one" and added that "Othello, although called a Moor, is, unequivocally, drawn as an Englishman." Finding few performances that satisfied his idealization, he even suggested that "matchless though it is as a piece of dramatic construction, the community, perhaps, would not suffer an irreparable loss if it were altogether relegated from the stage to the library." Yet often Winter admits that the very performances he denounced thrived at the box office. See *Shakespeare on the Stage* (New York: Moffat, Yard, 1911), pp. 252, 288, 301, and 270.

16. George C. D. Odell, *Annals of the New York Stage,* vol. 3 (New York: Columbia University Press, 1928), pp. 62–63.

17. Quoted in M. St. Clare Byrne, "Make-Up," in *The Oxford Companion to the Theatre,* 3rd ed. (London: Oxford University Press, 1964), p. 607. The evaluation of Rede's book is Byrne's.

18. Katherine Goodale, *Behind the Scenes with Edwin Booth* (Boston: Houghton Mifflin, 1931), p. 212.

19. George Vandenhoff, *Leaves from An Actor's Note-Book* (New York: D. Appleton, 1860), p. 109.

20. Winter, pp. 255–56.

21. Frederick Warde, *Fifty Years of Make-Believe* (New York: International Press Syndicate, 1920), p. 248.

22. Quoted from Herbert Marshall and Mildred Stock, *Ira Aldridge: The Negro Tragedian* (London: Rockliff, 1958), pp. 121 and 126. A remark in a third review seems to offer a rather heavy blow to any general acceptance of Kean's innovation. "Mr. Aldridge did not present us with so black a face as the representatives of Othello generally assume. His complexion is almost a light brown" (p. 122).

23. Representations of Kean as Othello that contrast with Fig. 1 can be found in Charles H. Shattuck, *Shakespeare on the American Stage from the Hallams to Edwin Booth* (Washington, D.C.: Folger Shakespeare Library, 1976), p. 41, and in Joseph Donohue, *Theatre in the Age of Kean* (Totowa, N.J.: Rowman and Littlefield, 1975), Plate 6.

24. Goodale, pp. 208 and 212.

25. Ellen Terry, *The Story of My Life* (New York: McClure, 1908), p. 222.

26. Miss Terry's memoirs offer evidence that Irving's makeup was quite different: "I am bound to say that I thought of Mr. Booth's 'protection' with some yearning the next week when I played Desdemona to *Henry's* Othello. Before he had done with me I was nearly as black as he" (p. 222). Henry Irving's biographer grandson, for one, confirms Irving's 1881 makeup as black: "He abandoned subtlety of costume and appeared as a gorgeously apparelled African and blacker than was the custom." In describing Irving's only other Othello performance, in 1876, he claims that Irving "modified to bronze the complexion of Othello which, by tradition, had become black." See Laurence Irving, *Henry Irving: The Actor and His World* (New York: Macmillan, 1952), pp. 277 and 272. Especially interesting here is the special pleading in ascribing originality—or courage—to Irving on both occasions. A mere five years separates the conflicting claims of black as "tradition" and "blacker than was the custom." A theater historian should not credit one as reliable and ignore the other, but the juxtaposed pair offers little help in determining the exact particulars of the onstage makeup of the nineteenth-century Othellos.

27. Carlisle has demonstrated some seeming internal inconsistencies in Lewes (*Greenroom*, p. 192), and I believe she is right in calling attention to the separability of "tawny" and "gentle" (p. 191). In isolation one sentence in her discussion would seem to anticipate my own interpretation: "Arguments over the Elizabethan meanings of 'Moor' and 'black,' [and] over the literal or dramatic interpretation of 'thick lips' and 'sooty bosom' . . .—these had flourished during the 'Bronze Age,' but they had left the stage largely untouched" (p. 194). I have referred elsewhere to the valuable achievement of this book (see *South Atlantic Bulletin*, 35 [Nov., 1971]: 95–100).

28. Discussion of costuming on early nineteenth-century American stages can be found in Grimsted, *Melodrama Unveiled;* Garff B. Wilson, *A History of American Acting* (Bloomington: Indiana University Press, 1966); and Richard Moody, *America Takes the Stage: Romanticism in American Drama and Theatre, 1750–1900* (Bloomington: Indiana University Press, 1955).

29. See especially Marvin Rosenberg, "The 'Refinement' of *Othello* in the Eighteenth Century British Theatre," *Studies in Philology* 51 (1954): 75–94. Matteo gives much attention to the cutting, including an appropriate corrective to Rosenberg's

emphasis on "atmosphere of sexuality" as grounds for much of the cutting (esp. pp. 197–8). See Charles H. Shattuck, *The Shakespeare Promptbooks: A Descriptive Catalogue* (Urbana: University of Illinois Press, 1965), pp. 354–79, for the surviving *Othello* promptbooks. One can determine cuts and preservations of individual lines in specific promptbooks, such as the "color" lines I discuss later, by using William P. Halstead, *Shakespeare as Spoken* (Ann Arbor: University Microfilms, 1977–1980); see vol. 11 for *Othello*.

Grimsted, *Melodrama Unveiled,* p. 128, discusses the cuts made in Philip Massinger's *A New Way to Pay Old Debts,* popular on nineteenth-century stages, cuts that include "several references to an impoverished hero's having lice and smelling bad." Grimsted's chapter "The Good Old Plays" provides a good, succinct discussion of older plays, especially Elizabethan, as they were used on the early nineteenth-century American stages; see also Shattuck, *Shakespeare on the American Stage.*

30. See *Nineteenth-Century Shakespeare Burlesques,* ed. Stanley W. Wells (Wilmington, Del.: Michael Glazier, 1978), 5 vols., and Henry E. Jacobs and Claudia D. Johnson, *An Annotated Bibliography of Shakespearean Burlesques, Parodies, and Travesties* (New York: Garland, 1976). Comprehensive theater histories give some attention to the parodies as one genre within the calendars of performances in nineteenth-century theaters, but the parodies are largely untapped resources of indirect evidence of the understanding of the plays. I know of no discussion of *Othello* as staged in the nineteenth century that refers to this derivative genre.

31. Quoted in Jordan, p. 405.

32. Carlisle, p. 192.

33. William B. Wood, *Personal Recollections of the Stage* (Philadelphia: Henry Carey Baird, 1855), p. 227.

34. Wood, for example, objected to cuts in act 4 made by "Many pretenders to this part" because the scene is "of the utmost importance to the progress of [Othello's] passion, and giving scope for the exercise of an actor's best talent" (pp. 203–204).

35. My guess about Baltimore Othellos comes from Reese Davis James, *Old Drury of Philadelphia: History of the Philadelphia Stage 1800–1835* (Philadelphia: University of Pennsylvania Press, 1932), which contains the calendar material from William Wood's "Daily Account Book," and from my reading of Wood's *Recollections.* "Records of Maryland's theatrical past are particularly sparse. Baltimore is certainly the most important theatrical center in the period without any stage history" (Grimsted, "Mirror for Nature," p. 530).

36. James Fennell, *An Apology for the Life of James Fennell Written by Himself* (Philadelphia: Moses Thomas, 1814), pp. 337–38.

37. I began my antebellum discussion with this review.

38. Dormon, p. 277. These phrases and the full diary entries are found in Maud and Otis Skinner, *One Man in his Time: The Adventures of H. Watkins, Strolling Player, 1845–1863 from his Journal* (Philadelphia: University of Pennsylvania Press, 1938), pp. 110–13. These pages also are the source of my biographical information. The Skinners have no comment about the "played dark" question.

39. Watkins was young and inexperienced. This was his first experience as manager of an acting company and, other than his post–Mexican War days in Texas, his first experience in the South. Ill-will toward Macon in particular probably began early, for its theater manager, sponsor of the tour, failed to supply travel money. For the 18th, four days before the *Othello,* his diary entry relates a pair of his troubles: "Had an angry discussion with Drew and his wife, the most unprincipled persons I've ever known. Being a favorite with the audience, she makes exactions that a man of any spirit would not submit to, demanding I shall play pieces to suit her vanity and

thinking I cannot do without them. . . . Fanny Mowbray . . . caused me wasted time and money, has by her conduct injured the business of the house. The steward of the hotel where we are boarding, one Mr. Hernandez, took a great fancy to Fanny and caused her room to be changed to another as her windows were too accommodating for the curiously inclined. It became town talk that Hernandez was constantly in her room. This has kept ladies from visiting the theatre."

Then Watkins reports the marriage of this "*happy* couple," the irony elaborated with "She I know to be a heartless coquette and everyone here says he is a villain and was the cause of his former wife's death." Fanny had been an old flame of Watkins; to gain victory over a rival suitor, Watkins had hired her and himself paid for her fare to Macon. Watkins's managerial and personal woes may blur his perspective and cast doubts on his *Othello* account.

40. See Hoole, pp. 187–88, for a list of *Othello* performance dates. Holbein, in the present volume, may alter that number slightly.

41. Frederick Warde, for example, recalled a tour in which he accompanied Edwin Booth. They played in Richmond, Charlotte, Columbia, Charleston, Savannah, Augusta, Atlanta, Macon, Montgomery, Mobile, Columbus, Chattanooga, and Nashville. In each city, *Othello* was a part of the repertoire. To illustrate the anachronisms that sometimes occurred because local theaters had only limited scenic resources, Warde cited an opening scene in *Othello* in which "the mansion of Brabantio" was "a small square set-piece about eight feet high and twelve feet long, painted to represent a rustic cottage with a door and window, the chimney appearing above a roof thatched with straw." The production's Brabantio, "mistaking the line of the roof for the ledge of the window, popped his head out of the chimney." Warde recalled a substitute Brabantio at the Charleston performance whose "speech was somewhat thick and uncertain—very suggestive of conviviality." But he managed to get through his part until he struck the world "preposterously," in the Senate scene, and that proved too much for him. He hiccoughed at the consonants and struggled with the syllables for some time but finally gave it up, sat down and fell asleep. *Fifty Years*, pp. 124 and 127–28. Generous sampling from Warde's recollections displays the absence of sensitivity to race or color.

42. See Alan S. Downer, *The Eminent Tragedian, William Charles Macready* (Cambridge: Harvard University Press, 1966), p. 295.

43. Quoted from Monique Davis Boyce, "The First Forty Years of the Augusta, Georgia, Theatre" (M.A. thesis, University of Georgia, 1957), pp. 110–12.

44. These reconstructions would include Grimsted, *Melodrama Unveiled;* Moody; Wilson; the "Introduction" to *Hiss the Villain*, ed. Michael Booth (New York: Benjamin Blom, 1964); and, though without any direct consideration of the American stage, Donohue; and Alan S. Downer, "Players and Painted Stage—Nineteenth Century Acting," *PMLA* 61 (1946): 522–76. On the other hand, most local theater histories accept each bit of primary evidence literally and let their apparently cumulative force stand unchallenged; for example, from them one could easily picture an audience hearing not a word, based on the accumulated evidence of "disturbances" and the absence of an understanding of participatory theater.

45. Moody, p. 46

46. See the introduction to the text of *The Gladiator* in *Dramas from the American Theatre 1762–1909*, ed. Richard Moody (Cleveland: World Publishing, 1966), pp. 229–40; and Grimsted, *Melodrama Unveiled*, p. 169.

47. Quoted in F. Garvin Davenport, *Cultural Life in Nashville on the Eve of the Civil War* (Chapel Hill: University of North Carolina Press, 1941), p. 129. Davenport makes no reference to performances of *Othello*.

48. Smither, pp. 141–42.

49. *Mississippi Free Trader* in 1836, quoted in William Bryan Gates, "The Theatre in Natchez," *Journal of Mississippi History* 3 (1941): 93.

50. Based on my interviews with Wallace Chappell, Artistic Director of the *Othello* production, and Bernard Havard, former Managing Director of the Alliance Theatre. Havard also made available the Alliance records, from which the subsequent attendance and box office figures come. I appreciate the considerable time and interest both men gave. For a fuller account of the entire production, see *Shakespeare Quarterly* 31 (1980): 218–220.

51. Winfield in an interview with Lawrence DeVine, the *Detroit Free Press* theater critic, published in DeVine's column on May 13, 1979.

52. John Bayles, "The Fragile Structure of *Othello*," *Times Literary Supplement*, June 20, 1980, p. 708. And in nearly a hundred pages dissecting the values and personalities of the major characters of *Othello*, Harold Skulsky made no mention of Othello's color; *Spirits Finely Touched* (Athens: University of Georgia Press, 1976), pp. 167–249.

PART II

Some Southern Shakespeare Festivals

"Bold To Play": Shakespeare in North Carolina

Larry S. Champion

The strong contemporary presence of Shakespearean productions in North Carolina has its roots in a vigorous theatrical tradition from the state's earliest days. Small touring bands of players performing on improvised stages in civic halls can be traced through public notices during the last third of the eighteenth century.[1] The State House in Raleigh, for example, was frequently used for "theatrical representations" and "sleight of hand performances,"[2] and a certain Robinson advertised in the *State Gazette of North Carolina* in New Bern (November 29, 1787) that he had made arrangements for an "elegant theatre" in Wilmington and planned to mount performances there for an entire month. Such improvised stages gave way to professional theaters as the towns grew sufficiently large to support them.[3] Apparently the first were in Wilmington, on the lower floor of Innes Academy around the turn of the century, and in Fayetteville, on the lower floor of the Masonic Lodge Building in 1801. Raleigh's oldest theater was not far behind; established in 1814, it also was located on the lower floor of the Masonic Lodge. Professional theater in all three instances can thereafter be traced in more or less an unbroken line. In Wilmington the Innes Academy was followed by Thalian Hall in 1858, the Opera House in 1871, the Academy of Music in 1902, and once again Thalian Hall in 1929; Fayetteville's Masonic Lodge gave way to a new theater in 1824 and to the Fayetteville Theater in 1835; in Raleigh a second theater in the City Hall above the City Market replaced the Masonic Lodge in 1840. Similar theatrical construction can be traced somewhat later in the Piedmont towns of Salisbury (Merony Hall in 1873), Greensboro (Benbow Hall in 1874), Winston-Salem (Brown's Opera House in 1880), Charlotte (the Charlotte Opera House in 1874), and somewhat later further west in Asheville (the Grand Opera House in 1890). Certainly the most thriving early theater was in Wilmington, where the already sizable population of 7,264 in 1850 grew steadily to over

20,000 by the turn of the century; Raleigh's antebellum population, by contrast, was only 2,244 in 1840. Thalian Hall offered 85 nights of entertainment in its first season of 1858–1859, and by 1863–1864 the number of performances had risen to 240.

Shakespeare from the beginning was a staple among Tar Heel theatrical fare, as varied as the spectators themselves. One reads, for example, of a performance in Raleigh in 1816 aptly described as "upwards of over 260 of the most wonderful and curious performances in Tumbling"[4] and, in all the larger towns, of the presentation of works like Bunyan's *Pilgrim's Progress*, the Book of Revelation, and Milton's *Paradise Lost* in the antebellum multi-media marvel of Phantascopal Illusions.[5] Nor are we denied glimpses into more titillating entertainments such as Madame Rentze's Female Minstrels in Greensboro, or Jack Gerard's Honey Moon Girls in Winston-Salem, or Mademoiselle Ninon Duclo's Sensational Blondes Revue in Wilmington. The latter was breezily reviewed in the *Morning Star* of October 19, 1877, as playing to an exclusively male audience that "appeared to admire the rigid economy observed by the 'Dizzies' in the purchase of their wardrobes"; the anticipated second night's large audience, who no doubt "will go just to encourage twenty modest maidens (all orphans) in their praiseworthy efforts to make an honest living," are forewarned that "opera glasses will not be needed—screens will be more appropriate."[6] On the other hand, a brief glimpse of the records reveals that well over two-thirds of Shakespeare's canon is prominently represented on these early stages. The actor-manager James H. Caldwell, for example, advertised "A Dramatic Olio from Shakespeare, Otway, and Morton" as the opening event for the Masonic Lodge Theatre in 1817.[7] And in Wilmington the opening season of Thalian Hall featured six Shakespearean plays, the following year presenting no fewer than nine along with Philip Massinger's *A New Way to Pay Old Debts*. The major comedies—*The Merchant of Venice, The Taming of the Shrew, A Midsummer Night's Dream, Much Ado About Nothing, As You Like It, Twelfth Night*—appear with some regularity; more surprising, perhaps, is a production of *The Winter's Tale* in Wilmington in 1899 or of *The Comedy of Errors* by the Ben Greet Players in

Asheville in 1912. Similarly, North Carolinians near the more populous communities had at least occasional opportunities to see the major tragedies *Romeo and Juliet, Julius Caesar, Hamlet, Othello, Macbeth,* and *King Lear.* Among the histories *Richard III* was far and away the favorite, but even *Henry V* was recorded as "a hit" in Wilmington's 1908 season. Even less traditional performances occasionally merited the early reviewer's mention, for example the Shakespearean readings by the three Celebrated Boon Children in Fayetteville in 1855 or the burlesque musical rendition of *Much Ado About Nothing* by the Chapman Sisters and the C. B. Bishop Company in Wilmington in 1871.

Not surprisingly many of these productions were built around established theatrical names such as Walter Keeble, Neil Warner, Edwin Forrest, Ernesto Rossi, Creston Clarke, Louis James, John Griffith, Charles Hanford, and Fritz Leiber. Among the more famous actresses were Madame Fanny Jananschek, Madame H. Modjeska, Mary Anderson, and Adele Belgarde. Warner, in the varied roles of Hamlet, Shylock, Romeo, Othello, and Richard III, was supported in Wilmington in 1869 by the Ford Company managed by John T. Ford, formerly owner of the star-crossed Ford's Theater in Washington. Forrest's Lear provoked unbounded praise: "Powerful, passionate, grand, and terrible is he while pronouncing his curse upon Goneril; distressingly passionate and pitiable is he in his despair; wild, raving, and awe-inspiring is he in the full tide of his madness."[8] The tone is similar eleven years later in an account of Rossi's Othello.[9] Rossi is described as an actor "of massive frame and commanding presence"; following Desdemona's death "the most terrible, agonizing remorse sweeps over him with fearful power, crushes his heart, and impels him to the fatal end. . . . We feel, when the curtain falls, that we have seen *Othello*—not acted but living." It was reported of the famous Polish actress Madame Modjeska that her Viola was most triumphant: "She throws her heart and soul into the piece, and holds her audience completely under her sway from the beginning to the end of the performance."[10] And her performance of the role of Portia over a decade later was cited as a "marvel and a revelation."[11]

In moving from such productions of earlier years to those of the present, I had hoped to be at least selectively more systematic by providing a summary of recent productions of Shakespeare in North Carolina and determining whether a significant number have been slanted in any way for particular regional appeal. To that end I wrote the drama departments of the 16 component institutions of the University of North Carolina, the 30 private senior institutions, the 8 private junior colleges, and the 57 technical institutes and community colleges. My concern, as I explained, was "not only with a list of productions, but also with the nature of the productions (traditional or modern setting, for example, or adaptations making use of Southern costumes, landscapes, music, or motifs). It may be that in some instances the plays have provided significant commentary about the South or have expressed certain Southern themes. My aim, in other words, will be to reflect both the wide variety of current Shakespearean production and also to attempt to relate this activity in some meaningful way to the Southern cultural, social, and political life."

The effort to solicit this information and to determine particular geographical emphases was in one sense admittedly a failure. Only 18 of the 111 institutions responded to my inquiry—7 public and 7 private senior institutions and 4 community colleges. Of those responding, 7 reported no Shakespearean productions, either local or imported, within the past several years. The remaining 11 institutions reported a total of 42 productions—25 comedies, 13 tragedies, 1 history, and 3 programs comprising selected readings or scenes from a variety of plays. *Macbeth* led the list with five productions; *The Tempest, A Midsummer Night's Dream,* and *The Merchant of Venice* were staged four times; *Twelfth Night, The Comedy of Errors,* and *Hamlet* three times; *As You Like It* and *Romeo and Juliet* twice; *All's Well That Ends Well, Richard III, The Merry Wives of Windsor, The Taming of the Shrew, Love's Labor's Lost, King Lear, Much Ado About Nothing,* and *Julius Caesar* once.

Admittedly these records are scanty, whether the consequence of indifference or of misdirected mail. Even so, the results do suggest a rather vigorous Shakespearean tradition. More specifically, the reports from only 16 percent of the institutions reveal that 18 plays (almost half of the canon of 37) have been staged within the past few years and that precisely half of the 42 were locally produced. Such a synopsis, moreover, makes no attempt to account for the not inconsiderable dramatic activities in the high schools and in the community theaters. Equally important, the productions reflect a healthy variety of theatrical experimentation. While such experimentation admittedly can lead to that which is merely trendy or gimmicky or philosophically incongruous, it can also discover the rich adaptability of the plays and explore the flexibility of staging characteristic of the Elizabethan age. The result, in any case, is a living stage tradition rather than the resurrection of a consciously archaic dramatic form. Admittedly, the settings of several ranged far from the traditional—a modern *As You Like It* by the Duke Players, a *Twelfth Night* by the Duke Summer Theater set in colorful beach cabanas, a mid-nineteenth century *Macbeth* and a turn-of-the-century *All's Well That Ends Well* by the Carolina Playmakers at Chapel Hill, and a wildly nontraditional version of *The Comedy of Errors* performed throughout the state by the Oxford-Cambridge Shakespeare Company. Set in Turkey in the 1920s, it was spiced with American songs of the period. Hoyt McCachren, chairman of the Department of Drama and Speech at Catawba College in Salisbury, writes of two recent experimental stagings. For a production of *A Midsummer Night's Dream,* the entire center section of seating in the small theater was covered and became one of three major acting areas (the world of the fairies, the lovers, and the handicraftsmen). With the audience seated in the two side sections and in chairs placed at the rear of the stage, the scenery was arranged to enclose the entire theater. A production of *The Tempest* utilized a similar arena style, with several traps removed and the audience seated on the stage itself. From David R. Batchelor, the director of theater at the University of North Carolina-Greensboro, comes news of interesting visual experimentation—for instance, emphasizing the magnitude of the sleepwalking scene in *Macbeth* through an extremely high stairway reaching from the floor of the fly gallery to the stage, or the use of an architectural set for *The Merchant of Venice,* or a formalistic style employing space staging for *Richard III,* or a uniform color scheme of black, red, and silver for *Twelfth Night.*

Certainly the most innovative and most controversial production is Arnold Wengrow's 1974 staging of *A Midsummer Night's Dream* at the University of North Carolina-Asheville. Influenced directly by Jan Kott, who envisions Shakespeare as a Beckett-like absurdist playwright trapped in a nihilistic universe and who describes life in the Forest of Athens as erotic, brutal, violent, and bestial rather than Arcadian, Wengrow—in the words of one reviewer—dredges in the "murky-Freud-frightened interiors for dark and despairing interpretations of what more innocent readers and viewers thought to be sunshine and fairy magic."[12] The program note explains that the staging—like John Hancock's production at the Actor's Workshop in San Francisco in 1966 (and subsequently at the Pittsburgh Playhouse and the Circle-in-the-Square Theatre in New York in 1967) and Peter Brook's production for the Royal Shakespeare Company in 1970—is a reaction against the lush, romantic extravaganzas suffered under directors from David Garrick in the eighteenth century to Max Reinhardt in the twentieth. As Wengrow himself described his artistic task,

> Any production of *A Midsummer Night's Dream* must, consciously or unconsciously, contend with the ghosts of the old, romantic tradition and the new tradition of Kott and Hancock and Brook. This production is quite deliberately indebted to Kott for an initial impetus, although it departs from him radically in many respects. For example, Kott says, "I imagine Titania's court as consisting of old men and women, toothless and shaking, their mouths wet with saliva, who sniggering procure a monster for their mistress." It will be obvious how our interpretation differs. Knowing the Hancock and Brook versions only by reputation, the director has not knowingly reproduced any of the pyrotechnics from those theatrical feasts [Puck swinging from an overstuffed red satin heart suspended from the flies, Hippolyta wearing a leopard-skin bikini and confined in a bamboo cage, fairies as glow-in-the-dark animated puppets, a neon-lighted Wurlitzer jukebox blaring "Tenderly," a totally white space in which actors in rehearsal costumes imitate acrobats in a gymnasium]. Every director, of course, hopes to make some unique contribution to the interpretation of a famous play, and it is in the conception of Theseus and the supernatural beings that this production strives to make a new statement.[13]

This conception, apparently, was built upon a dream within a dream suggested by doubling within the various strands of plot and by the dimly lighted vision of Theseus brooding dreamily over the action in which he was not involved. The mammouth set, described by one reviewer as something resembling the human brain[14] and by another as "organic, a somewhat abstract form, . . . at once cave, palace, woods, and a collection of human forms, perhaps even heaven and hell,"[15] contributed effectively to the subliminal mystery of Shakespeare's (in this case) not-so-happy romantic comedy.

Many critics, playgoers, and readers alike will understandably react with horror to the superimposition upon Shakespeare of a *Weltanschauung* basically alien to that of the Elizabethan age; to many it is not a question of making Shakespeare relevant so much as destroying or distorting his fundamental perceptions of life. At the opposite end of the spectrum, for instance, is Charles Martin's 1976 production of *Twelfth Night* at North Carolina State University, which stressed the traditional values of romantic love. The program notes describe the care and concern for authentic costuming; a member of the Department of Speech Communication worked with each cast member for over six weeks on Shakespearean dialogue, the director researched aspects of the play in England with members of the Royal Shakespeare Company, and the incidental music— played on recorders and a viola de gamba—was Elizabethan.

Aside from this variety of activity at the collegiate level, and aside from the numerous city and community theatrical activities, at least two dramatic groups are expressly dedicated to Shakespearean production in North Carolina—the one on a relatively local level, the other on a statewide basis that holds the genuine promise of developing into a major Shakespeare attraction in the southeastern region. The Montford Players Company, sponsored in part by the Asheville Department of Parks and Recreation, has produced nine plays in its eight years of existence—*As You Like It, A Midsummer Night's Dream, The Taming of the Shrew, The Merchant of Venice, Twelfth Night, Love's Labor's Lost, 1 Henry IV, Othello,* and *Macbeth.* Performing in a racially mixed neighborhood, this company draws a healthy cross-section of local citizens and tourists. One of the most delightful rewards of playing Shakespeare in Appalachia is the constant reminder of the close similarity between contemporary mountain speech and the Elizabethan idiom. As Hazel Robinson, director of the Montford Players, writes, the sixteenth-century language is surprisingly intelligible: "Doubtless, in other parts of the country such locations as 'down in the neighbor bottom' and 'he drew a dial from his poke' may be puzzling, but in Appalachia they are still part of everyday speech. Aside from the vocabulary, the rhythms and rhetoric are still familiar here. Brought up on the King James Bible and the rolling periods of sermons modeled on it, the audience and actors (local and amateur) find a familiar music in Shakespeare's speech."[16] Robinson notes further the effectiveness of utilizing a broad version of local "country" pronunciation for the comic dialects of such rustics as Corin, Audrey, the Athenian handicraftsmen, Costard, and Launcelot Gobbo. Reviewing a recent production of *1 Henry IV*, William Moore observed that, "to anyone raised in these mountains, watching a Shakespeare play is like going home"; and he catalogues locutions like "nary," "scot and lot," and "horrible afeard" that are "straight out of the local idiom."[17]

The most significant Shakespearean news, without a doubt, is currently coming from High Point, the home of the newly formed North Carolina Shakespeare Festival. The rapid artistic maturation of this company along with the prudent economic policies guiding each stage of its development makes it an excellent model for other states interested in developing such cultural programs. The festival grew out of the North Carolina Theater Ensemble, a professional theater in Winston-Salem that produced fifteen plays in 1975–1976. Directed by Mark Woods and Stuart Brooks, who, though relatively young, brought a wealth of theatrical experience from Boston and New York, the company was chartered in 1977, chose the High Point Theatre and Exhibition Center as its home base, and offered three plays (*Henry V*, *The Taming of the Shrew*, and Moliere's *The Miser*) during the first summer season. Each play was performed eight times in repertoire. For the second season *Much Ado About Nothing*, *The Merchant of Venice*, and Robert Bolt's *A Man for All Seasons* were selected, and the run for each play was increased to eleven. In 1979, with matinee performances included for the first time, the productions included *A Midsummer Night's Dream, 1 Henry IV*, and Richard Brinsley Sheridan's *The Rivals*. In 1980 the offerings were *Macbeth, Twelfth Night, The Comedy of Errors*, and Moliere's *The Imaginary Invalid;* and in 1981 the company staged *Hamlet, As You Like It*, and Noel Coward's *Hay Fever*. With the run for each play increased to fifteen, the 1982 season featured *King John, Romeo and Juliet*, and Feydeau's *A Flea in Her Ear*.

In 1978 the North Carolina Shakespeare Festival expanded into a full-season company called the Festival Stage Company, offering the work of such playwrights as Wilde, Miller, Goldoni, Knott, Gillette, Williams, and Goldsmith. The artistic director of the winter company, Malcolm Morrison, dean of drama at the North Carolina School of the Arts, has now assumed a similar responsibility for the Shakespeare Festival. Based at the High Point Theater since the fall of 1978, the Festival Stage Company lengthened its season in 1979–1980 by adding residencies in Charlotte and Greensboro. Remarkably, the North Carolina Shakespeare Festival—Festival Stage Company, in its expansion from a ten-week season of three plays in 1977 to a seven-month season of eight plays covering three markets in 1980–1981, has emerged as a truly regional full-season theater company—the only one in North Carolina and one of few in the nation. Instead of a fall residency in the three particular locations in 1982–1983, the company projected an extended touring season following the summer productions in High Point, in this way making performances of Shakespeare available to an even wider segment of the population of the Southeast; at the same time, Mark Woods adds, "It is hoped that this will increase NCSF's visibility, stimulate greater attendance for future seasons, and substantially increase income."[18]

Such success obviously does not come without sound fiscal planning. Uniquely, for one thing, the company does not depend upon box office revenues for operational expenses in that particular season. That is, the budget for the 1977 season ($92,500) was entirely in-hand before opening night; all box office revenues were placed in escrow to serve as basic budget support for the succeeding year.

Even as the budget has increased to $173,260 in 1978, $295,000 in 1980, and $412,000 in 1982, the policy has remained the same; thus, no deficits can occur because no expenditures are based on estimates of ticket sales. As observed by Howard Hall, managing director until 1981, "Such fiscal accountability is unprecedented in American professional theater and is the best assurance to benefactors that their gifts and grants will be used for the benefit of the region by an arts organization combining artistic fields of endeavor."[19] Public support, too, has exceeded expectations. Attendance at the twenty-four performances in 1977 was over 11,000 (72 percent of capacity), and approximately 27 percent of the 1978 budget was generated and placed safely in reserve. For the Shakespeare Festival productions in 1978, 1979, and 1980 attendance increased by more than 20 percent to well over 13,000 (24,000 including the Festival Stage Company), and revenues are up more than 50 percent. Obviously, spiraling expenses have posed many problems through this period of growth, but a conscious effort has been made to keep ticket prices at a level that makes the plays fully accessible to the general public. And it has worked. "We estimate," notes Woods of the first season, "that about fifty percent of the people who came, came from the ranks of the population that you just wouldn't expect to attend. And I think that was because we made a sincere effort to get those people to this theater."[20]

Most importantly, of course, solid entertainment attracts its public, and the Shakespeare Festival Company is establishing a sound and well-deserved reputation for good theater. There are flaws, to be sure—momentary lapses in pacing and an occasional uninspired or labored interpretation. The recent production of *The Rivals,* for instance, suffered the imposition of about fifteen minutes of trendy, upbeat music; and *I Henry IV* seemed, on opening night at least, for the first several minutes to bore the very actors themselves, a quality from which the title role never fully recovered. But the reviews have been positive from the beginning; such phrases as "superb production," "high calibre," "rich in flavor," "outstanding success," "wonderfully funny," "utterly delightful," "a first-rate troupe," "spectacular and thrilling" occur far too consistently to be provincial, self-serving, or whimsical. The productions, moreover, are steadily improving. Seasoned actors were selected for the opening summer, and the success and enlargement of the program have made possible the retention of a core company that has grown artistically through close association. There is relatively little annual turnover in the membership; six actors, in fact, have been with the group since opening night and have been cast in each of the plays.[21] One of the most impressive characteristics of the young company has been its genuine diversity of styles—ranging from the mannered comedy of Sheridan and the broad farce of Moliere to the romantic fantasy of *A Midsummer Night's Dream*, the "Fellini-Godfather" quality of *The Taming of the Shrew*, the 1920s flapper version of *Much Ado About Nothing*, and the solidly traditional conceptions of *1 Henry IV* and *Henry V*.

The 1980 season was the festival's most ambitious effort, with productions of *Macbeth, Twelfth Night*, and Moliere's *The Imaginary Invalid*. The demands of these three plays tested the strength and versatility of the company, and for the most part it successfully met the challenge. *The Imaginary Invalid* was staged as a rollicking farce charged with frenetic energy, while *Twelfth Night* possessed an autumnal lyric quality. The festive world of Illyria verged at times upon the melancholy, whether in such touches as the decrepit, lame Feste or the visible misery of Belch's hangovers or the moments of Viola's and Sebastian's poignant remembrance of a sibling's presumed death; the conclusion is deliberately ambiguous as Aguecheek and Antonio and Malvolio stand outside the charmed circle of reconciliation and resorption into normal society, sad examples of the transiency of life described in the Fool's parting song. Perhaps least successful was the staging of *Macbeth*, the company's first effort at tragedy. If there was nothing flatly incompetent about the production, it lacked the sparkle of first-rate ensemble acting. Both Macbeth and Lady Macbeth established such intense levels of delivery at the outset that there was little room for development as their lives spiraled toward bloody destruction. There were touches, though, of convincing agony in Macbeth, genuine remorse, for example, at the moment of the decision to assassinate Banquo or his sense of frustration that each bloody deed committed him more irrevocably to a villain's role that ran counter to his nature. Certainly the most striking aspect of the production was the dark massive throne with twelve ascending steps which vividly established the crown and its power as the dominant concerns of the play. At times the throne divided and opened to become a foreboding and foggy cave from which the witches entered amidst lightning and the rumble of thunder.

The production of *As You Like It* in 1981 provoked mixed responses from an audience increasing both in size and in expectations. The setting was stunning, with Duke Frederick's palace a solid white and the Forest of Arden a montage of lush green and blurred pastels. The secondary roles of Touchstone and Jaques, almost contrapuntal in nature, were also memorable. But Garson Stine experienced difficulty with the characterization of Orlando; at one moment he was the credible infatuated wooer awash with hyperbolic rhetoric, while at another he appeared thoroughly embarrassed by and uncomfortable with the amusing inanities of the Arden poet-lover. But, if the staging of *As You Like It* was a qualified success, the 1981 production of *Hamlet* established without question the competency of the company to perform Shakespeare's most demanding works. The open set effectively maintained the flexibility of Elizabethan staging, while the costumes, as reviewer John Moehlmann observes, "suggestively integrated Roman cloaks and stormtrooper uniforms of Nazi Germany."[22] And virtually without exception the cast exhibited intensity and enthusiasm. The character of Hamlet was especially well conceived by Eric Zwemer, an excitingly capable young actor who returned as Romeo in 1982 for a second season with NCSF following three years with the Folger Theatre Group in Washington. His Dane dominated the stage in a manner not unlike Derek Jacobi's in the PBS production. More precisely, Hamlet—conscious not only of his stage role but of his feigned posture within that role itself (his madness, his disdain for Ophelia)—tended to step out of character during his soliloquies. Instead of our eavesdropping or seeming to overhear the protagonist's inner thoughts as a part of the ongoing dramatic action, he

The North Carolina Shakespeare Festival production of *Macbeth*, 1980
Courtesy North Carolina Shakespeare Festival

spoke directly to the audience, leading and directing our attention to particular characters or issues. His lines following the player's speech on Priam's slaughter, for instance, as well as his later "to be or not to be" soliloquy, were delivered directly to the actual spectators, stage forward, in quiet, almost intimate, terms. At another moment, chiding himself for lack of action, he would assume the conscious actor's role, addressing first one, then the other, side of an imaginary audience. In the play-within-the-play scene he suddenly rushed onto the stage within a stage, standing among the actors as he explained the source of the play to Claudius and assured him that there was "no offense i' th' world" in it. Described by reviewers as "a cauldron of hot-blooded, youthful anger"[23] and as an "idealistic youth . . . troubled with an energy and a passion,"[24] this Hamlet, in a word, at one moment functioned as a choric figure to his own plot line, at another as a director moving in and out of the action of the play-within-the-play, at another as a protagonist whose interaction with Claudius and Gertrude was dictated by their response to the inner play. Those in the audience observed Hamlet in these multiple roles from, of course, their higher level of awareness, since they were forced to interpret all of this through their own perceptions of the conflicting emotions in Hamlet and of the impact of his actions on the surrounding characters. The result was a chilling theatrical experience that stressed Hamlet's sense of entrapment in a situation from which neither emotional interaction in his play world nor objective intellectualizing of his stage role could win release. Director Malcolm Morrison admittedly was attempting to focus on the unacceptability of private behavior when it spills over into the public domain. "In the moments of courtly formality the revelation of private, personal grievance is shocking, embarrassing, and frequently inflammatory."[25] For director and actors alike, the tragedy—whatever the incidental flaws—was a remarkable success, clearly the company's highest artistic achievement to this point.

Despite the ravaging effects of inflation on production costs, the future appears bright for the North Carolina Shakespeare Festival. Morrison, British-born and trained, ultimately envisions a year-round activity involving brief residencies in several cities and a supplementary touring season. The heart of the program will continue to be the summer Shakespeare productions in High Point, and the intention is to produce the entire canon within a reasonably brief period. But his vision extends beyond North Carolina to a chain of regional theaters that will constitute a national theater with individual productions moving from one state to the next. "I don't see the National Theater being one building in Washington as it is in London. I think it would be a network of perhaps ten theaters in various parts of the country. Productions would be sent from one to another, while actors would travel between them. This country is so large that it is easier to move the mountain than to move Mohammed."

Morrison adds with a twinkle in his eye that he is delighted to be producing the plays in the South where people "listen better" and still "speak in complete sentences."[26] He insists, furthermore, that the style of speech need not be imported, that it should not create an unnecessary barrier between our contemporary audiences and the poetic force of Renaissance drama. "Americans speak English; English speak British—so America should hear its own form of speech." He insists, in fact, that productions can assume a new life and vitality when the director and actors pointedly do not ape the English. "You walk through Stratford. Sure, what you're experiencing is history, but don't forget that history permeates a lot of the thinking and activity in England. Every time you deal with something, you deal with heritage. And sometimes that can be very stifling."

Shakespeare, in a word, is available in North Carolina in a wide variety of forms—whether traditional, period, or modern; whether amateur, semi-professional, or professional. While academic programs admittedly play to a somewhat captive audience, arguing the need to expose the student to the best of his cultural heritage, other programs are successfully depending upon the level of interest and support among the general public. And, to a significant extent, this public represents a cross section of the state's pluralistic society. If the question of Shakespeare's relevance was effectively addressed in 1623 by Ben Jonson, who described the playwright as "not of an age, but for all time," the ability of his work to teach and to delight, to absorb and transcend the contemporary, must be discovered anew by each generation.

NOTES

1. See Richard Walser, "Strolling Players in North Carolina 1768–1788," *Carolina Play-Book* 10 (1937): 108–9; also Archibald Henderson, *North Carolina, The Old North State and the New* (Chicago: Lewis, 1941), 1:643.

2. David L. Swain, *Early Times in Raleigh* (Raleigh: Hughes, 1867), p. 7.

3. See a series of articles on early professional theater in North Carolina by Donald J. Rulfs in *North Carolina Historical Review* 28 (1951): 119–36, 316–31, 463–85; 29 (1952): 344–58; 31 (1954): 125–33; 35 (1958): 328–46; 36 (1959): 429–41.

4. *Raleigh Register*, Nov. 22, 1816.

5. *North Carolina Standard*, July 3, 1850.

6. *Wilmington Morning Star*, Oct. 19, 1877.

7. *Raleigh Register*, Mar. 5, 1817.

8. *Wilmington Daily Journal*, Oct. 27, 1870.

9. *Wilmington Daily Review*, Dec. 20, 1881.

10. *Wilmington Morning Star*, Jan. 31, 1884.

11. *Wilmington Messenger*, Jan. 30, 1894.

12. "A Critic's Diary," *Asheville Native Stone*, May 2, 1974, p. 8.

13. UNC-Asheville Playbill, *A Midsummer Night's Dream*, Apr. 25–27, 1974.

14. *Asheville Native Stone*, p. 8.

15. Martha Abshire, "Innovative Shakespeare by Theatre UNC-A," *Asheville Citizen*, Apr. 26, 1974, p. 26.

16. Letter received from Hazel Robinson, Oct. 11, 1979.

17. "Do You'ns Remember?" *Asheville Citizen*, Feb. 2, 1979, p. 8.

18. News release, "The North Carolina Shakespeare Festival Revises Program Format," May 24, 1982, p. 2.

19. "Prospectus on Continuing the Development of the North Carolina Shakespeare Festival and the Festival Company into a Regional Theatre," Apr., 1979, p. 4.

20. Jim Eldridge, "A Tar Heel Interview with Mark Woods and Stuart Brooks," *Tar Heel* 6, no. 4 (1978): 36.

21. Personal interview with Malcolm Morrison, Apr. 18, 1980.

22. "*Hamlet* Full of Relevancy, Imagery," *High Point Enterprise*, July 18, 1981, p. 3A.

23. Jim Shertzer, "*Hamlet* Puts Demands on Audience and Cast," *Winston-Salem Journal*, July 19, 1981, p. 1B.

24. Abe D. Jones, Jr., "Festival's *Hamlet:* Flawed but Fine," *Greensboro Record*, July 18, 1981, p. 12A.

25. North Carolina Shakespeare Festival 1981 Playbill, p. 7.

26. Personal interview, Apr. 18, 1980.

The Alabama Shakespeare Festival

Carol McGinnis Kay

The 1981 Alabama Shakespeare Festival (ASF) season concluded the first decade of an astonishingly successful Shakespeare festival. "Astonishing" because it is one of many current festivals, most of which are struggling financially; because it exists in a southern town of fewer than 80,000 people that is over an hour's drive from the nearest city, Birmingham; and because it developed from a shoe-string budget smaller than most, i.e., the director borrowed $500 from his mother. "Successful" because it has grown to regional, indeed, national, prominence among playgoers, critics, and scholars; because it now attracts over 20,000 persons annually for the six-weeks season; and because it has repeatedly offered superbly staged productions.

When Martin L. Platt, a graduate of Carnegie-Mellon, arrived in Anniston, Alabama, in 1971 to direct the local little theater group, he was soon struck by the void of professional theater in the region, and at the same time he admired the excellent technical facilities offered by the newly built Anniston High School theater. Platt decided that he might be able to fill this void and fulfill his own desire to direct classical theater, specifically Shakespeare, by initiating a Shakespeare festival. He borrowed from his mother and won the support of many townspeople, particularly Josephine Ayers, now executive producer, who gave financial assistance, time, energy, and even room and board to the actors for the first ASF season, all of whom performed without salaries. It is a tribute to the perseverance and devotion of all concerned that after an opening-night audience of twenty-four in an unairconditioned theater and a first season deficit of $32 (after a total budget of only $8,000) they did not throw up their collective hands and quit on the spot.

Instead, fortunately for those of us who love live theater, the planners took bigger risks the next year and achieved several major turning points—such as moving into the new theater, opening the 1974 season with a beautiful, vibrant, enormously popular *Midsummer Night's Dream*,[1] incorporating Equity actors for the first time in 1976, adding a managing director in 1977, going on a regional tour in 1978, becoming the state theater in 1976, gaining national recognition from the *New York Times, Washington Post,* and *Shakespeare Quarterly* in 1976, being accepted by the Foundation for the Extension and Development of the American Professional Theater in 1980, and developing substantial financial increases from local, state and federal sources so that by 1980 the season's budget was over $500,000—all of which seem to have put the ASF on a sound enough artistic and financial basis for us to expect good things for years to come. As Frances Teague observed in her insightful account in the *Southern Quarterly,* "Simply by assuming that first-rate Shakespearean productions are possible with good will and hard work, the Anniston Shakespeare Festival has, in fact, been able to achieve excellence in the past and will likely continue to do so. If the festival were to advertise in its own program, it might use the Shakespearean line, 'Thinking makes it so.'"[2]

During its first ten years the ASF has presented twenty of Shakespeare's plays, some more than once. The season is normally six weeks of repertoire staging, with Shakespeare's plays alternating with one, or occasionally two, non-Shakespearean plays, e.g., *The Country Wife, Tartuffe, Rosencrantz and Guildenstern Are Dead, Private Lives,* and *The Importance of Being Earnest.* Roles are doubled, so that each actor may play up to five parts in a season.

Amusing or interesting behind-the-scenes stories are typical of any dramatic company: The 1976 *King Lear* costumes, fur and leather creations weighing up to forty pounds each, arrived full of fleas, a fact which was made increasingly evident as the dress rehearsal progressed; Bill Kellog, who was playing William in the 1973 *As You Like It,* was tripped by Touchstone so enthusiastically at dress rehearsal that he broke his wrist and the tripping was changed to a pratfall on the rear for the actual production; throughout the first act of the 1972 *Hamlet,* seamstresses were frantically sewing Hamlet's third act costume; and an actor's illness in 1980 meant that the actors playing Tybalt (Bruce Cromer) and Iachimo (Terry Laycock) stepped into their demanding roles less than two weeks before opening night. The reason for our interest in such anecdotes is that they show us the tricks behind the magic, the human being behind the mask, and the appeal of them is usually in proportion to the success of the magic perpetrated on the stage. In the case of the ASF it is considerable magic indeed.

As the ASF has developed, its productions have come to have certain hallmarks: little tampering with the text (usually the Arden edition of a play); gorgeous costumes; spare, effective sets on a thrust stage; a rapid pace, and exuberant sophisticated staging of the comedies.

Martin Platt seldom alters the lines *per se* with anything more drastic than condensing a play, such as cutting approximatley 700 lines from the 1980 *Cymbeline*, an abridgment which was perhaps too conservative for so large and unwieldy a play, because the 3½ hour production was still wearisome for the audience. Cuts are usually made to avoid problems or simplify matters for a contemporary audience. In the final scene of *King Lear* (1976), Lear did *not* ask for a mirror or a feather, both old devices for determining whether someone is breathing; "Where is Fancy bred" was deleted from *The Merchant of Venice* (1978), and the 1979 *Macbeth* omitted the description of Edward the Confessor curing scrofula, an omission which most Elizabethan scholars would decry because the central panel in the act 4 triptych that shows the impending healing of Scotland's ills is lost. Similarly, a thematic point was lost in *Richard II* (1975) by the removal of all references to the threatened revolution by Aumerle and company, thus eliminating one of Shakespeare's points that we have come full circle politically as the play ends. Such efforts to remove passages that don't advance the plot do occasional violence to Shakespeare's tonal or thematic points, but they are perhaps the inevitable consequence of staging plays from earlier periods. Whenever the meaning of a line depends on knowledge or earlier topical events, or people, or ideas, or words, the contemporary actor, whether English or American, faces the problem of how to make that line intelligible to the audience. For instance, most persons in a modern audience would not understand the physician's presence in *Macbeth* because we have essentially lost the Elizabethan analogy of King = Physician that was an important part of the Renaissance concept of world order. Sometimes the play's program may be used to give background information about such concepts; sometimes lines may be acted out so that the meaning is made clear through gestures or props; and sometimes, as was the case in *Macbeth,* the actor and director chose the easiest way out and cut the whole section.

Such rationalization, however, does not seem to be behind all deletions by the ASF. For example, in *King Lear* (1976) Cordelia's asides in act 1, scene 1, were omitted, as was the later explanation of France's absence from the battle.

Exceptions to this fairly conservative policy have been made in several plays, usually comedies, and occasionally the histories. Apparently Platt thinks the history plays are too difficult for his television-trained audience to comprehend without a lot of help, because he keeps giving them on-stage history lessons. Both *Richard II* (1975) and *1 Henry IV* (1981) opened with long voice-overs, the former giving the pertinent passages from Holinshed and the latter the "Let us sit upon the ground" speech from *Richard II.* And every time anyone mentioned the English soil in *Richard II,* someone rushed downstage and let a handful of dirt run through his fingers. If Platt could trust his audience to be more perceptive than he does and could trust Shakespeare to know what he's doing in creating credible characters, then the ASF histories could reach the level of excellence currently achieved in the comedies.

Some of the comedies apparently offer irresistible opportunities for textual embellishment. In *Twelfth Night* (1975) some thirteen or fourteen lines were *added* that exaggerated the farcical quality of that production: for instance, Antonio's arresting officers were puny things, clearly no match for him, and as they were attempting to drag him away, one officer feebly hit the back of Antonio's head with his night-stick, causing Antonio to look up into the sky quizzically and say, "Pigeons?" The laughs garnered by such additions are clearly at the expense of the play itself, as all the additions to *Twelfth Night* emphasized the zany atmosphere of the play as a cross between Keystone Cops and the Pirates of Penzance, and thereby undercut the romantic strain of Shakespeare's play.[3] Similar gimmicky additions were made in the 1974 *Taming of the Shrew*, in which the Italian strolling players swore vigorously with opera titles, "Cosi Fan Tutte" and "A-iiida."

Undercutting of the romantic element was also achieved by an addition of sorts in the 1979 *Comedy of Errors*, in which the opening scene with Egeon's lengthy account of disasters at sea became hilarious. As Egeon (Charles Antalosky) told the Duke of Ephesus (Earle Edgerton) his sad tale of shipwreck and a separated family, the story was transformed into a Saturday morning at the movies, complete with a lantern show upstage center, popcorn for the Duke and the jailer, and a huge map dotted with Egeon's travels. The "entertainment" was so well received that the jailer contributed a coin to pay for Egeon's release, and, as he left, Egeon started his story again. Egeon knew a good thing when he saw it and at every possible—or impossible—moment during the rest of the play he tried to recount his story, "In Syracuse was I born and wed. . . . " The line is Shakespeare's, of course, but the repetition of it is not, and the reaction from most theatergoers acquainted with Shakespeare was mixed. On the one hand, the repetition was hilarious, a funny piece of business that was its own justification. On the other hand, it did prevent our responding sympathetically to Egeon and his history, and the whole clever stage business surrounding the repetition captured our attention so completely that the story was difficult to follow. I doubt that anyone seeing the play for the first time understood the exposition at all.

The cleverness of the additions in *Love's Labor's Lost* went beyond a single word or line. The play was moved to the South of France on precisely April 10, 1932, according to the playbill and the copy of "Le Figaro" lying on a table on the patio. Set, costumes, music, and elaborate stage business quickly established an artificial world of Noel Coward elegance. The trellised terrace of the King of Navarre's summer home, overlooked by French windows and decorated with wrought-iron tables, chairs, a bar, and, of all things, a grand piano, formed the perfect background for the Bright Young Things who quipped their way through life in this play.

Even before the first line was spoken, the actors were very busy. The maid (Jaquenetta) dusted everything in sight, including the butler when he found a speck of dust on a chair; Sir Nathaniel, brandishing a huge white net, pursued butterflies around the breakfast table; servants set up the bar and laid out the morning newspaper and the chauffeur (Costard) chased the maid around, and even under, the piano. Throughout this bustle a young man with brilliantined hair played the piano and looked mildly bemused. After some ten minutes Dumaine, Longaville, and Berowne entered, one at a time, each man picking up the rhythm of the music and breaking exuberantly into a soft-shoe routine. Finally, the King of Navarre strolled out, said "Good Morning," and the play proper began.

The entire production reflected the fun everyone seemed to be having with it off-stage as well as on. The *dramatis personae* listed someone called "Jacques Marivaux, former Marquis de Brillot," a name invented for Bruce Hoard, who played the piano throughout the play, singing occasionally, but never speaking a line. Whenever Constable Dull entered, Hoard played the Marseillaise, and while Berowne chased Costard all around the stage he played Keystone Cops music. Allan Almeida as Moth gave a wonderful rendition of "Mad about the Boy" in Armado's honor, while Armado sipped champagne, nodded agreement with every compliment, and hugged himself in appreciation. During the intermission Costard, Jaquenetta, Moth, and the butler sang "What shall we do with a drunken sailor?"[4]

This transformation in time and place for *Love's Labor's Lost* typifies a consistent pattern in ASF productions: most seasons have had at least one production, usually a comedy, sometimes a romance, that was relocated from the original setting. The opening season's *Two Gentlemen of Verona* was moved to the eighteenth century. The second season began with *Much Ado About Nothing* set in the antebellum South and featured a Dogberry who was, in the words of one reviewer, "a sort of Italianate Gomer Pyle," and strains of "Dixie" and "Zip-a-dee-doo-dah" filled the air.[5] The 1973 season also offered a rock musical version of *As You Like It*. The 1976 season gave us a *Winter's Tale* that opened in early nineteenth-century dress against a stylized set of silver panels. The Sicilian household wore white, with the women in beautiful, frilly empire gowns, and Polixenes later wore flashing black satin with a red sash. Dress was not, however, consistent, for there was a curious mixture of empire and Victorian formal garb, medieval monastic robes for Polixenes and Camille in disguise, shepherd costumes of no identifiable period, and even Mexican peasant dress for the rustics.[6] More emphatically and consistently nineteenth century in set and costume was the 1978 *Measure for Measure*, for which the playbill listed the time as 1871. The stage bristled with pointed helmets and betassled Victorian dress. Upstage, narrow stone arches flanking a statue of Justice suggest a law court. Angelo (Philip Pleasants), as he awaited the return of Isabella, wore a silver cravat and a crimson lounging jacket trimmed with pink satin, and he sipped apricot brandy poured from a crystal decanter.[7] The 1979 *As You Like It* was reminiscent of the recent BBC production in mounting the play as a beautiful, languid Gainsborough painting. The time was 1780 and costumes featured tri-cornered hats, walking sticks, plum velvet frock coats, pink ribbons, and curly wigs. Guest director Jay Broad shifted his 1981 production of *Much Ado* to some unidentified Arabian Nights world of shifting lights, temple bells and Indian drums, bejeweled turbans, and scimitars. This exotic Indian-Persian-Bedouin world was a languid place of latent and potentially destructive power barely held in check by the thoughtful and witty characters of the play.

While these shifts in locale may not be called tampering with the lines *per se,* they often constitute considerable tampering with the concept of the play as a whole. As may be obvious from the references to the 1978 *Measure for Measure,* when the play is reduced to melodrama the play has been quite thoroughly eviscerated. Gone is the ambivalence of a complex Angelo who is surprised to find that he is capable of lust, who hates himself for that lust, and who yet cannot stop. Gone, in fact, is the whole complex psychological probing of the play as Shakespeare wrote it, and in its stead we have a stock Victorian "Will-the-wicked-villain-violate-the-heroine?" melodrama.

In the case of *Measure for Measure,* moving the play to the nineteenth century seems an easy way to avoid the play's problems. In the case of the 1972 *Much Ado* set in the Old South the movement seems pointless, indeed, disruptive and silly. The play became a "catch that allusion" contest; in *The Winter's Tale* and *As You Like It* the relocations also seem pointless but harmless enough. The movement of the 1981 *Much Ado* to an unspecified fantasy world was quite effective in creating a half-familiar, half-strange land where anything can happen and can be accepted. In the case of *Love's Labor's Lost,* I would go further and argue that the relocation was conceptually valid, indeed, brilliant.

By transferring the play to France in 1932 the ASF production gained the contemporary audience's immediate recognition of the play's world. They knew precisely the sophistication, artificiality, and wit to expect in this Noel Coward world in a way they would not if the playbill had said "Navarre in the sixteenth century." The "era of Noel Coward and Cole Porter, of luxury, almost decadence among the well-to-do, seems to me," said Platt in the 1977 program, "to parallel that luxurious court of the King of Navarre" of Shakespeare's play. Moving the play to the 1930s and peopling it with characters from English and American musical comedies of the period irritated several theatergoers, but the fact remains that most members of a contemporary audience are unaware of Navarre's reputation at the end of the sixteenth century. When a director moves the world of a play to one that reinforces the play's original atmosphere and is immediately comprehensible to a contemporary audience, it seems to me that he is within his legitimate rights as an artistic creator himself.

Platt apparently wanted to create a similar instant recognition for *Measure for Measure:* he said that the political problems of late nineteenth-century Austria seemed to him to be quite analogous to those of the early seventeenth century.[8] Perhaps so, but I suggest that most contemporary audiences are as little familiar with nineteenth-century Austria as with seventeenth-century Austria and that the production in this instance has therefore gained nothing by being transplanted in time.

For only two relocations in ten years to be an unqualified success says something about the value of directors' hunting for "new" ways to stage Shakespeare. We all know instances of directors' doing considerable violence to plays in the name of freshness or contemporaneity. Platt is less offensive in this way than many, but even he succumbs occasionally. About this Old South *Much Ado,* he said, "In Beatrice and Benedick I saw flashes of Scarlett and Rhett, in Claudio and Hero, Ashley and Melanie. Immediately I set in a Civil War framework *without the setting distracting and distorting the play*" (italics added).[9] Platt's own words make it clear that the move in this case was not intended to add anything or to make a point, but merely to be different without damaging the play if possible. It didn't work.

Three major turning points in the history of the festival—at least from the theatergoer's perspective—were the building of the thrust stage, the arrival of Lynne C. Emmert as Costumer in 1974, and the addition of Michael Stauffer as set and lighting designer in 1978. Designed by John Ross, at University of Alabama, the stage was built by Phillip Evolas in the Anniston Little Theater and moved to the high school auditorium. Constructed in twelve pieces, the stage was finally dismantled in fourteen pieces when the movers discovered that some pieces would not fit through the little theatre door. The thrust stage gives excellent sight lines from anywhere in the 1,000-seat auditorium and is flexible enough in size and proportions for imaginative staging. As is currently typical in staging Shakespeare, most ASF sets are clean and spare: a shuttered arch formed the background for both *Merchant of Venice* and *Othello* (1978), shallow green platforms, a tree, and a dappled shade were the set for *As You Like It* (1979), and panels of silver shimmered behind the actors in *The Winter's Tale* (1976). When the ASF sets get more elaborate, as in the case of *Hamlet* (1977) or *Macbeth* (1979), both characterized by stone stairways that must have been the devil to play on, the productions were not very successful, although I would hesitate to suggest a causal relationship, especially because a few of the more elaborate sets have marked extremely successful plays, e.g., *Twelfth Night* and *Love's Labor's Lost.*

Elizabethan devices of staging are still used, that is, much of the scenic impact lies in brilliant costuming and effective props—a point which takes us back to Lynne Emmert and her costumes. As the budget has grown, the ASF has come to depend less on commercial costume houses and more on construction of its own costumes under Emmert's ingenious directions. To describe accurately the costumes in any recent ASF production would make a reviewer susceptible to cliché-mongering: the costumes are simply stunning. I especially think of the world of Belmont (*Merchant of Venice,* 1978) with its burnt orange, melon, soft blue, and dark brown Elizabethan costumes in velvets, taffetas, and brocades, with pearl-encrusted caps, feathers, lace, and jewels galore. Morocco (Sydney Hibbert) and his train wore red velvet and gold lame, gold turbans, and brocade pointed slippers. Aragon's men wore gold and orange velvet. Jessica's dress was brighter in each successive scene at Belmont until she had been nurtured in the humane warmth of Portia's world to the point of flowing in white in the final scene. In spite of a costume budget that is still quite low (some $12,000 in 1980) Emmert manages to create a lavishness of color, texture, and line that makes simply looking at ASF productions a pleasure.[10]

The fact that most of my references to specific plays thus far have been to Shakespeare's comedies may say something about my own interests, but I think it says more about the ASF's strengths and weaknesses. As the festival has developed as a repertoire company with its own brisk style, it has come to be known more for its success with the comedies than with the romances, histories, or tragedies. (The ASF has not yet staged any of the Roman plays.) The reputation may be explained in part by the fact that approximately twice as many Shakespearean comedies have been staged as all his other genres combined, and that the non-Shakespearean plays have almost always been comedies. Perhaps the festival board thinks comedies will attract a bigger audience, perhaps Platt is more comfortable directing in the world of sight gags and slapstick, or perhaps he assumes that his television-oriented audience is more comfortable in such a world where the visual can predominate over the aural effect. Whatever the reasons, the number of ASF successes is higher for comedy than for all other types of plays combined. Even those two early plays *The Comedy of Errors* (the 1978 version) and *The Two Gentlemen of Verona* (1980) were excellent, thanks to a fast pace, endearing, credible characters, and a few perfect pieces of stage business, such as Silvia's slapping Valentine in the final scene of the latter play.

This is not to say, however, that the ASF cannot stage a serious play well, only that such success is rare. Many reviewers liked Mathew Faison's Hamlet in 1977. Platt staged *Hamlet*, as he himself said, quite straightforwardly, as a revenge play, with the result that, in my view, another complex play was reduced to only one perspective.[11] Likewise, many theatergoers praised Phil Pleasants's Macbeth in 1979 especially for his portrayal of ambition run amok. But I found his exaggerated mannerisms reducing a complicated figure to a single note. Because Pleasants's Macbeth began the play already committed to evil, there was no building of tension in the early scenes, no growing sense of horror on either Macbeth's part or ours, no chance for development of his character. Instead, we watched a static figure bent on murder do his bad deeds and then get caught.[12] Most other reviewers and I agreed that *Richard II* fizzled, largely because the subtlety of the central character's mind was lost amidst cockney-speaking gardeners trimming incongruous blue-and-green crepe paper topiaries.[13] And every member of the audience that I have talked with hated Sydney Hibbert's Othello in 1978. Hibbert, a slight man, not only did not look the part, but also his Jamaican accent and constant wrong emphases on words made him not sound the part, and finally his limited skills made him not act the part.[14]

The two bright spots in this pejorative litany are the 1980 *Romeo and Juliet* (not to be confused with the interminable 1974 one) and more especially *King Lear* in 1976. The recent *Romeo and Juliet*, largely uncut, had a fine Juliet in Michele Farr, and an atmosphere of crackling tension created in large part by Bruce Cromer's Tybalt. But the production had a serious flaw in having an unconvincing, rather irritating, short, balding Romeo. Any production of *Romeo and Juliet* in which the audience is pulling for Paris is in trouble.

The unqualified jewel among ASF's tragedies is *King Lear*. Yes,

Lear, perhaps the most difficult of all Shakespeare's plays to stage, because of its confusions, its unrealistic elements, its number of diverse characters, its epic, symphonic proportions, and on and on. Yet the ASF did it. In my review in *Shakespeare Quarterly* I wrote that Charles Antalosky's Lear would be the standard by which I would judge all future performances and I still stand by that statement.[15] Perhaps a small part of my delight was that it was so unexpected. Charles Antalosky is the only actor to have been with the festival from the beginning and he usually plays the great comic roles, Falstaff, Sir Toby Belch, Bottom, Touchstone, and Don Armado.

Antalosky is round-faced, raspy-voiced, and not very imposing, but his Lear was imposing indeed. No gimmicks, no succumbing to tricks, just fine, fine acting. Antalosky's Lear was old, foolish, weak, and strong—all at the same time. And he grew in self-knowledge as his psyche received shock after shock. The pattern of his maturation was almost stylized as he responded to each buffet with uncomprehending fury, then incomplete self-control, and finally a calmness, born of exhaustion, or madness, or acceptance. Antalosky's great scenes were Shakespeare's great scenes: the ousted Lear, accompanied only by his Fool (Bruce Hoard), walking slowly downstage while lightning flashed, thunder rumbled, and white fog poured over the stage; the resurrected Lear awakening to a quietly beautiful reconciliation with Cordelia (Judith Marx); the strong but defeated Lear carrying Cordelia onstage and then turning slowly to look into each courtier's eyes as he cries, "Howl . . . howl . . . howl." Antalosky's Lear moved his audience to pity, but, significantly, he moved us even more to an appreciation of man's strength and his potential for growth, knowledge, and sensitivity.

Antalosky received admirable support from a fine cast, fur and leather brown and black costumes which make the characters look like ominous creatures of prey, a spare set which typified the barren world of this play, and a coherent directorial concept of the spirit.

The Arden text typically was little altered and some gestures were added that helped to resolve textual problems or illuminate the text. In the opening scene Edgar (Stefan Cotner) stood by Cordelia, mute

The Alabama Shakespeare Festival production of *King Lear,* 1976
Courtesy Alabama Shakespeare Festival

but supportive, thus giving each sister a male analogue or supporter.
The Fool also appeared in the opening scene, listening and silently
responding to everything as he huddled by the throne, clasping his
bauble (with his face on one side and Lear's on the other). His
distress over Lear's foolish banishment of Kent and Cordelia was
both funny and sad; thus he guided our response to Lear even before

he spoke. Later in the storm scene the Fool collapsed after making his prophecy; Lear first supported, then carried him, only to abandon him for the "learned Theban" Edgar. The Fool, carried into Gloucester's farmhouse by Kent, tried desperately to recover Lear's attention and affection, but in vain. After lying down at Lear's feet to "go to bed at noon," he simply did not awaken again, a victim of exposure, stress, and loss. It was a neat explanation of the Fool's disappearance after act 3, scene 6, but the frenzied competition between Edgar and the Fool reduced the objectivity of the Fool as Lear's teacher and encouraged us to see Lear as heartless at the very moment when Shakespeare shows him responding to the needs of the human heart. Other nontextual gestures that have become almost commonplace appeared here also: Oswald (Robert Rieban) and Regan (Elizabeth Schuette) made love on a huge bear-skin rug throughout Act 4, scene 5.

One of the major reasons for the success of *King Lear* was the fast pacing, the sense of building rapidly and inexorably to a holocaust with smaller climaxes of villainy along the way. Both the pacing and the gestures mentioned above reinforced the idea that no human being is ever static, that change is life's one constant, that the moment of decision for good or for evil comes and disappears with dazzling rapidity. In the opening scene, Goneril (Leslie Blake) and Regan (Elizabeth Schuette) were only monsters in embryo. They grew in the craft of evil as wickedness spawned a larger wickedness. Regan was encouraged somewhat by Goneril, clearly the dominant sister, but even more by her husband Cornwall (Lester Malizia). From the opening scene, when he kept encouraging her to con her father, to his final scene, when he encouraged her to stab his attacker, Cornwall fed her growing appetite for power and blood. The signal that the monster was fully hatched came as Regan helped her husband in Act 3, scene 7, by slicing the back of the servant's neck. Afterward she looked consideringly at the bloody knife and the servant's crumpled body and then stabbed the servant once more. Her expression of surprised pleasure was terrifying.

The brilliance that characterized *King Lear* in concept and execution has not, unfortunately, been the norm for most ASF attempts with the more serious plays. The histories have typically been stolid and pedestrian, with even the plum roles of Falstaff and Hotspur reduced to one-dimensional stick figures. Yet, the company and director are clearly capable of comprehending the whole tonal range of the Shakespeare canon. This is, after all, the same repertoire company that can portray complex, ambiguous nuances even in the most stereotypical characters in the comedies. The ASF frequently has the courage to explore the serious counterpoint in the comedies, 1981's *Midsummer* and *Much Ado* being two examples, and as soon as the company develops the courage to explore the comic and lyric in the serious plays with similar enthusiasm, it can be the top Shakespeare festival in the country, not just the Southeast, as it is now. From those early productions in which a few professional actors with varying skills were set amidst amateurs with marked southern accents and little experience with blank verse, the ASF has come to the current point of offering over forty professionally trained actors in performances of the highest quality. During a six-week season of three or four Shakespeare plays and one or two non-Shakespearean ones, the ASF can now offer live theater consistently of a caliber comparable to the best theater nationally and occasionally internationally. Scholars and theatergoers may argue about the interpretation of a character, the reading of a line, or the concept of a play, but we are arguing about aspects of what has come to be widely recognized as a highly skilled professional repertoire company in a part of the country where such is far too rare.

Not since the national touring companies came through Alabama during the nineteenth and earlier twentieth century have Alabamians and playgoers from nearby states had the opportunity to see Shakespearean plays with any regularity. Certainly Platt does not intend the ASF to be state or even regional in focus and his productions only occasionally show anything that one may suspect is aimed for southern appeal, and even then the motive is scarcely demonstratable. Southern conservatism may account in part for Platt's decision to delete a considered bit of sexual stage business, but the ribald 1975 production of *Twelfth Night* makes it clear that Platt does not hesitate to let his actors be as sexy as they want on occasion. It may also account for the lack of touching by Othello and Desdemona in the 1978 *Othello*, but Shakespeare himself suggests only one embrace by the couple, so whose motive is more operative?

The only *genuinely* regional characteristic of the ASF productions that I note appears to be a kind of warm enthusiasm from an audience that does not have the same opportunity as, for example, New Yorkers, to see live theater. Standing ovations are frequent. This is not to be patronizing about southern audiences: the opposite is the case. Again, even this emotional response of the ASF audiences is very Elizabethan, and it must give the actors a special stimulation to play to such appreciative audiences. The ASF's growth from an opening night audience of twenty-four in 1972 to a season total of over 22,000 persons in 1981 is ample testimony to the artistic and business skills of Martin Platt, the ASF staff, and to their supporters throughout the state and region. Such growth is also valid witness to the fact that Shakespeare can still be viable commercial theater— when given the chance.

NOTES

1. For detailed accounts of this significant production see Kenneth Paul Shorey's "Shakespeare at Anniston," *Birmingham News*, July 28, 1974, pp. 1E and 8E; and Randy Hall, "Midsummer has Offering of many Riches for All," *Anniston Star*, July 21, 1974, p. 2A. Because the 1974 season was perhaps pivotal for the ASF, retrospective reviews of the entire season are useful. They include Bruce Cook, "What Light through Yonder Window Breaks, Y'all?" *National Observer*, Aug. 24, 1974; Randy Hall, "Festival Plays Improved," *Anniston Star*, Aug. 20, 1974; and Pat Guy, "Huge Success Scored by Shakespeare Festival," *Anniston Star*, Sept. 15, 1974.

2. Information about the history of the festival and backstage anecdotes comes primarily from personal interviews with Martin Platt and Lynne Emmert, costume designer, in July, 1976, and Aug., 1980. Additional sources are the 1980 ASF program, the seasons' reviews cited in the previous and subsequent notes, and Frances Teague, "The Alabama Shakespeare Festival," *Southern Quarterly* 19 (Winter, 1981): 43–53.

3. For further information, see my review, "The Alabama Shakespeare Festival, 1975," *Shakespeare Quarterly* 27 (Winter, 1976): 68–71.

4. For further information, see my review in "Alabama Shakespeare Festival," *Shakespeare Quarterly* 29 (Spring, 1978): 243–44.

5. See Kenneth Paul Shorey's review in *Birmingham News*, July 16, 1973, p. 8A.

6. For further information, see my review in "Alabama Shakespeare Festival," *Shakespeare Quarterly* 28 (Winter, 1977): 221–22.

7. Cf. my comments in "Alabama Shakespeare Festival," *Shakespeare Quarterly* 30 (Spring, 1979): 206–7, with those of Randy Hall, "'Measure' May be ASF Sleeper," *Anniston Star*, July 30, 1978, p. 2D.

8. Personal interview, July 20, 1980.

9. Reported by Kenneth Paul Shorey in his review of *Much Ado* in *Birmingham News*, July 16, 1973, p. 8A.

10. Cf. Randy Hall, "'Merchant of Venice' Triumph for Festival," *Anniston Star*, July 17, 1978, p. 2A; and Helen C. Smith, "As you Like It in Anniston," *Atlanta Journal and Constitution*, July 20, 1980, pp. 1E and 7E.

11. Compare the high praise offered by Kenneth Paul Shorey, "Anniston's Hamlet Strong, Intelligent, Thoughtful," *Birmingham News*, July 24, 1977, pp. 1E and 4E, with the mixed comments of Randy Hall, "'Hamlet' Solid if not Exciting," *Anniston Star*, July 24, 1977, p. 1D, and my own negative remarks in "The Alabama Shakespeare Festival," *Shakespeare Quarterly* 29 (Spring, 1978).

12. Compare Robert Fulton's comments in "Alabama Shakespeare Festival," *Shakespeare Quarterly* 31 (Summer, 1980): 224–25 and my comments in *The Tuscaloosa News*, July 25, 1980, Punch Section, pp. 1 and 4.

13. Cf. Cody Hall, "Richard II a Pageant of Contending Royalty," *Anniston Star*, July 27, 1975, p. 10A, and my comments in "The Alabama Shakespeare Festival, 1975," *Shakespeare Quarterly* 27 (Winter, 1976): 66–68.

14. Cf. Randy Hall, "'Othello' Inspires Mixed Feelings on Opening Night," *Anniston Star*, July 25, 1978, p. 1D, and my comments in "Alabama Shakespeare Festival," *Shakespeare Quarterly* 30 (Spring, 1979): 206–7.

15. Cf. my comments in "Alabama Shakespeare Festival," *Shakespeare Quarterly* 28 (Spring, 1977): 220, 222–23, plus those of Roy Reed, "Anniston, Ala., Hears the Bard's Voice," in *New York Times*, Aug. 12, 1976, p. 87.

Shakespeare at the Globe
of the Great Southwest

Earl L. Dachslager

On the face of it Odessa, Texas, seems an unlikely place to be the home of what is by nearly all accounts one of America's—indeed, at the moment one of the world's—most authentic reproductions of Shakespeare's original Globe theater.[1] Located in far west Texas near the New Mexico border, in the heart of a vast oil-rich region known as the Permian Basin, Odessa (with its twin city, Midland) has a population of 150,000, which makes Odessa not a small town but, at the same time, not exactly the sort of large urban center one might assume to be the home of an annual and well-attended Shakespeare festival. Further, Odessa, compared with other sites of annual Shakespeare festivals—for example Ashland, Oregon; San Diego, California; the two Stratfords—could hardly in itself be considered one of the nation's top tourist attractions. In fact, were it not for the presence there of the Globe Theater, it would be fair to say that Odessa, not too far from the middle of nowhere and, for the most part, hot, flat, and dry, would attract relatively few of the nation's tourists.[2]

Yet in spite of its unlikely and somewhat bizarre locale (at least in comparison with the sites of other Globe "replicas," not to mention the site of the original Globe!) the Odessa Globe, or The Globe of the Great Southwest (to use its specific name), has become a major attraction for Texas and the Southwest. And while no doubt many of the Globe's annual visitors (several thousand each year) are curious to see an Elizabethan theater on the flatlands of west Texas, the Globe of the Great Southwest is more than just a curiosity—in fact, it is a great deal more. The one person to whom most of the credit goes for the existence of this remarkable southwestern institution is a one-time English teacher, lifelong devotee of Shakespeare, and an indefatigable money-raiser for the Odessa Globe: its founder, Mrs. Marjorie Morris.

The story, now legend in Odessa and its environs, of the Globe's origin begins in 1948 when Mrs. Morris was teaching at Odessa High School. In the course of her students' study of Shakespeare, one member of the class brought in a model of the original Globe and talked about how exciting it would be to have a "real" Shakespearean theater in Odessa so that students could see how the plays were "actually" performed in Shakespeare's day. Mrs. Morris evidently agreed that such a theater would indeed be a good thing for her students to have, and from that day determined that she would build an authentic Globe theater in Odessa, Texas. To have even considered seriously the possibility of a Globe replica in west Texas seems startling; to have accomplished it seems only slightly less, if less, than miraculous. But from such stuff Globes, as well as dreams, are made on. That it would take very nearly two decades from the inception to the completion of the Globe of the Great Southwest is something that Mrs. Morris could not have known when she first decided to put up her theater in Odessa, but in talking with her one gets the feeling that the time it took was not important; doing it was. "I knew that if I worked hard and kept my faith it would eventually be completed," Mrs. Morris has told me.

Following her decision to build a Globe replica, Mrs. Morris went on to study Shakespeare and the early Elizabethan theaters at North Texas State University, where she wrote her M.A. thesis, under the direction of Arthur Sampley, on the topic: "The Proposed Globe Theater at Odessa, Texas." She continued to study Shakespeare and his Globe theater further at the Folger Shakespeare Library, the University of Southern California, and the University of Birmingham in England. During her studies at Birmingham she worked with Allardyce Nicoll, then of the International School of Shakespeare, who told Mrs. Morris that if she completed her theater she would, in his words, "have the most nearly authentic replica of Shakespeare's own Globe anywhere on earth."

Once Mrs. Morris resolved what she wanted to do and felt that she had acquired enough knowledge and authority to do it, the first step—more accurately, obstacle—for realizing her dream was, as we might expect, raising the money to begin construction. To this end Mrs. Morris literally went around knocking on doors; she solicited funds from private citizens, corporations, and foundations, a task which she has kept at consistently and insistently over the years and still continues to this day. Whatever it took to get the money from the folks of west Texas to put up a Globe theater in their neighborhood, faith and perseverance to say the least, Mrs. Morris managed to do it. A triangular piece of land on the campus of Odessa College, where Mrs. Morris was then teaching, was donated for the site of the theater, and in 1958 construction was started, ten years after she first dreamed her improbable dream.

To design and supervise the construction of the building itself, Mrs. Morris engaged the services of J. Ellsworth Powell, an architectural designer, who first became intrigued by the prospect of building an authentic Globe when he had been asked by Mrs. Morris to illustrate her thesis. Powell's plans for the building were based on Mrs. Morris's research which, in turn, was based on the work of John Cranford Adams. "The Globe was a challenge to me," Powell has said. "I became very interested in Marjorie Morris's thesis and read all the books I ran into for ten years after. No drawings, as such, existed after the burn-out of Shakespeare's Globe. . . . The John Cranford Adams' plans are widely accepted by Shakespeare authorities and the most authentic was the octagonal design. The original had no roof and the thatched roof was not profitable. We used a simulated redwood shaker shingle roof and a unique band of concrete that holds the entire building together. It is doubly strong with eight steel beams."[3]

For fifteen years Powell supervised the Globe's bit-by-bit, piece-by-piece construction. When funds were available, construction went ahead; when money ran out, construction was halted until more cash could be raised. In this way the Globe was kept out of debt and built on a strictly cash basis.

Along with the roof, the wooden areas under the stage and the stairways leading to the upper levels were treated with a fireproof

substance to prevent the Odessa Globe from meeting the fate suffered by the original. The open-thrust stage was built of 3″x 6″ pine
and, we are told, is strong enough to support an elephant. (Are there
any Elizabethan plays in which elephants appear?) The total playing
area covers 30′x60′, slightly less than the size given by Adams. In
Powell's words, "I had plenty of time so I used it. The wood was
seasoned and put up slowly before the stucco was applied and there
are no cracks." Though far smaller than the original Globe's seating
area (seating capacity is 418), the Odessa Globe's seating area is
solidly set on an earth-filled footing. It was allowed to set for two
years in the weather, and its tiers are set upon solid earth. The
timber beams throughout the building were personally handhewn
by Clyde Scott, the building contractor, and his brother. The walls
are 14″ thick with 1½ inches of plaster. According to Powell, the
building "will last forever."

Genuinely worm-eaten pecky cyprus was imported from England
for the foyer and other interior parts of the theater and is one of the
most effectively authentic features of the building. Even the lanterns
hanging inside the Globe were modelled after English lanterns of the
sixteenth century. And although some of the original plans for the
theater have yet to be completed, such as tiles for the entry and a
moat with a removable drawbridge for pre-show activities, the building as it now stands is, for all practical purposes, the accomplish-
ment of the day nearly thirty-five years ago when one of Mrs.
Morris's high school English students metaphorically laid the foundation for the Globe of the Great Southwest. When the Globe was
completed in 1966, eight years after construction started, Howard
Taubman wrote: "Mrs. Morris's dream brought to reality is a jewel.
With the help of J. Ellsworth Powell . . . she has reincarnated the
spirit of Shakespeare's theater in an unlikely setting. Curiously
enough, her Globe, standing on a disused oil field on the edge of
Odessa College's campus, looks as if it belongs. . . ."[4]

Yet neither the history of the Odessa Globe's origin nor its physical and architectural features nor even its unexpected location—its
quaintness, as we might call it—is, finally, what is really important
about this unique theater. What is important is that the Globe of the

The Globe of the Great Southwest

Great Southwest is not only a model theater but also a practical, working theater, one which has for fifteen years achieved a high and uniform level of competence in its Shakespearean productions. The Odessa Globe had its first professional season in the spring of 1966—eighteen years after Mrs. Morris was inspired to make the theater a reality—when Paul Baker and his Dallas Theatre Company put on six performances of *Julius Caesar* (previously, the Globe had been used just once: by the Permian Playhouse for a production of *Kiss Me, Kate*). Three years later, in the summer of 1969, Charles David McCally, the Globe's first full-time producer-director, inaugurated the annual Shakespeare Festival, a series which has continued to the present.

McCally, a native of Fort Worth and a professional actor—he has, for example, performed on all three major television networks—more than any other person has been responsible for the basic format and tone of the Globe's Shakespearean productions—at least until his resignation in 1978 to try other professional interests. In addition to his directorial and acting chores at the Globe (he played the prince in the Globe's 1970 production of *Hamlet*), McCally has also directed at the Dallas Theatre Center and Trinity University's Ruth Taylor Theatre. Of his work as director, John Velz wrote, "his productions are inventive and physically alive . . . full of subtle and effective stage business. . . ." Referring more specifically to the combination of McCally and the fabrication of the Odessa Globe, Velz further observed, "The Globe is the right theater for McCally's talents; the stage thrusts into a 400-seat house, offering great flexibility and good intimacy. The sight lines are excellent and the acoustics near perfect."[5] Along the same lines, Anne Englander, writing about the Sixth Annual Shakespeare Festival—"a striking success" in her words—noted that "McCally, more than anyone, has made the 'live program' at the Globe a success and an event worthy of national attention." Of McCally's *Macbeth* (1974) Englander wrote "Never have I seen a production which made more extensive and effective use of visual and aural effects; in fact, the barrage of stimuli was so overwhelming that I felt positively weak by the end of the performance."[6] Without a doubt McCally's effective productions of Shakespeare at the Odessa Globe have been due in part to the physical structure of the theater itself.[7]

Looking over the list of the thirty-one Shakespeare plays presented at the Globe's annual Shakespeare Festival over the past fourteen years, we can draw a number of more or less obvious conclusions about Shakespeare in the South, or at least about the Globe of the Great Southwest.

The comedies (twenty productions counting repeats) are easily the most popular of Shakespeare's plays at the Southwest Globe, not a surprising fact considering the largely regional, essentially student and family audience, the Globe caters to. Whatever may be true of other southern Shakespeare festivals (or national, for that matter), this type of audience has clearly proved to dominate (if not necessarily influence) the Southwest Globe's Shakespearean offerings, especially since the festival was moved, in 1980, from a late summer schedule to an early spring one. The reason for the move was practical necessity, economic as well as logistic. Attempts to stage classical drama (in the broad sense) year-round at the Odessa Globe have proved in the past to be less than satisfactory, again perhaps not too surprising for a theater as far from nowhere (as Shakespeare festivals go) as the Globe of the Great Southwest.

Here, geography joins with culture—by and large, socially and religiously conservative—to create a unique and very special situation (literally) for a Shakespeare festival. As Alice Boggs Berthelsen wrote in her review of the Twelfth Annual Festival (1980), "The Globe of the Great Southwest has struggled continuously to rationalize its existence on the barren plains of West Texas. For several seasons a year-round program proved an exercise in futility, owing to the small demand for classical theater in one of the nation's richest oil fields."[8] In short, the Globe of the Great Southwest, by geography as well as demography, is literally and figuratively miles from Shakespeare festivals such as those in New York, Houston, Dallas, San Diego, Ashland, or the two Stratfords, all of which can count on large and relatively cosmopolitan populations or a large influx of tourists or both. None of these conditions holds true—or at least *as* true—for Odessa's Globe Theater, and to that extent it is remarkable that the Southwest Globe has not only managed to survive for fourteen seasons but, beyond survival, shown signs of new verve and vitality.

As always, much of the credit for the Odessa Globe's persistence has to go to Marjorie Morris, and also, since 1980, to the Globe's business manager, David Weaver. In addition to the beginning of Weaver's tenure, 1980 saw some significant and, as it has turned out, salutary changes in the Globe's scheduling and productions. In that year festival dates were switched from late summer to early spring to coincide with the school year in order to take advantage of a "captive" student audience (in addition to area public schools, Odessa is the site of Odessa College, a two-year junior college, and the Permian Basin branch of the University of Texas, with a combined student population of close to two thousand). No doubt even more important was the institution during the 1980 season of the practice of using a professional company, The National Shakespeare Company, in addition to student and other largely amateur groups, to stage Shakespeare's plays. The "happy result," to again quote Berthelsen, "was a program of higher quality than had ever before been attempted at the Globe."

For the 1980 festival the National Shakespeare Company performed two plays at the Globe: *Much Ado about Nothing* and *Julius Caesar;* a third, *A Midsummer Night's Dream,* was staged by students from North Texas State University's drama department. Thus we find, given the site of the Globe and its audience preferences, that the comedies have proved twice as popular as the tragedies or, even, tragi-comedies, a ratio which has held true from the Globe's beginning. Of the comedies produced at the Globe, the most popular over the years has been *A Midsummer Night's Dream,* with three separate productions, followed by (with two apiece), *The Merry Wives of Windsor, Much Ado About Nothing,* and *Twelfth Night.* Indeed, if the tentative schedule for the 1983 (Fifteenth) festival holds true (*King Lear, Hamlet, The Merchant of Venice*), it will be the first season in which noncomic plays outnumber comic ones. Obviously, Shakespeare's comedies are not less valuable or inferior to the tragedies or histories (a popular notion but I think a perverse one); nor is the overwhelming popularity of the comedies at the Odessa Globe evidence of condescension to the Globe's patrons (again, one suspects that the comedies are *generally* more popular than the tragedies or histories, in the South or elsewhere, although I have never seen any statistical evidence on this matter). In any case, the fact that the comedies make up half of the canon is no doubt pertinent to the number of overall performances given. Finally, the popularity of the comedies does not mean that they are somehow easier to stage than the other genres; this also is a very misleading notion, since some comedies (e.g., *Love's Labor's Lost* or *The Merchant of Venice*) are extraordinarily difficult, indeed treacherous, to perform, although not necessarily, as with the two examples given, for the same reasons. As always with Shakespeare, the play *is* the thing.

But whatever the reasons for their popularity—regional tastes, director's or manager's preferences, audience demands—the comedies have fared well at the Globe of the Great Southwest. In fact, all of Shakespeare's comedies have been staged at the Globe (discounting those two rarities *Pericles* and *The Two Noble Kinsmen*) with the exception of *The Winter's Tale,* a somewhat surprising omission considering the strong spiritual overtones of that play as well as its highly theatrical qualities, which at least equal if not surpass those of *Cymbeline.*

Several notable productions of the comedies deserve brief comment, beginning with the 1980 staging by the National Shakespeare Company of *Much Ado,* which, along with the same company's production of *Julius Caesar,* proved to be a dramatic (in all senses) turning point in the Globe's history. These two productions, Alice Berthelsen told her readers in the *Odessa American,* surpassed "all previous efforts at the theater, both directorially and dramatically."[9] Of the production of *Much Ado,* Berthelsen observed that "the professional cast portrayed each character with sensitivity and subtlety that captivated every member of the opening night audience," clearly implying that this was the kind of play and production ideally suited to the Globe's needs and interests.

The Odessa Globe's 1978 production of *Love's Labor's Lost,* the only time that play has been attempted at the Globe, turned out to be mostly, if not wholly, successful, which is saying something for that thorny play. Here, as so often, the flexibility and contemporary sensation of the Globe's physical structure helped, as perhaps did director Regina Walker's decision to cut some of the play's poetic prolixities. Or, as Waldo McNeir put it, "The problem of rhymed and mannered verse was solved by cutting the most high-flown of the 'taffeta phrases.'"[10] That such surgery needs to be performed on Shakespeare's first comedy (perhaps his first play) was made clear to me during the 1982 production of the play by the Houston Shakespeare Festival, a production that went on and on until the viewer felt that the author either forgot to end the play or did not know how. In any case, the fact that the Globe (meaning of course the director, staff, and players as well as the theater) managed an effective production of what McNeir calls "Shakespeare's most feminist play" is certainly testimony to its commitment to bring Shakespeare to the Deep and Far South, meaning, for Odessa, the South and the West.

What is perhaps the most famous regional adaptation of a Shakespeare play at Odessa is the 1972 "western" version of *The Taming of the Shrew*. Often cited for its innovations, this production transformed Petrucchio's Padua to a Texas ranch.[11] The western theme, costumes, and setting are clearly captured in the photograph.

Of the tragedies presented by the Odessa Globe over the past fourteen seasons, only *Julius Caesar, Macbeth,* and *Romeo and Juliet* have been given more than one production; here again the choice of these plays for repeats is not surprising since they are all widely taught in public schools and colleges and are certainly, along with *Hamlet,* the most familiar Shakespearean tragedies. The potential dangers—or one potential danger—of performing only the more popular plays, and especially for student audiences, became apparent during a 1981 performance of *Romeo and Juliet* by the National Shakespeare Company. In the words of the *San Angelo Times* reviewer, the performance was "hampered by giggly high school youngsters who probably thought they would be served popcorn. . . ."[12] But in spite of the "giggly" youths, or perhaps because of them, the 1981 season turned out to be the most successful ever in the Globe's history, with over 4,800 visitors attending the festival during the month of March, including over 2,800 out-of-towners, quite an achievement for a Shakespeare festival on the windy plains of west Texas. In addition to the National Shakespeare's *Romeo and Juliet,* which played to SRO audiences for each of its five performances, North Texas State University's musical version of *A Comedy of Errors* and Texas Christian University's *The Merry Wives of Windsor* also played to packed houses, demonstrating again that when it comes to Shakespeare in the Southwest, the comedies and the more popular tragedies spell success.[13]

The tragedy that is most conspicuous by its absence from the list of Globe productions is, of course, *King Lear*. While the play is perhaps the least popular of the major tragedies, it is also the one usually designated as the greatest of all of Shakespeare's tragedies (a duality which does not necessarily imply a cause-and-effect relationship). One wonders if this notable omission is due to the play's reputation (well-deserved) for being difficult to stage and perform or

Western version of *The Taming of the Shrew*, 1972
Courtesy Globe of the Great Southwest

to its being too somber, pessimistic (and pagan?), or to both reasons.[14] Somewhat less conspicuous by its absence from the list of tragedies—at least in comparison with the absence of *King Lear*—is *Coriolanus,* long the least-often performed (except *Titus Andronicus*) of Shakespeare's Roman history plays and, if we also except *Timon of Athens,* the least-often performed of any of Shakespeare's tragedies—a standing due perhaps to the combination of the play's strong political, antirepublican bias, the ambivalent character of the play's hero, and the relatively static action of the plot. In a word, it is a perverse play which, given the realities of where and for whom the Odessa Globe stands, has been perhaps prudently untried by the Globe thus far.

Of the so-called tragicomedies, two out of the usual three have been played at the Globe; the one that still remains to be done turns out to be *All's Well That Ends Well*. Once again, the omission is not too surprising, although George Bernard Shaw once referred to the countess's role as the greatest old woman's part ever written. In spite of this play's general unpopularity (partly, I believe, due to a bad critical press and partly due to its rather randy sexuality— although no worse, or better, in this regard than *Troilus and Cressida* or *Measure for Measure*), I suspect that *All's Well* would be in certain ways an ideal play for the Globe of the Great Southwest or, for that matter, any regional Shakespeare festival, particularly in the South. The reasons for my suspicion have to do with the character of Helena, "the loveliest of all of Shakespeare's heroines," as Coleridge said of her, and also with the predominantly courtly quality of the play, which somehow strikes me as southern in its adherence to tradition, honor, good manners.

But what is perhaps most surprising of all—indeed perplexing— taking the Odessa Globe's record of Shakespeare performances as a whole, is that none of the English history plays has ever been staged at the Globe. True, the histories are the least performed of Shakespeare's plays and certainly the least frequently taught in high schools and colleges; nevertheless, it does seem strange that an annual Shakespeare festival completing fifteen years of performances has not attempted one of Shakespeare's versions of his nation's roots—at the very least, one of the more popular versions: *Richard II, Richard III*, or, especially, *1 Henry IV* (we may take some consolation in knowing that Falstaff has appeared on the Globe stage, if only in *The Merry Wives of Windsor*). But no Hal or Hotspur, Gloucester or Bolingbroke? That the Globe of the Great Southwest should have for whatever reasons neglected to "cram" "A kingdom for a stage, princes to act, / And monarchs to behold the swelling scene" within its "nearly-authentic" confines seems as ironic as it does regrettable. While the lack of any of the English history plays surely imparts a feeling of incompleteness to the Globe's sustained record of Shakespeare festivals, all in all, however, it seems fair to say that to date—and keeping in mind the practical requirements of selling tickets and gaining the patronage, financial and otherwise, of its local supporters—the Odessa Globe has done well by Shakespeare: thirty-one plays in fourteen seasons, ranging from *The Comedy of Errors* at one end to *The Tempest* at the other.

Mention of *The Tempest,* as it invariably does, brings us finally to the end of the Globe's revels, although there is no doubt at all that the Globe will go on bringing Shakespeare to the people of Texas and the Southwest—indeed to anyone who gets to it—for many years to come. In conclusion, what needs to be stressed is the uniqueness of the Southwest Globe, as a Texas institution, a southwestern institution, a national institution. That a reminder of a playhouse which once stood on the south bank of the Thames 350 years ago now stands on the site of a dried-up oil well in Odessa, Texas seems passing strange. Yet, for someone attending a performance at the Globe of the Great Southwest, sitting in the upper level, watching, say, *Macbeth* or *The Taming of the Shrew,* the enormous distance in time and space between the first Globe and the Globe in Odessa becomes temporarily meaningless. In the end, one can only agree that the play, the players, the audience, and the Great Globe of the Southwest itself "are such stuff as dreams are made on."

NOTES

1. In addition to the Odessa Globe, three other annual Shakespeare festivals are held in replicas of the original Globe: Hofstra, Utah, and San Diego. The theaters at Ashland and the Folger Library are, strictly speaking, reproductions of Elizabethan playhouses rather than of the Bankside Globe. For an excellent survey of Shakespeare festivals and festival theaters, see *Theatre Crafts* (Mar./Apr. 1973), a special issue devoted wholly to this subject. Glenn Loney and Patricia MacKay, in their review of Shakespeare in North America, *The Shakespeare Complex* (New York: Drama Book Specialists, 1975), seem skeptical about the authenticity of the Odessa Globe; they refer, for example, to its "bogus Tudor decor" (p. 71). Since no one knows what a real "Tudor decor" was, and since everybody, including the management, understands that the Odessa Globe is a replica and not an exact duplicate of the original Globe, their disclaimer strikes me as petty. In any case, two separate projects to create "faithful" reconstructions of the original Globes (Globe I, 1599–1613: Globe II, 1614–1644?) are now underway—one under the sponsorship of Shakespeare's Globe in America, the other under the International Shakespeare Globe Theatre Center. For more on Globe replicas, see *Shakespeare Newsletter* 28 (Sept., 1978, and Nov.–Dec., 1978), and C. Walter Hodges, S. Schoenbaum, and Leonard Leone, eds. *The Third Globe: Symposium for the Reconstruction of the Globe Playhouse, Wayne State University, 1979* (Detroit: Wayne State Univ. Press, 1981).

2. Unless otherwise indicated, the background material and references come

from Mrs. Marjorie Morris, the Globe's founder, who patiently answered my questions, supplied me with programs and other material on the Globe's productions, and made my visit to Odessa enjoyable as well as informative. I also thank David Weaver, the Globe's business manager, who supplied me with detailed information about the operation of the theater; and finally I acknowledge the Department of English of the University of Houston for supplying me with the necessary funds to visit the Globe.

3. Some of Adams's, and hence Powells's, plans for the Globe have since been modified, or at least challenged, by later students of the design and construction of the original Globe. Hodges, for example, questions Adams's design and use of the so-called inner stage as well as the exterior shape of the building, although Hodges believes the shape was certainly polygonal (not a "wooden O") if not in fact octagonal. See C. Walter Hodges, *The Globe Restored: A Study of the Elizabethan Theatre* (New York: Coward-McCann, 1968), pp. 4, 47, *et passim*.

4. *New York Times*, Apr. 14, 1966, p. 66.

5. *Shakespeare Quarterly* 24 (Autumn, 1973): 435.

6. *Ibid.* 25 (Autumn, 1974): 425; 428.

7. For a sketch of the Globe's early productions, and, especially, the work of McCally, see Glenn Loney and Patricia MacKay, pp. 68–71. The two-hour time limit on Shakespeare productions, referred to by Loney and MacKay (p. 70), no longer holds, if it ever did. For example, the 1979 production of *Antony and Cleopatra* was done in an uncut version that ran for 3 hours, although the production was later shortened by the director more for dramatic than technical reasons. See Alice Ann Boggs Berthelsen, "The Globe of the Great Southwest," *Shakespeare Quarterly* 31 (Summer, 1980): 248.

8. *Shakespeare Quarterly* 32 (Summer, 1981): 241.

9. *Odessa American*, Mar. 2, 1980, p. 18c.

10. *Shakespeare Quarterly* 30 (Spring, 1979): 224.

11. The production was reviewed by Loney and MacKay in their *Shakespeare Complex* and in the special Shakespeare festival issue of *Theatre Crafts*.

12. *San Angelo Times*, Feb. 27, 1981, p. 8B.

13. In addition to plays by Shakespeare, the Odessa Globe often stages other classical dramas, for example, *The Miser, Cyrano de Bergerac, The Imaginary Invalid, She Stoops to Conquer, The Glass Menagerie*, and, scheduled for fall of 1982, Sheridan's *The Rivals*. Along with plays of this caliber, the Globe annually stages a religious drama during the Christmas season (e.g., *The Life of Christ, The House of Saul, Elijah*), a policy in keeping with the predominantly family and regional audience which patronizes the Globe. Although to my knowledge, the Globe has never staged any of Shakespeare's plays with a particularly southern setting or flavor (though its 1972 production of *The Taming of the Shrew* was done "western-style" and the 1981 *Comedy of Errors* was set during the California Gold Rush), the regular performance at the Globe of Biblical drama (to be accurate, one should say "Christian" drama since no doubt the Old Testament is treated as prefiguration to the New) does, I think it is fair to say, impart a southern quality to the Globe's overall theatrical program, southern in at least a fundamentalist sense if not necessarily a geographical one, although the two of course are connected.

14. An outstanding 1980 production of *King Lear* was given by the Houston Shakespeare Society as part of its Summer Shakespeare Festival put on each year free of charge in Miller Theater, an outdoor amphitheater in Hermann Park. This production, directed by Sidney Berger and featuring Dan O'Herlihy in the title role and with a supporting cast from the University of Houston drama department, can stand as witness to the fact that *Lear* can be effectively and compellingly staged for a general, largely local, audience.

Shakespeare—Dull and Dusty?
Some Revolutions in Central Florida

Stuart E. Omans
and
Patricia A. Madden

In the summer of 1979 the National Endowment for the Humanities and the University of Central Florida cosponsored a program entitled "Shakespeare in His Age: An Interdisciplinary Institute." Conceived by Stuart Omans and two other professors and involving an international faculty from eleven institutions including The Royal Shakespeare Theatre and the University of Warwick, the Institute's student body was composed of some forty teachers and would-be teachers, who for eight weeks were involved in both the theoretical and practical study of Shakespeare's art. Their focus was music, literature, theater, dance, and history as an amalgam of the culture in which Shakespeare created his plays. After two intense months of reading, attending lecture-demonstrations, learning and rehearsing dances, designing and sewing costumes and wigs, studying the theory of Renaissance music, composing and performing music, designing, building, painting a set and props—in short, after totally immersing themselves in every dimension of Shakespeare's art—the students presented a concert of Elizabethan music and dance on August 9, 1979, and a major production of *A Midsummer Night's Dream* on August 10, 11, and 12. Both performances took place in The Bush Civic Theatre in Orlando, located twenty-five miles from campus. The performances were attended by overflow SRO crowds. In central Florida, where theater is usually struggling to breathe the air left behind by football fans and where Shakespeare is generally regarded by the public as wonderful but dreary, the success of the project seemed little less than remarkable. That the audiences at the performances became so excited they demanded midnight repeat performances is little short of a southern miracle.

278

The adults, children, and teenagers who attended the Institute's productions experienced the fun and excitement of Shakespeare. But we are getting ahead of the story.

In reality, the National Endowment for the Humanities Institute grew out of a seed planted seven years earlier in a much less ambitious program. It began in a course designed by Stuart Omans in which university students from outside the traditional arts and humanities were encouraged to enroll; it was a new, thematically-based Shakespeare course.

The course began with a reading of Shakespeare's plays in one category (history, comedy, or tragedy), with most attention directed to themes that seem repeatedly to have interested Shakespeare. In the history plays, for example, the students kept finding themselves involved in discussions of the reasons men seek power and the methods by which they try to retain it. After careful study Omans administered the students their first of many shocks: they were to focus on a dominant theme which the class would later present for high schools in central Florida in an original show to be written by everyone in the class. The show was to be aimed at that segment of the high school community which normally would twist away at the very mention of Shakespeare. Omans told the students that he wanted them to select a theme which demonstrated the "simplicity" of Shakespeare and not his "complexity," because they would have the task of presenting the shows to junior high school and high school students in rural communities. It was at this point that many students–would-be actors–musicians–writers quietly sneaked off into that good night called "Withdraw with Pass." Ironically, once the remaining students came to terms with this task, they began to see that the brilliance in the plays comes through Shakespeare's understanding of what makes men fundamentally human, and they also began to realize how clearly and how deeply Shakespeare managed to convey our humanity, and that most often his ability to speak simply and clearly of human activity was his greatest gift.

After carefully working through the plays, winnowing through scenes, arguing, sifting through again, and finally agreeing upon which scenes within the plays most clearly enlarged on the extended meaning of the chosen themes, the students began to discuss possible formats for the presentation of their Shakespearean motley. Omans asked them to think especially about what kind of narrator might most vividly accommodate this, their own Shakespearean world. In their first show, "To Know Thyself," the students created the narrator as a young girl who was to appear like the students in the audience, at first somewhat smug and complacent, satisfied with her shell. After all, she is there to formally present a group of actors who can "put on" a few Shakespearean scenes about self-identity and personal happiness. She is there to give the sweaty multitude a little culture—and rub elbows with them as little as possible. During the show, her separatist plan does not work. Her understanding deepens and she is pulled into Shakespeare's world and sees through other eyes the possible consequences of not trying to understand herself more fully. As she asks a series of rhetorical questions about self-understanding—"How can a man learn to deal with himself?"—at the show's outset, a fool appears from nowhere (in this case, the back of the hall). As he works his way up through the audience delivering lines to them, moving closer and closer to her space, he offers more answers than she had bargained for. It is clear that his speech alternates between cliché and wisdom. It is also clear that he does not belong here. By the time the fool is directly in front of the stage and speaking to the narrator, he now, uncomfortably for her, changes his attitude and quietly advises her. The narrator listens, first, with raised eyebrows, superior and amused. But she is not without questions and not without being a little frightened. However, she is still enough her former self to go on and tell the students her story of Shakespeare's first comedy about identity, *The Comedy of Errors*. Still very much separated from Shakespeare's world, she explains that from the beginning of Shakespeare's career he explored the comic possibilities of the "deceptively simple" maxim "Know Thyself." She then begins to go on with her glib explanation—only to be faced by the jester again, this time in a more serious mood, who repeats to her, "yes, know thyself" and again disappears. She pauses now, a little more shaken but still removed, and she continues, this time with some annoyance and bravado: "Identity yes, that's the ticket! But it's always easier to say than do, especially when a man is dog tired, after touring the world, searching for his long lost twin brother (who unknown to him has been living here in this strange town for over twenty years). Add to this the fact that his servant's long lost twin brother is living here too and is the servant of *his* brother. Well, the problem of knowing himself can get very comically complicated" says she, "very comically complicated indeed." At this point, the action moves to Act 1, Scene 2, of *The Comedy of Errors,* with the narrator withdrawing down stage left to observe from a slightly raised platform. The scene proceeds until it cuts to the entrance of Adriana, who is frantically waving to the man she believes to be her husband. The narrator steps forward and assures the audience that just before the new lady's appearance, the visiting Antipholus was feeling better. Less upset, he now again knew who he was and who Dromio was. But this new lady had shaken him by recognizing him, using his name, and claiming to be his *wife.* As the narrator withdraws again, to observe Adriana's dilemma, Adriana, looking around, realizes that someone is missing from the scene Shakespeare wrote for her. It is her sister Luciana! She simply picks up the closest possible female substitute and it is the narrator, who now finds herself smack in the middle of Shakespeare's scene. The first lines of Adriana are addressed as much toward her "sister-in-law" as they are to her "husband." The stage picture suggests for the first time that the narrator has been pulled away from her complacent and safe definition of self into an exploration—by entering the world of the plays. As the show progresses, she too progresses and changes, and along with her the audience, which itself is physically included more and more in the fiction, as they all are invited to experience the comic consequences of not trying to explore more fully and, therefore, understanding themselves.

The narrative character is crucial not only to the success of the performance but to the student performers' education in Shakespeare's art as a man of the theater. They learn to understand *from the inside* why a play by Shakespeare is a great vehicle for a performer. The student performers quickly realize that the narrator must be consistent in characterization, ideas, and even to some extent in language with Shakespeare's own characterization, theme, and language if the show is not to bore the audience. In fact, as the narrator more and more enters Shakespeare's world and then returns to observe other scenes, class members insist that her language grow richer, more metaphoric, more in tune with the rhythms of the scenes. "To Know Thyself" moves on through *The Comedy of Errors* to *The Taming of the Shrew, A Midsummer Night's Dream,* and finally to *Twelfth Night.* At each progressive step the students insist that the narrator's sense of language become richer. In this show she eventually sees Kate and Petruchio as "two blunderbuss characters—a lady who believes she can defeat any man because of her wits, and a man who can beat any 'little lady.'" In inventing their Shakespearean narrator, the student writer-actors begin more clearly to realize that every word a character says must be motivated and, as a corollary, they begin to have a fuller understanding of what stage motivation means in Shakespeare. *They see audiences respond.* Subsequently, they learn why editing Shakespearean scenes is so incredibly difficult. When the actor who is trying to realize the character of the narrator in rehearsal complains that a section of character "droops for her" and therefore will do so for the audience, or that it simply "makes no sense," the student writers must defend the section by actively demonstrating how it works or else recognize that in action it has no defense and thus must be revised until the character does work. The lesson is fundamental, and it suggests the way revisions of text probably were done in Shakespeare's own rehearsals.

The tears and sweat of their own dramatic revisions make the students more sensitive to the principles of editing Shakespeare for presentation. Most important is the excitement that comes to a student who recognizes why it is so excruciating to edit a Shakespearean scene for presentation. They must edit for the new context because public school schedules are inflexible; the shows we present may take a total of only one and one-half hours of performance time. Because the students are forced to combine their talents as students of literature with their growing talents as working dramatists and actors, they see the play from both inside and outside.

In "To Know Thyself," for example, the students agreed after much discussion and some trial performance that the material from *The Comedy of Errors* was running too long. First they identified the least damaging cut, deciding that the deleted lines describe, through Elizabethan punning, actions that could be theatrically delivered through stage movement. Through their close *contact* with the scene, the students realize how complex editing is by having to confront Shakespeare's language and its relationship to his stage-craft in an *active dramatic situation of their own making*. This proc-ess of making, of discovering, through integration with the audience, of *becoming*, emerges most clearly when a student actor confronts his or her character. These encounters are all experiments in con-frontation. Their reality eventually makes its way to the young audi-ences in Florida; they respond by standing and yelling for more. "I've never seen actors love a play so much. I've never seen this in theater," says a teacher. "I thought it would be boring because I'm not too crazy about Shakespeare. But there wasn't one minute that I could stop laughing at those crazy wonderful people. Especially Kate. What a woman! Give me her number!" says a high school roué.

From its first experiments with "To Know Thyself," the Simply Shakespeare program has now conceived and produced five other shows: "The Magic of His Web: Shakespeare and Man's Imagina-tion"; "It's a Man's World, Isn't It?"; "All the World's Our Stage"; "The Chain of Power"; and "Liars and Soothsayers." With each production both the concept and audience reaction have grown more favorable and, in repeated situations, more gratifying. Perhaps the best illustration of the success of the method came one day on a football field. A 190-pound high school football player in full gladiatorial regalia approached a referee and shouted, "Hey Sir Toby Belch! You 'member what y'all told me about Re'sance Man? Well I look'd it up, and I got me in *Othello*, and to tell ya the truth I don' care who likes it." The referee, a burly cast member of Simply Shakespeare who weeks before had played Belch *and* Iago, after the show had been accosted by this student from the audience, demand-ing to know who the actor *really* was, and why he hated Othello. The student-actor explained that a part of him was Belch and probably, a part that he hated, was Iago and that it was Iago, not he, that hated Othello. He went on to explain that Shakespeare showed us through such characters more about the roots of racial hatred than most modern books. The troupe member explained that he played in *Othello* to more fully understand his own potentials and limits, that being a football coach, sociology student, and referee was not enough; he dreamed of being a Renaissance man. The kid apparently listened very well. The referee watched, smiled, murmured, "Excellent devil of wit!" and blew his whistle to start the game. A tiny glimmer of a new self took over in that student. Football was no longer enough.

Reactions to the Simply Shakespeare programs were positive but also sometimes confusing. When Omans started he was afraid that the strongest resistance would come from the kids in the audience, but this proved not to be the case. The problem came from teachers' reactions. They were convinced that the plays or even parts of the plays would be too hard for their more basic students, and despite Omans' pleas they insisted that they wanted to "weed out" the "less capable or slower students who could not possibly appreciate" Shakespeare's world. Omans realized that often it was the teachers' ingrained attitudes he was fighting, not the students'. The Simply Shakespeare performances went on, but new plans went forward as well. It was six years after the first performance of Simply Shakespeare that the first Shakespeare Institute came into being. We realized that the teachers "venerated" Shakespeare but often only with lip service. Robert Ornstein's warning, "undergraduates are not as excited or absorbed by the study of literature as they once were" and "the situation in high school" is even "unhappier," had slapped us full in the face.

And so we proposed an institute that would expand the approaches of Simply Shakespeare and would appeal to a selected group of some forty students—practicing secondary teachers and graduate students preparing to teach. These would be chosen from mixed disciplines—English, speech, drama, humanities, as well as history and music. For the first time in most of their careers the teachers were to be provided a matrix for developing and exchanging creative ideas about literature while engaged together in the preparation of a Shakespearean production, *A Midsummer Night's Dream* and a Renaissance music concert.

Shakespeare would be presented not as the speaker of musty wisdoms glowering at them and their students with forbidding words from atop a marble pedestal, but as a genius who was able to unite art, music, dance, history, and poetry into the most brilliant amalgam of theatrical presentation ever created. Our premise was again simple. We were convinced that it would be *only* by enacting plays and bringing them to life that they could become meaningful and that new ways of presenting them to adolescents could, in turn, become possible. Because of the questions which could arise only in production, our teacher-participants would be able to revise their own methodologies as the result of their intense study of the plays, not merely as poetry but as realized drama in which actors and audiences provided insights into character, language, action, and theme.

We emphasized that in Shakespeare's plays the action is embedded in the text, with only rare stage directions to guide the interpreter. As such, the intelligent student of these plays must enact the scenes so that the meaning in the lines is realized and the significance of the scenes can be interpreted fully. We made it clear to our teachers that watching filmed versions or listening to the taped performances of professional actors was not a viable alternative to total involvement. *Participation was seen to be the key to the curricular innovation that was the Institute's ultimate goal.* The National Endowment for the Humanities thought we should be given the chance. And we began.

For eight weeks students attended class demonstrations dealing with seven of the plays but always focusing on *A Midsummer Night's Dream*. The literary and theatrical approaches to the plays were combined. Students were asked to attend Medieval and Renaissance dance classes and also to partake of music classes in which they learned to read and sing Renaissance vocal music and to play replicas of Renaissance instruments. A costume shop, run by Sandria Reese, a member of the Royal Shakespeare Theatre wardrobe department, involved students during their "free" hours in the

theory and construction of Renaissance costume. Every stitch worn
by the *Dream* cast was made by members of the Institute. Every
wig, every beard, was built from scratch by members. Even the
design for costumes came mainly from the students themselves.

Students in the music theory courses were encouraged to com-
pose original music for the production and, in fact, the basic theme
for the fairy sections used in the production was composed by the
student who played Starveling, Craig Alexander. Indeed, he wrote
and scored music for the entire play. He determined to separate
"fairy land" from Theseus's court, the lovers, and the mechanicals.
To do this he employed a tritone, a musical device he felt compelled
to defend because in theory he had learned it was probably used
only rarely by the Elizabethans. The tritone consists basically of an
interval span of three whole steps on an augmented fourth. The first
two notes of the tune "Maria" from *West Side Story* illustrate the
tritone. The feeling evoked is a kind of etherealness. So our *A Midsummer Night's Dream* had an original score marked by a tritone,
which imposed itself in the opening measure of the "fairy song" to
mark the division between "fairyland" and Theseus's court. Alexander added an aural mood change to complement the technical
changes created by costume, lighting, and the full three-level Renaissance set constructed by the student-actors.

Theseus's court was given a simple but rich melody to be played
on a sackbut. The background was to be portrayed by a clavichord,
suggesting the air of a fanfare. The lovers were to be orchestrated as
well, with music that displayed vacillation through most of the
piece, ending with a sweet melody that musically sang "they lived
happily ever after." Finally, Alexander proposed mechanicals'
music: six mechanicals, but only five themes since Alexander insisted that Bottom and Quince are Shakespeare's versions of the
straight and the funny man. They would chase each other forever
and not ever catch up, like a dog chasing its own tail.

Alexander finally suggested, as his contribution, the additions of
incidental music, including harp, psaltery, finger cymbals for "fairy
magic," and a sackbut to awaken the lovers.

Alas, the plan was too ambitious for our novice Renaissance musicians. Our musicians (used on stage and in a gallery during the production) sagged during rehearsals under the weight of so much musical ambition, and we finally settled only for the haunting tritone fairy theme. Other music for the production was chosen from simpler existing scores. But the point is easily made: the production was fully the result of the Institute fellows' new understanding.

Every other dimension of our production reflected Alexander's concern that the music capture the essence of each character group. The teacher actors discovered that there could be no *a priori* intellectualizing, no intellectualizing that has not grown out of, or through, *doing*. Our Puck kept trying to analyze her character and was in misery until she realized that she had to stop intellectually searching for the "right voice" or the "right walk." They were all there implicit in the lines. She had to make the lines her own. Puck was trying to tell her but as a teacher she was, at first, afraid to listen and then to *do*. Sent on an errand by Oberon, Puck replies, "I'll put a girdle round the earth in forty minutes." Another time Oberon demands, "Be here again ere the leviathan can swim a league." Similarly the spirit is in Puck's, "How now, spirit! Whither wander you?" Here is the quickness of the repeating vowel sounds in the first half of the line as well as the alliteration in the second half. But only when our Puck determined to do her lines while turning a cartwheel did she find her character. She could not create the unworldly speed Shakespeare suggests but she could be nimble, she could fly. She learned that she had to discover by *doing*. In fact, she had to get involved with the emotions and circumstances of the character or the performance would not fly.

The emphasis on *doing* carried the Institute *Dream* to this review in the *Orlando Sentinel* (Aug. 12, 1979), p. B8.

"A Midsummer Night's Dream" turned out to be a dream of a production, charmingly staged, well acted and imaginative. . . , Although very few of the Fellows had previous acting experience, they acquitted themselves more than acceptably. . . . Perhaps the crowning touch in the staging, which really invoked the fairyland fantasy the play aims for, was the use at the end of glowing, phosphorescent wands by the young fairies flitting about on the darkened stage like fireflies, followed by Puck's final speech to the audience from a swing high above the audience. . . . Connie Foster, an Osceola High School teacher from Kissimmee. . . . accomplished something of a tour-de-force in playing Bottom, the weaver. Puck, played by Jennifer Reeves of Westridge Junior High in this production, has undoubtedly been done by a female before, but this was probably a first for Bottom in a regular production of the play.

With a beard and her rambunctious interpretation, Ms. Foster emerged triumphant. Ms. Reeves, who had to scamper about on her various Oberon-directed missions, could not always be understood in her peregrinations but suggested the sprite quite adequately in what is perhaps the most difficult role in the play.

In short, the Institute fellows accomplished a very difficult task—they gave themselves to the play. They *did,* and emerged triumphant. Shakespeare could never be the same for them. It would never be the same for the audience or their students either.

The Institute's results did not end with the productions. The fellows produced *The Practical Bard,* a 200-page interdisciplinary guide for the teaching of Shakespeare. Currently in its second printing, the book already has been distributed to libraries and educators in Alabama, Florida, Georgia, Illinois, Kansas, Maryland, New York, and Virginia. New courses were initiated. An example of one of the most innovative is entitled Shakespeare for the Emotionally Handicapped. Schoolwide Shakespeare festivals sprang up. An example was the one held at South Seminole Middle School involving everyone from the gifted children to those in the vocational classes. And perhaps, most important, teachers began to stage their own productions. Connie Foster, our trend-setting Bottom and one wondrous teacher at the Osceola High School, staged a community production of *A Midsummer Night's Dream,* with players ranging from kindergarten children to residents of a retirement home.

Plans for a second Institute are now underway. We will use the same intense interdisciplinary approach but plan to expand our goals. We believe that despite its successes the Institute missed an important dimension of its potential: the play's capacities to make us explore our own prejudices.

In the second Institute the question of the outsider will be our focus, recognizing that it has been the root of major American social problems. Our rationale is that every society, including Shake-

The Simply Shakespeare Company's production of *A Midsummer Night's Dream*, 1979

speare's, has produced this figure. But the treatment of the figure—be it the outsider by virtue of race, religion, birth, nationality or age—varies according to the society's definition of the outside group. Shakespeare's idea of "Moor" or "Jew," for example, is obviously different from our own. It is in these subtle differences that the plays will provide an important focus for our second program. We will use some of Shakespeare's plays which examine the outsider as a way of analyzing our own attitudes and definitions. We will continually move between Shakespeare's art and our own world.

We feel that this theme is particularly appropriate for central Florida, since students in this state's schools are still very much divided despite the history of busing. (The recent riots in Miami and Orlando indicate the severity of frustration and anger in the minority communities.) Students in the schools are still tracked, with majority students being exposed to college preparatory subjects like theater, music, and English and the minorities being placed in lower, "more appropriate" classes. The teachers themselves are as isolated and frequently find themselves limited to teaching only basic or uninspiring courses. The circle of frustration is obvious. Frustrated teachers teaching frustrated students are separated from meaningful contact with each other or with the work of great writers such as Shakespeare, writers whose insight into the very roots of frustration are neatly sealed away in airtight compartments from those who could use them.

Our rationale for the second Institute proceeds along the following lines. From the beginning of his career, Shakespeare was fascinated by the problems of the outsider. Even in his first play, *The Comedy of Errors,* being an outsider (a foreigner) is used, but mainly as a means for organizing a rollicking farce. Shakespeare's expanded interest in the outsider is evidenced in such plays as *Romeo and Juliet, King Lear, The Merchant of Venice,* and *Othello,* which respectively treat a person who is an outcast partially as a result of his innocence of social prejudice, his birth, his religion, and his race. Finally, in *The Tempest,* Shakespeare's treatment of the theme has become much more complex and provides the play with its central focus. It has thus developed from simply a means of organizing a play to an exploration of the deepest facets of the human experience. The Institute will focus on demonstrating this progression.

Throughout the Institute, students will work together to produce *Othello,* confronting the intellectual, emotional, social, and artistic questions it raises. Here, Shakespeare's treatment of the outsider, a Moor in a predominantly white society, most closely approaches our own problems.

For this second Institute, a group of fifty students, at a nearly equal balance between teachers who traditionally are considered insiders (majority) and outsiders (blacks), will be recruited. We expect these students to be in residence at the University of Central Florida for the duration of the Institute.

The cross-cultural nature of the student group will be reflected in the faculty as well. A minority artist-in-residence will participate in the core course, teach acting classes, and take the role of Othello in the final production. A team of two master teachers (white and black) will work with the student-fellows throughout the course to crystallize ideas about the plays and to adapt these to the high school curriculum.

Our second Institute is predicated on the belief that by bringing the teachers together in residence and study, by involving them *actively* in the pursuit of these plays, by asking them to work with total commitment in producing Shakespeare's greatest play about the outsider, we can begin a lasting dialogue and professional commitment that will carry into their school communities. More concretely, though, the Institute can have a number of exciting results:

1. The Institute format can break down fears of open discussions of prejudice.
2. A study of Shakespearean insights can illuminate our own continuing problems.
3. New teaching strategies can be developed.
4. Cooperative dramatic productions can grow (e.g., interracial high school companies).
5. Existing literature and theater classes can become the forum for sensitive, informed, and open treatment of segregation issues.
6. The "elitism" associated with "drama" can be dismantled.
7. A second Practical Bard and a continuing newsletter can provide written forms of dissemination and lead to similar results in other parts of the country.

We recognize that the second Institute is very ambitious, perhaps to the point of hubris. But we are heartened by another recognition: seven years ago in central Florida, there was little interest in watching or doing dusty, dull Shakespeare. We are certain there is interest now.

Notes on Contributors

Arnold Aronson is assistant professor of theater at the University of Virginia.

Larry S. Champion is professor and head of the Department of English at North Carolina State University.

Earl L. Dachslager is associate professor of English at the University of Houston.

Woodrow L. Holbein is associate professor of English at The Citadel.

Carol McGinnis Kay is dean of the college at Randolph-Macon Woman's College and professor of English.

Philip C. Kolin is professor of English at the University of Southern Mississippi.

Charles B. Lower is assistant professor of English at the University of Georgia.

Waldo F. McNeir is emeritus professor of English at the University of Oregon.

Patricia A. Madden was a performer in Simply Shakespeare at the University of Central Florida.

Sara Nalley is instructor of speech and theater at Columbia College.

Stuart E. Omans is professor and head of the Department of English at the University of Central Florida.

Linwood E. Orange is professor of English at the University of Southern Mississippi.

Joseph Patrick Roppolo is emeritus professor of English at Tulane University.

Christopher J. Thaiss is associate professor of English at George Mason University.

Mary Duggar Toulmin is a retired reference librarian from Mobile.

Index